A NEW DAWN:
*Society and Politics
in the Light of Initiatic Science*

Newly translated from the French
Original title: LE VERSEAU ET L'AVÈNEMENT DE L'ÂGE D'OR
Title of first English edition:
AQUARIUS, HERALD OF THE GOLDEN AGE

© Copyright Prosveta S.A. 1999. All rights reserved for all countries. No part of this publication may be reproduced, translated, adapted, stored in a retrieval system or transmitted, whether privately or otherwise, in any form or by any means, electronic, mechanical, photocopying, audio-visual or otherwise, without the prior permission of author and publishers (Law of March 1957 revised).
Prosveta S.A – B.P.12 – 83601 Fréjus CEDEX (France)

ISBN 2-85566-777-1
1ère édition : ISBN 2-85566-163-3
édition originale : ISBN 2-85566-086-6

Omraam Mikhaël Aïvanhov

A NEW DAWN:
Society and Politics in the Light of Initiatic Science
Part 2

2nd edition

Complete Works – Volume 26

P R O S V E T A

By the same author:
(translated from the French)

Brochures:
301 — The New Year
302 — Meditation
303 — Respiration
304 — Death and the Life Beyond

Daily Meditations:
A thought for each day of the year

Cassette:
KC2510A — The Laws of Reincarnation

Readers will better understand certain aspects of the lectures published in the present volume if they bear in mind that Master Omraam Mikhaël Aïvanhov's teaching was exclusively oral and that the editors have made every effort to respect the flavour and style of each lecture.

The Master's teaching is more than a body of doctrines; it is an organic whole, and his way of presenting it was to approach it from countless different points of view. By treating certain aspects in many different contexts he constantly reveals a new dimension of the whole, and at the same time throws new light on the individual aspects and their vital links with each other.

Omraam Mikhaël Aïvanhov

TABLE OF CONTENTS

1. Principles and Forms 11
2. The True Religion of Christ 37
3. The Concept of a Pan-World 103
4. The Cosmic Body 131
5. The Kingdom of God and His Righteousness .. 165
6. The New Jerusalem 225

Chapter One

Principles and Forms

I

The important thing in life is to put the same heart and soul, the same tireless love into everything you do and never to give up, for it is the things that endure that must have priority. If something is to last, however, its particles must continually be renewed, and this means that if you are unwilling to clean out and discard the dusty remnants of your old ways of thinking and feeling, you will never create anything durable. Of course I know that it is going to be difficult for you to appreciate the importance of this truth, because the person who says it is a nobody. You think that only those who are learned or famous can reveal the truth. But that is not so; you should be able to recognize and appreciate a truth whoever may say it, be it a child or a beggar.

If something is to endure, it must constantly renew itself. And if the Church is disintegrating today, it is because it fails to renew itself; it continues to cling to old conceptions which are no longer valid and which need to be replaced. Of course I am not talking about the basic principles on which Christianity is built; no one will ever find principles more perfect than those of the Gospels. But why does the Church still burden itself with obsolete practices which no longer serve their purpose? Many people abandon the Christian religion because they think that science contradicts and nullifies the truths of the Gospels. This simply shows they have not understood the first thing about it, for it is just the opposite: the discoveries of science actually corroborate and emphasize the truths of the Gospels.

I can show you—in fact I have often done so—that the discoveries of science prove the truth of initiatic science, but this is something that neither scientists nor religious people have ever understood. For me there is no contradiction between science and religion; they go hand in hand. In fact they go hand in hand with art too, for the three are intimately related. From science mankind receives light, from religion warmth, and from art activity. Why have human beings separated these three realms that were created to coexist and work together in nature and in human beings? Initiates have never separated science, religion, and art, but today there is a gulf between them, and the result is that religion no longer has a hold on scientists; they reject it out of hand. They reject it, of course, because they do not possess the one true science. Their science focuses only on the physical, material world. They know nothing of the true science on which all religions are based. As for art, it fluctuates uncertainly between the two, in conflict first with one and then with the other.

The true religion is initiatic science. In nature, I repeat, religion, science, and art are one. If they are not one today it is because human beings have separated them, and as long as they continue to separate them, they will never understand anything. Science, religion, and art form a unified whole, thanks to which everything can be understood and explained. Science corresponds to a need of the intellect, religion to a need of the heart, and art to a need of the will, which seeks to express something, to create and build. These three needs are closely related, for we begin by thinking something, but we have to feel it before we can make it a concrete reality.

As a matter of fact, many initiates of the past have reincarnated today as scientists. Yes, many contemporary

Principles and Forms

scientists were once high priests of the ancient Mysteries. Those who discovered radio and television, for instance, were once initiates in ancient Egypt, and they have simply applied the knowledge they acquired in the distant past to the material world. Our era is connected in many ways to Egyptian civilization, and the science of ancient Egypt will soon be known and will manifest itself in many technical applications.

But let us get back to this idea that the Church should change some of its ideas and attitudes. Take just one example: the other day somebody sent me an article about a recent speech by the Pope in which he deplored the activity of the devil who, he said, was poisoning the work of the Church by sowing doubt in the minds of the faithful. Yes, for centuries the devil has been blamed for everything that was wrong. Even now in the 20th century the faults and errors of human beings are still said to be the work of the devil. It is still the devil who moves human beings to act. Do you hear me talking constantly about the devil? Certainly not. Why is he still so conspicuously present in the discourses of religious leaders? In the Middle Ages the devil was present day and night in people's lives. Everything began and ended with him. Nothing else mattered. Even God took second place to Satan. It was he who was held responsible for all miracles and prodigies. It was he who was said to heal the sick and utter prophecies. When a man or woman manifested exceptional gifts or talents they were always said to be inspired by Satan, never by God. Nobody ever said that it was God who was omniscient and all-powerful. No, the all-powerful one was Satan. And the extraordinary thing is that even today, if someone works a miracle or achieves something truly unique, the Church is never very eager to acknowledge it as the work of God or of his angels; it is always suspicious, always ready to see the hand of the devil in everything. But believe me, the more you talk about the devil, the more you nourish and strengthen him and make it possible for him to act.

It seems that people need to fear something, so the devil is held up as the great 'bogeyman'. But this is ridiculous, for the only result is that people get so used to him that they no longer fear him (just as birds get accustomed to an old scarecrow and no longer fear it). Now I am not saying that the devil does not exist; he does. But the less we talk about him the better. If you tell people you have done something really astounding they will often exclaim, 'The devil you did!' Why? What has the devil got to do with it? To invoke the name of the devil—and even the fact of being afraid of him—are forms of black magic by which you attract his attention.

It is time the Church had a more intelligent grasp of esoteric science and stopped seeing the hand of the devil in everything. As it is, instead of acknowledging that people are abandoning religion because its representatives are unworthy of their calling, it blames the devil, saying that the devil has infiltrated the Church. How often I have explained to you that if you refuse to entertain the elements that attract the devil and keep your doors resolutely closed to him, he is powerless. This law is absolute. But instead of explaining this, the Church allows the faithful to think that he has the power to enter their inner being and that there is nothing they can do to stop him. We are asked to believe that human beings are so shoddily made (the Lord obviously did not do a very good job.) that, however pure and saintly they may be, the devil can always get into them. Well, this is simply not true. It is the knowledge contained in initiatic science that is lacking in the Church.

Christianity is in need of major transformations, for it is still living in antiquated traditions that are no longer suited to our day and age. Mankind would be much better off today if religion as the Church understands it were really enough, but since it is little more than a series of empty forms, is there any wonder that most people cannot take it seriously any longer?

In any case, people are more and more inclined to think things out for themselves and question what others tell them.

Principles and Forms

In the past they were ready to swallow whatever the Church said because for them the Church was the authority; it was the Church that thought for them, that made decisions for them. But today nobody wants others to do their thinking for them, so they leave the Church. This shows that Christianity will be forced to accept the new forms that are being suggested to it by the invisible world. And the day will come when these new forms will wear out in their turn and will have to be replaced by others. Only principles endure, not forms. Cosmic intelligence has decreed that physical forms should not be permanent. The only function of a form is to keep the contents intact; it is a container, a boundary, a limitation. It is also a prison; and if the contents within a form are not to congeal and become rigid, that form must be broken open and the contents poured into a new, subtler, more flexible, more transparent form. This is why nothing that exists on the physical plane can be eternal. One day everything, even the great pyramids, even the sphinx, will disappear.

Time cannot affect principles, but it does affect forms. To say that all things are corroded and destroyed by time is true only in regard to forms, and Christians have not yet understood that the forms in which their religion was given to them centuries ago cannot last for ever; they are going to have to change them. But Christians are stubborn; they are unwilling to change anything. The teaching of the Universal White Brotherhood offers no new principles, only new forms; that is to say, new methods, methods that allow the content, the spirit, to express and manifest itself more perfectly. The Universal White Brotherhood has no desire to introduce new principles, for principles are eternal; it wishes to renew only the forms, because forms are subject to the wear and tear of time. Remember this one thing therefore: only principles are eternal.

When people are happy about something, they say, 'Long may it last!' Lovers for instance always want their love to last for ever, but unfortunately this is impossible. Why? Because they cast it in fragile, perishable forms. If you want to express your love eternally you are going to have to change its form. Let me give you an example: if you express your love through your lower nature, your personality, even your eyes will reflect the desire to indulge your appetites without a thought for the good of the other person or the effect your actions will have on them. The only thing you want is to satisfy your own hunger and thirst. This is a coarse, cruel, selfish form of love, and the eyes of one who loves in this way become bloodshot and swollen with lust; they express something slimy, impure, and violent.

But when human beings express their love through their individuality, their higher nature, beauty, light and transparency shine from their eyes because such love is selfless. It asks for nothing in return; it wants only to give and to help and enlighten others. This is the most beautiful form of love... and yet most women prefer to see the flame of desire in a man's eyes. When they see this, the poor things are pleased because they imagine that such a love is so intense, potent, and expressive that it will last for ever. The one thing that women long for is a love that will endure—and of course they are right to do so. The only trouble is that they are blind; they do not realize that a sensual look speaks of a love that cannot last. The fire they see is a flash in the pan that will die down as suddenly as it flared up. Why do women have so little discernment?

It is up to you now to cultivate a broader outlook and, above all, to intensify your desire to evolve. For what is evolution? It is simply a change of form. The natural sciences have always had a keen interest in the question of evolution: some say that it is forms that evolve, while others say that forms are predetermined from all eternity and that beings migrate from one form to another. It is this second theory that is correct; forms do not evolve. All forms—whether of animals, insects, or plants—pre exist in the world of archetypes, and individual creatures assume these forms for a

Principles and Forms

time and then discard them and move on to others, exactly as actors put on a new mask for each new play. So the form in which the spirit is clothed is always different, but forms themselves do not evolve. They were created from all eternity, and the future forms of plants and animals that are still unknown to us already exist as archetypes.

New forms have been prepared and are ready and waiting for human beings as well. As our evolution progresses we shall assume these new forms, for we must constantly cast off the old forms and assume new ones that are, purer, more flexible, and more luminous. When we assume a new form we also acquire new and better means of action and manifestation. To remain tied to our old forms would be to limit our progress; we would never get any further. This is what Christians fail to understand. They try to perpetuate the form, but that is not possible. Their attitude is diametrically opposed to the decrees of cosmic intelligence.

Cosmic intelligence has no need to perpetuate forms on the physical plane; they are already eternal. Yes, but they are eternal only in the higher realms, in the world of archetypes. On that level all forms are eternal because they are there to serve cosmic intelligence. It is when men try to perpetuate them on earth, when they cling obstinately to one particular form, that the invisible world is obliged to set them free by taking its sledge-hammers and smashing that form. Human beings are scandalized by what they take to be cruelty on the part of cosmic intelligence, but how could they be free if they were permanently bound to the same form? Are you still not convinced? Very well, but think about what happens to human beings from one incarnation to the next. More often than not they change their sex. If you were a woman in a previous life, it was in order to learn to manifest the qualities of the feminine principle, and now that you are a man you must learn to manifest other qualities.

This apparent cruelty on the part of the invisible world,

which shatters old forms in order to create new ones, is not yet understood by the Church. But whether it understands or not I guarantee that its old forms will be destroyed. However hard Christians try to save their old forms, the invisible world is going to demolish them in order to set them free and oblige them to move on. Human beings always have a tendency to cling to their old ways, and this is precisely what they should not do. What is a materialist? A materialist is someone who clings to material forms. This is why materialists will also be broken, smashed, and wiped out—so that they may be freed.

One day an angel, wishing to study the ways of animals and humans at first hand, decided to come down to earth in the form of a pig. He adapted himself so well to his new state that life in a pigsty seemed to him to be all that was most desirable. He stuffed himself with acorns and pigswill, he took a wife and was soon surrounded by innumerable offspring, and his happiness was complete. Nothing could induce him to abandon such bliss. In the meantime his brother angels were getting very worried about him and tried to decide how to get him back to heaven, for he was enjoying his life as a pig so much that he ignored all their messages. Finally, as a last resort, they decided that there was only one solution, and that was to send him to the slaughterhouse. Well, when the angel was released from his animal form and saw the carcass being roasted for a banquet, he was astounded that he could have forgotten his own identity so completely and was full of gratitude to his fellow angels for rescuing him. Unfortunately a great many human beings are like that angel; they too have become 'pigs', and they too are destined to be butchered. All the philosophies, all the systems, all the traditions that fail to evolve are going to be shattered; only the principles will remain, and they will assume new forms.

The Universal White Brotherhood is a new form of the religion of Christ. Oh, I know, Christians are going to exclaim in horror and take up arms against us to show that they are faithful to the traditions they have inherited. But this is a battle they will not win, for the invisible world will intervene to show them that they are wrong. A new form is going to appear, and it will last for a certain time before it too makes way for yet another more perfect form. As you see, I am being perfectly fair and honest with you, I have no wish to deceive you by telling you that the forms introduced by our teaching are eternal. There will always be new expressions; expressions that will become more and more perfect and luminous.

When people tell me that as Catholics they cannot accept the teaching of the Universal White Brotherhood, I say, 'Very well, if you feel more at home in the Church, stay there. But as for us, we are going to move on.' I ask you, what can you learn from all those sermons that explain nothing at all? Who is to blame if people listen to them and then go on doing all the things they should not do? They leave the Church because it has no answers to their questions, no words with which to allay their anguish. Their sermons are very poetic and also highly moral. Yes indeed, very pretty and very pathetic. I entirely approve of what they say, but you cannot learn much from their words because they contain no real understanding of the meaning and goal of human existence, the laws that govern it, or how to behave in harmony with those laws. It is all words, words, words; no mention of how to put those words into practice. Do you really believe that Christendom has ever put the Gospels into practice? No, the facts speak for themselves. For my part, I am in favour of radical changes; and such changes are coming. You will see them for yourselves.

All those who decide to work with the eternal, unchanging principles of Christ belong to the Universal White Brotherhood. They are not destroying anything; they are not working against Christ; they are not trying to promote a new religion. No, they are simply working to promote new forms. And those who cling to the old forms show that they have not understood the principles. They rely on forms to save them, and they sleep soundly at night in the security of their protection. Yes, those who rely on forms fall asleep; whereas those who rely less on forms and work more with principles evolve very rapidly. Is this not a far better, far more beneficial ideal? Jesus himself tells us how magnificent it is, for we read in the New Testament: 'The letter kills but the spirit gives life,' and that is exactly what I have been trying to explain. I am constantly urging you to turn toward the spirit that gives life.

So, as I say, all those who give the priority to principles belong to the Great Universal White Brotherhood; not to the Brotherhood here on earth, but to that glorious Brotherhood that embraces all the most luminous creatures in the universe. Our role in the world is simply to provide these perfect beings with means and possibilities for action so that the kingdom of God may be established on earth. It is in this sense that the Universal White Brotherhood can be seen as a new form of the religion of Christ, and this is why I say that those who work with the principles of Christ belong to that great Brotherhood. They may not even know of our existence, but that does not matter; they are still members of the Universal White Brotherhood.

Why do human beings cling so stubbornly to forms? The answer is that they are lazy. All their spiritual activity is dead; all that is left to them is to wave the banner of form. Take the case of all those people who wear a cross, for instance: their cross will not save them if they wear it only externally without any participation of the spirit. But if they cling to the principle behind the material cross and try to understand what it means and apply it to their lives, then it can help and protect them. Keep certain forms if you wish, but never lose sight of the spirit behind them, otherwise you too will be lost. Wear a cross if you like, but attach yourself to the spirit, for behind that form is the spirit. For me the cross is a fantastic symbol (a three-dimensional cross is composed of twenty-two planes, corresponding to the twenty-two letters of the Cabbalah with

Principles and Forms

which God created the world). But the Christians of today are really to be pitied; they have no desire to learn. They oppose change in the belief that they are being faithful to Christ; whereas in reality they are only being faithful to human beings, to idiots, to people who are sick.

We must be faithful to God, not to men. If you insist on being faithful to men, very well, that is your own business. I have no objection, but you will end up as dust. What was so special about all those people who ruled the Church for so many hundreds of years? What did they stand for? As often as not they were no different from all the other poor wretches on earth. In fact if any of them manifested a higher degree of understanding they were immediately banished, excommunicated. Look at the historical record and you will see for yourselves: all those who really wanted to reform things were cast out and rejected. Yes, for the sake of forms. But form is not very productive; all it can do is imprison human beings. Form is a perfect prison. If you are a prisoner of form you can never escape.

A form should be preserved only as long as necessary, as long as it is indispensable or simply useful. As soon as it becomes obsolete it means that a new phase has begun and we must either replace it or reach a much more profound understanding of it. There are a certain number of rites, such as Baptism, Marriage, the Mass, and Communion, that are founded on eternal laws and a knowledge of magic. This is particularly true of the Mass, which is pure magic. In fact it would be true to say that it is thanks to the Mass that the Church has endured until today. The sad thing is that a great many priests do not realize the profound significance of what they are doing when they celebrate the Mass. If they understood it, the power of the Mass would be even greater.

Then there is the custom of lighting candles and votive lights in church. Take the example of the Easter ceremony in Orthodox churches: everyone in church holds a candle and the celebrant begins by lighting his own candle. He passes on the flame to the candle of the priest or deacon standing next to him, who passes it in turn to the person beside him. And so it goes on, each one receiving light from one neighbour and handing it on to another until the whole church is ablaze with light. Symbolically speaking, this means that there must be someone who begins by lighting his candle, that is to say, his intelligence, his mind. Once he holds a lighted candle others will come and light their candles, their intelligence, from his, until all the men and women in the world form a multitude of lighted candles. The symbolism of the votive light is identical to that of the candle except that a candle is a masculine symbol whereas a vigil light is feminine. But this is such a profound and sacred question that I dare not tell you any more than that.

Man has a candle and woman has a votive light, but neither of them knows that they have something that needs to be set alight. Christians automatically light candles and votive lights, but I have never seen one who knew anything about the mystery involved in this act, who knew how and why they should be lit. And yet what great transformations they could work in themselves if only they knew. This is why I say that Christians have not yet begun their real work. Even if they go to church, light candles, bless themselves with holy water and receive Communion, they have still not begun, because they have not yet done these things inwardly. They hang a little icon of the Virgin Mary in their homes and imagine that whatever they do the Virgin will always be there to protect them, but this is nothing but superstition. They count on this and believe in that, but belief and faith are two quite different things.

Most people who think they have faith actually have nothing but a collection of beliefs. Yes, because they are too attached to forms. They do not realize that even prayers can be no more than forms. There is a story about a monk who was in the habit of paying secret visits to the wine-cellar every evening. It was his péché mignon, his favourite weakness, and

Principles and Forms

he was incapable of giving it up. Every night he would say his prayers and ask God to forgive him and then sleep soundly with a clear conscience—as though by mumbling an act of contrition he could put everything right. One night he was rudely awakened from sleep by someone shaking him and saying: 'Wake up, wake up! You forgot to say your prayers.' And whom did he see beside his bed but the devil himself. All of a sudden he understood that the devil had taken the trouble to come and remind him to say his prayers, because it was the devil who benefited from them, not he. If he continued to say his prayers in the belief that he was automatically forgiven, then he could go on drinking. It was certainly not the Lord who had come to wake him up. The Lord does not hear a drunkard's prayers. So you see, often enough it is the devil who hides behind forms and urges you to go to church, light a candle, say your prayers, or receive Communion. In this way he helps you to become more and more deeply entrenched in these old forms.

I have nothing against Communion. The only thing is that I see so many Christians who receive Communion all their lives long, who have already swallowed wagonfuls of hosts and drunk barrels of wine, and who are still as vicious, aggressive, slanderous, and unjust as ever. Whereas if you communicate with the perfect, living host of the sun as it rises every morning and with the wine of life that flows from it, it will not be long before you find that you are obliged to transform yourself. Yes, because the sun is alive. This is what Jesus meant when he said, 'Unless you eat the flesh of the Son of Man and drink his blood, you have no life in you. Whoever eats my flesh and drinks my blood has eternal life.' [1] At the time Jesus said this people were incapable of understanding such advanced ideas; this is why they had to be given bread and wine. But that era belongs to the past; today we must go much further. The fact

---

[1] See *Complete Works*, vol. 1, chap. 5.

that a man can be a regular communicant and still continue to beat his wife or slander his neighbour is surely proof that this kind of Communion is not very effective. Communion can help, of course; if you have faith, it can help. However, in spite of your faith, in spite of the strength of your convictions, and in spite of the priest's blessing, the sun is more potent than any number of hosts.

The blessing given by a priest is very important, that is true; but the quality of his blessing depends on his own elevation, purity, and faith. I am afraid that many priests are so sick of repeating the same gestures over and over again every day that they mumble the words of consecration without putting their soul or spirit into what they are saying. So the bread and wine are blessed, but with a blessing that is not very potent. Besides, even if a priest puts his whole heart and soul into the blessing I feel like asking: 'If you believe that the words of consecration are so powerful, could you not just as well consecrate some wood shavings or scraps of metal and distribute them to the faithful?' The truth is that in blessing bread a priest is blessing something that has already been blessed by the Creator. The wheat from which the host is made is alive, and this means that it has already been blessed by God. The blessing it contains is life itself.

To conclude, let me repeat that it is time to do away with the old forms that you still stand up for and try to defend. You think I am exaggerating, but I know that once you see the question more clearly you will not only agree with me, but you too will find these old forms irksome and intolerable and be anxious to free yourselves from them.

The Bonfin (France), August 11, 1972

II

I want to add a few words today to what I have already told you about forms and principles, for it is important that the question should be clear to you. You must not think that I am against all forms—certainly not. Forms are useful and necessary but they must not be expected to last for ever. After a time they need to be changed.

As I have said, a form is simply a receptacle, a container. This is easy to understand. Take the example of the clothes we wear: does a man wear the same clothes, the same trousers, shoes, or shirts, from the age of two to the age of ninety? Of course not. He always needs trousers, shoes, and shirts, but at intervals, as his size and shape changes, he grows out of his old clothes and needs new ones. And just as each human individual grows and changes, so the world itself evolves and needs new forms that correspond to that evolution. Centuries ago mankind was like a new-born baby, but today that baby has begun to grow out of its swaddling clothes; it needs to exercise its arms and legs—and in doing so it claws and bites and kicks out in all directions.

The only real question is which forms to retain and which to change. As long as you are on earth you have to preserve and even protect the form of your physical body. You have to keep it healthy, well-groomed and expressive; but for how long? Only until the day you depart for the next world. There always comes a moment when this form has to be cast off like a threadbare garment. Perhaps you are wondering why the ancient Egyptians tried to preserve the physical forms of the pharaohs, and why our museums are still full of their mummies. In reality, the ancient Egyptians knew very well that forms cannot be preserved. They mummified the bodies of their pharaohs for purposes of magic, for they were very advanced in the knowledge and practice of magic.

It would take far too long to mention all the different instances in which forms change, but the example of dress is very significant. Only a few years ago the well-dressed man wore a carefully pressed suit, carried a walking stick and wore a hat, gloves, and even spats. And today? Today there are no more walking sticks, no more gloves, and men's trousers are all crumpled. These are the new forms. And women are in even more of a hurry than men to abandon old forms. Every year, several times a year in fact, fashion obliges them to change forms. This is why I must address myself particularly to women, because women are the first—the only ones—to take this question of changing forms seriously. Ah, women, the marvellous creatures! How they love to change their hats, their shoes, their dresses. Just wait and see how many new forms there will be next year. Nobody ever criticizes the leaders of fashion for bringing in new fashions every few months, and yet when I speak about changing forms everyone is up in arms against me. I ask you, is that fair? Dress designers are applauded when they change forms, but when I suggest that some forms should be changed everyone is against me. How unjust people are!

Of course, many of the forms that still exist served a useful purpose in the past, because when they were first developed, human beings could not understand anything more advanced.

Principles and Forms

But they must not be allowed to last for ever. We have to see how nature deals with this question; it is nature that leads animals and men to adopt certain patterns of behaviour and then, after a while, it is again nature that urges them to change their ways and behave differently because times have changed. Take the example of fear: nature has cultivated the reflex of fear in animals for their own protection. Fear is a healthy reaction in an animal because it warns it to flee when it is in danger. But if human beings are to attain a higher degree of evolution they need to rid themselves of fear, and replace it with other, nobler sentiments. There always comes a time, therefore, when nature recognizes the need to change patterns that she herself defined hundreds and thousands of years before. There are many different kinds of fear: the fear of public opinion, the fear of falling ill, the fear of financial ruin, and so on. But we must no longer be ruled by fear. It was necessary for our own self-preservation at an earlier stage of evolution but today it is a serious obstacle to spiritual progress.

Fear is a very striking example of something that was necessary or useful in the past and that may no longer be useful today. It is nature herself that has taught me this, for I continue to study in her school. Unfortunately, Christians never turn to nature to learn how she envisages things and how long she intends them to last. They think that something that was decreed by human beings in the past must remain valid for all eternity. The trouble is that human beings are not qualified to foresee everything; they do not know what life will be like a few centuries from now. Scientists are always making predictions about the future and telling us what is going to happen, but the only way to be sure is to go and find out from cosmic intelligence; for it is cosmic intelligence that planned things a very long time ago.

For centuries, the Church taught that a life of poverty and destitution was a spiritual ideal. It is true that poverty can be a good exercise; it can help you to become stronger. In other words it can be good for a period of training, but cosmic intelligence has not designed us for a life of perpetual deprivation. Our heavenly Father is not poor and destitute, and there is no reason why we should be. So poverty can be a good exercise for a time (in fact, when the sages first taught the practice of poverty it was as an exercise to counteract certain excesses), but it should not be seen as an ideal in life. The Lord wants us to be as rich, as beautiful, and as powerful as he is. If he has created us in his image, it is not so that we might eat rotten, mouldy fruit and live in the midst of filth and disease, wear hair shirts and flagellate ourselves. Human beings can no longer be expected to abide by such rules of life. A life of poverty can no longer be held up as an ideal, and people are less and less ready to believe that it is a good thing.

Heaven has a curriculum, an itinerary mapped out for us, but it is a course, a route to be followed, not a permanent abode. The plans of the invisible world are not what human beings imagine. Many saints and prophets acted on orders from heaven and carried out their assigned tasks faithfully and well, but special missions of this kind were only valid for a certain period; they were designed to encourage people to develop certain faculties which they still needed. Once those faculties were acquired, the next phase of the curriculum was waiting for them. As far as poverty is concerned, therefore, there is no reason why it should not be practised for a limited period as an exercise. For my part, almost half my life has been a life of poverty—of destitution, in fact. But does this necessarily have to go on for ever? No. On the other hand there is no necessity for me to go to the opposite extreme, for in doing so I would lose all that I had gained by the practice of poverty. Well, there is a great deal more that could be said about this question, but it will have to wait.

Even if you possess all the gold in the world, you still need light. You also need to know what to take for yourself and how much to take, where to stop. There was once a Turk, a member of the Sufi sect of Whirling Dervishes, who lived in Bulgaria. The Dervishes lead very frugal lives, and when they ask for something people are happy to give it to them immediately, for they are much loved and well known for their integrity. One day, when this Dervish asked a rich man for alms, the man offered him his purse full of money, but the Dervish took just one coin, enough to cover his basic needs for that day. This is what you should do, too. Even if you possess great wealth you should only take very little, the strict minimum, for yourself.

And now let me tell you frankly that the reason why so many religious orders and spiritual movements are in error is simply that they fail to understand the Lord's plans for mankind; they cannot see things from his point of view. The tragedy is that human beings always see and judge things with their own limited intellects, and in this way they distort reality and hinder the Lord's plans. The truth is that they are not concerned about what the Lord has in mind for us, but only about precepts which were formulated by human beings centuries ago and which are now obsolete. God manifested himself through Jesus, true, but he had already manifested himself through Moses. If Moses accomplished so much that was extraordinary, it was because God was with him. But by the time Jesus came, the intransigence of the Law of Moses was no longer appropriate to the plans of cosmic intelligence for the development of mankind.

Human beings find it so difficult to discard old forms. The different religions still treat those who are not of their flock with hostility and intransigence; they still think of them as pagans, infidels, sinners. Why should these old forms, which are an impediment to the coming of the kingdom of God, not be replaced with new ones? I tell you, it is the Churches that stand in the way of the kingdom of God. Fortunately, young people are getting rid of many of the old forms. They are eager to travel to other countries, to love all human beings, to understand and help everyone. However, new forms have yet to be found for these manifestations, for they often degenerate and slip back into the old forms. If new impulses are forced into old forms, the old forms split open. Jesus said: 'No one puts new wine into old wineskins; otherwise, the skins burst, and the wine is spilled, and the skins are destroyed.' And this is exactly what happens with young people: they have a new wine that is foaming and fermenting, but they put it in old wineskins. Young people want to love freely, and this is magnificent, but why do they think that they can only do so by sleeping together and wallowing in sensual pleasure? New and better forms must be found.

How can we find these better forms? Well, they will certainly not be found by the blind groping of ignorant human beings. Or rather, they could be found in this way, but the process would take hundreds and thousands of years and involve a great many mishaps on the way. The best way is for an initiate to explain things, for only an initiate knows how mankind is destined to mature and blossom in new, innocent forms. The trouble is that human beings are not willing to accept the opinions of the initiates; they want to find their own solutions, and the results are always disastrous. Even when they do find a solution, they are incapable of putting it into effect because it is always too late; they find it only when they have already wasted their energy in futilities. They are already old, worn out, human wrecks. And if they try to tell other people what they have learned from their painful experience, nobody listens to them: 'How can you imagine that you have anything to teach us? Just look at yourself in the mirror.'

Cosmic intelligence has other plans for mankind today. There was a time when disciples had to swear that they would never divulge the secrets revealed to them by their initiator. But then the Marquis of Saint-Yves d'Alveydre, a well-known French spiritual writer, published his book 'The Mission of India' in which he tells of how one of the leaders of Agharta saw in his meditation that the pyramid of light that shone over

Principles and Forms 33

Agharta was split in two. When he asked cosmic intelligence what this meant he was told that although the mysteries had traditionally been hidden from non-initiates, the time was coming when they would be revealed to all those who were capable of understanding them. Incidentally, the Bible also says that the time will come when all that was hidden will be revealed; and that time is now upon us, so there is no cause to be astonished if you see that many great secrets are revealed in the Universal White Brotherhood.

In the past, the truths of initiation were revealed very sparingly and only at the price of terrible trials. This is why those who received them could use them to become extraordinarily powerful. But now that people receive them without having to make any effort of their own, they are incapable of using them to become powerful. They are like those who have a lot of money without having earned it: they waste it; they have no true appreciation of its value. Whereas those who have to earn their living by the sweat of their brow are fully aware of the value of money. How true this is. However, in spite of all this, the great mysteries must gradually be revealed, for that is the will of heaven. Actually, you yourselves already know far more than even the sadhus and yogis of India. Their knowledge is not very extensive, but they use the little they know to acquire great powers; whereas you who know a great deal are not capable of achieving very much.

In our times also, initiation will take a different form. In the old days it was given in the temples, and candidates had to endure trials by fire, air, water, and earth. Nowadays, it occurs in the course of everyday life: an initiate places his disciples in certain situations, confronts them with certain problems, and observes their reactions without their even being aware that he is doing so. All your trials occur in the ordinary course of life; the four elements are present in your lives. It is in your everyday lives that you have to show that you have overcome fear, concupiscence, egoism, sensuality, and so on. Yes, there are many trials in everyday life, and this is particularly true for those who want to advance towards initiation. They can be sure in advance that their desire will be granted, but they can also be sure that they will be put to the test. When they are least expecting it, in the ordinary course of their lives, they will be tested. The trials of initiation are part of life; every minor event of our lives can be a testing. In fact it is precisely because people underestimate the importance of these little things and expect their trials to take the shape of a major event that they often fail.

When you have advance warning that you are going to have to confront great difficulties you are better armed, better prepared; you can plan for what lies ahead. But when you are taken unawares it is much more difficult, so it is up to you to be awake and on your guard. You must constantly remind yourselves that every little event or circumstance can be an initiatic test. And your response will be judged by beings in the world above—and perhaps also in this world if you have a master on earth. If you pass the test you will be awarded a diploma, but not the kind of diploma that you get at a university and that can fade or be torn, burned, or stolen. The diplomas of the invisible world adhere to your face and your whole body; nobody can ever take them away from you. And the spirits of nature, who know how to read these diplomas, will welcome and appreciate you if you have one. Otherwise, wherever you go throughout the whole of space, if they see that you have not earned your diploma they will have no respect for you. They will even persecute you because they will consider you to be a weak, ignorant, useless creature.

I could point out thousands of examples of forms in which human beings have become bogged down. Take the case of medicine. It is reduced to nothing but forms: pills, capsules, drops, surgical operations, all these are forms. What has happened to the spirit? There is no life in these things, nothing to trigger or evoke something spiritual, something divine.

Principles and Forms

No, it is all forms. This is why people never get any healthier, why they are always weak and sickly.

Those who cling stubbornly to the same old forms become fossilized and lifeless because they dam up their inner spring. One often sees people like that, people who always have the same blank, wooden expression. It is dangerous to cling always to the same form. In fact this is one of the reasons why so many marriages break up. The man and wife are sick of seeing always the same gestures and expressions, of hearing the same words every day. They never see anything new or expressive in each other. In the long run they cannot bear it any longer, and they both go off and look for new forms. Many couples have never thought about this, and yet it is often the reason why they separate. If you are always the same, other people will get bored with you and begin to dislike you. Always try to renew yourselves therefore; be alive and expressive and no one will ever want to leave you, because you will always be sparkling with new life, always expressive.

But women have never understood this—neither have men for that matter. A woman faithfully does her duty by her husband: she takes care of him, washes his clothes, irons his shirts, cooks his meals—and even keeps him supplied with the little confections he loves—and then one fine day he leaves her for another woman. She cannot understand it at all. What has happened? Everything she did was for him. Yes, but she was always the same and her husband got bored with her.

One day a woman came and complained to me that her husband had deserted her. 'And yet,' she moaned, 'I always did everything I could to make him happy. I was always so devoted, so loving.'

'Ah, yes, and what is the other woman like?'

'Oh she's cold. She's a block of ice.'

'Well, there you are; you were always too warm and he has gone off with that other woman because he needs to cool off.'

So you see, it is not good always to be too warm, otherwise your partner will have to go and find someone cooler.

You must know how to have variety in your life, but variety in the forms, not in the principles. You must always adhere to the same principles, always be animated by the same love, the same light, the same nobility, the same ideal; but you must not always manifest them in the same way. What an extraordinary thing the Universal White Brotherhood is. What extraordinary power it has to vivify and exalt us, to fill us with awe, wonder, and enthusiasm. The great clairvoyant Rudolf Steiner saw this. He said, 'When I have gone, someone else will appear whose work will be marked by enthusiasm.' The keynote of Steiner's work was not enthusiasm; it was philosophy, science. I know nothing about either philosophy or science—or anything else for that matter—but I am capable of firing you with enthusiasm.

And now, in conclusion, always remember that everything in life is the product, the result of the relation between the two opposite poles: spirit and matter, principles and forms. Human beings are not capable of living only with principles; they need the support of forms. The spirit incarnates in the form of a body in order to manifest on the physical plane. When it returns to the higher regions it no longer needs this form, but here on earth it does need it. We have to remember, however, that the form cannot last long. God has not given eternal life to forms. This is why heaven sends an initiate or a great master every now and then to change the forms. Yes, but forms only; never the principles. The principles are unchangeable because they are the spirit, the soul, the virtues; they are love, wisdom, truth, and sacrifice. These principles are immutable; they will be valid for all eternity.

The Bonfin, August 17, 1972

Chapter Two

The True Religion of Christ

I

When I say that the teaching of the Universal White Brotherhood is bringing a new religion to the world, it is not that I think that this teaching is an improvement on the religion that Jesus gave us. That is impossible. Jesus truly represents the summit; nothing can be more perfect than the law of love and sacrifice that he came to teach. It is only in the methods, applications, and interpretations of that law that we can go further. The Gospels do not say it all; there are still so many things that are obscure and unexplained. And this is what the teaching of the Universal White Brotherhood can bring us: the explanations we still need.

Also, when I say that it is time for a universal religion, it is because Catholicism is not fully universal. Of course, the word 'catholic' means universal, but the fact remains that the Catholic religion is not universal. In the first place it is far from being practised by all human beings, and, above all, by rejecting many essential truths such as reincarnation, the laws of karma, and the primordial role of the sun in man's spiritual life, the Church has cut itself off from universal truth and become a sect. For a religion to be truly universal it must accept the whole truth and it must reach all men.

As it is, no religion in the world is founded on principles

that are accepted by all human beings. Only a solar religion can be the universal religion, because all human beings accept the sun. We all seek the sun and understand what it is. Everything else interests some but not others; suits some but not others. In fact, if there are so many different religions, it is because each one is adapted to a particular mentality. If the claim of the Catholic Church to be universal is true, if it embraces every aspect of truth, why do I never see Catholics who are truly fulfilled spiritually? A great many Buddhists are far more advanced. They have such faith in the immortality of the soul that they are capable of throwing themselves into the flames. They have no fear of death. Whereas Christians are so timid, so lacking in courage, that they tremble at the slightest threat and scream in terror if they are in danger of death.

As I have said, a universal religion must embrace all the knowledge and all the practical methods human beings need in order to reach the Lord. When Christianity refuses to teach reincarnation it makes it impossible for people to understand God's justice. Is there any wonder that nothing makes sense to them any more? They cannot see the underlying reason for what happens to them; everything seems illogical and unfair. In the face of evil or suffering, Christians can only say, 'It is the will of God.' The amazing thing is that they consider themselves to be blameless, above reproach. They have done nothing to bring misfortune on themselves; it is entirely the Lord's doing. But this means that God behaves without rhyme or reason; his decisions are completely arbitrary.

For centuries their refusal to believe in reincarnation has barred Christians from advancing. The doctrine of reincarnation explains everything: from one existence to the next, every cause triggers a corresponding consequence. When we know this we know that it is no longer the Lord who is to blame for what happens to us, but we ourselves. By choosing to follow a certain path, to manifest ourselves in a certain way, it is we who are responsible for our destiny, not God. God's sublime greatness, his splendour, perfection, and justice are untouched, unsullied. Whereas if you reject reincarnation you have to put all the blame on God. It seems to me that if Christians were really concerned about the glory and perfection of God, the least they could do would be to accept reincarnation. They are so stupid that they do not even recognize the consequences of their attitude; they do not realize that the image of God they hold up to the world is a monstrous caricature. God gave human beings free will. He tells them, 'Do whatever you like, but remember that if you break the law you will suffer. But that does not matter; you have all eternity ahead of you. You will have plenty of time in which to repent and make reparation. I am patient.'

Take a man who is miserable because he is married to a shrew, a veritable Xanthippe, and he has no idea why he has such a wife. He thinks she must be a punishment from heaven. Not at all. It was he himself who sought her out, who chose her. Yes, like Socrates. But Socrates knew what he was doing when he married Xanthippe; whereas this poor fool chose a shrew without knowing what he was doing, and now he regrets it bitterly. Socrates never complained; he put up with everything patiently. One day, while he was talking to a friend, Xanthippe was muttering and scolding in an upstairs room and ended by pouring a pail of slops over him. The friend was very indignant, but Socrates only remarked, 'Oh well, after the thunder comes the rain.' He was not so easily put out. He had chosen to marry Xanthippe, and thanks to her he developed great patience and indifference in the face of criticism and insults. So my advice to you is to find a Xanthippe for yourself. Why do you want your wife to be perfect? You would only go to sleep and stop evolving if she were; but think of what progress you would make with a Xanthippe by your side. You see what excellent advice I always give you!

By refusing the reality of reincarnation the Church is portraying the Lord as a monster and a tyrant. In any case, quite apart from this, there is much to object to in the image the Church presents of God, for it has inherited the Old Testament notion of a jealous, vengeful, terrifying God, always ready to punish and chastise human beings. And I say that this view is false. God is not like that at all. Why did the Old Testament present him in this way? The answer is that the human beings of those days were at a stage of their evolution where they needed the discipline of fear. They needed to envisage a stern, ruthless God with whom Moses could intercede to soothe his wrath and turn him away from the destruction of his people. The truth is that God never punishes anyone; he is not concerned with punishment. He spends his time up there in the midst of song and music, banqueting in the company of his angels and archangels while divine nectar and ambrosia flow in abundance. Do you imagine that the Lord has nothing better to do than to follow human beings around day and night, writing down in his little notebook all the filthy, revolting things they do, whether openly or in secret? Poor Lord, what a job. Think how disgusted he would be.

No, I do not believe a word of it. I think that if human beings have invented machines to record and do their calculations for them, it is because such machines already existed in nature and therefore within us also. It is these machines that record our thoughts, feelings and actions, and as soon as we overstep the mark, in whatever area, the machine cracks down on us. But it is not God who punishes us. On the contrary, God is always ready to welcome us to his banquet.

Let us suppose that you are being pursued by enemies (you may remember that I spoke to you about this one day), and in order to get away from them you run and run as fast as you can until you get to heaven. And there, breathless, covered with dust, your clothes all tattered and torn, you suddenly find yourself in the midst of a magnificent assembly of angels and archangels. Dumbfounded, you gaze at these beautiful creatures as they sing and rejoice with the Lord, who is seated

The True Religion of Christ

in their midst. Nobody says, 'What are you doing here, you dirty ruffian? Away with you. This is no place for you.' On the contrary, as soon as he sees you the Lord says to his servants, 'Give him water to wash with, dress him in fine clothes, and let him come and share in our banquet.' But the enemies that were pursuing you will not be allowed in. They are made to wait outside, and as the banquet lasts a long time they finally lose patience and go home. Yes, this is how it works. Have you never realized that? You have all known days when you were overwhelmed and besieged by your inner enemies, and then you started to pray and pray and pray... and within a few minutes you had a wonderful feeling of happiness and release; your enemies had left you. You must try to understand what this image means.

Do not think that I have come to destroy the Church, not at all. It is just that I possess a light that the Church does not possess at the moment, but I am very willing to collaborate with it. In fact I have already tried to do so. I have often met priests, Dominicans and Franciscans, and others and have tried to talk to them, but I have never had much success. Oh, perhaps I succeeded with two or three of them, but not with the others. The trouble is that their minds have been so deformed by their seminary training that there is nothing anyone can do now to persuade them to accept the light of these great truths. This is why I prefer to deal with atheists, unbelievers, and anarchists; I am much more successful with them. But with the religious? My word, how rigid, bigoted, and narrow-minded they can be! I have every confidence that this will change one day, but not before they have had to endure all kinds of tribulations and been forced to reflect.

If the Lord is in the process of creating a new heaven and a new earth (and this is what the Bible tells us), why should there not also be a new religion? New in exactly the same way as heaven and earth can be new. Of course the expression is symbolic; I have already explained to you that you must not take it literally. If you did, you would have a very bad impression of the Lord and would feel quite safe in saying that he was neither wise nor omniscient. It would mean that he had used second-rate materials when he built heaven and earth, and now they are rusting and wearing out. This is why he has to start all over again... and while he is rebuilding, all the inhabitants of heaven and earth are going to be out in the rain without a roof over their heads. No, that is just nonsense. The truth is that the new heaven and new earth refer to us; it is within us that God is creating them. The new heaven is a new mentality, a new philosophy, a new point of view, a new understanding of things; and the new earth is a new behaviour, a new way of doing things. This is how you should interpret this image of the new heaven and the new earth. To understand it any other way would be to slight the Lord. It would mean that he did not know the properties of the elements that he himself created and now he finds that they are rotting and wearing out. Whereas if you interpret this image as I have shown you, the Lord's greatness, immensity, and infinite wisdom remain intact.

Of course, I know that you will not accept what I tell you, but you must at least try not to cling rigidly to your own opinions until you have made quite sure that they really correspond to the truth. There are still a great many of you who hold obstinately to your own point of view. Instead of trying to understand what I tell you, you think to yourselves, 'Oh no, that is not true. It cannot be. It is monstrous. I know how it should be.' But there comes a time in life when you simply have to ask yourself whether your own point of view is really correct, really flawless. Unfortunately, so many men and women prefer to cling to their point of view, to defend it all their life long, without ever trying to find out to what extent it is realistic and true. And that is very dangerous. Many people's lives end in disaster simply because they insist on defending their mistaken philosophy at any price. Yet those same people

The True Religion of Christ

find it normal to go for a physical check-up from time to time. They get a doctor to examine their heart, stomach, liver, spleen, or intestines and tell them what is wrong with them, but they would never go and ask a spiritual master to tell them what was wrong with the way they felt and understood things. They consider that in these areas they are in perfect health: their thinking is all right, they see things clearly, their judgement is impeccable, they reason perfectly. But what proof do they have that all this is so perfect? The proof of their misfortunes, sorrows, and failures. Yes, and yet they continue to believe that they are impeccable.

The whole world will one day come to the Universal White Brotherhood. At the moment you do not believe me when I say this, because there are more and more new teachings and new sects—not to mention all the ancient practices that had died away and are now being revived. Every one of these groups and philosophies has some good in it, but they all lack one essential element: none of them gives priority to the necessity of living for the collectivity, for brotherhood, for universality. Their members work for themselves, for their own advancement. And does mankind benefit from all that knowledge and power? It does not. Indeed, they themselves are often very unhappy people. So you must leave all those things alone and work only to bring peace, happiness, joy, and light to the whole world. True power and true knowledge are given to those who work unselfishly for the whole world. You will not know exactly how these gifts come, but they will come to you and dwell within you. It is when one stops thinking so much about oneself that one becomes truly formidable, because in this way one widens the circle. This is the new teaching that we are bringing to the world.

The Bonfin, August 11, 1974

II

All religions set aside one day of the week as a holy day, a day of prayer, but they have not all chosen the same day: for the Christians it is Sunday, for Jews, Saturday, for Muslims, Friday, and so on. But is there any real difference between the days of the week? No, none at all. Every day is sacred; every day is divine. Friday is the day for doing good; Saturday is the day for doing good; Sunday is the day for doing good. In the Universal White Brotherhood every day must be sacred. Otherwise just look what happens: for six days in a row men and women break the law, and on the seventh they go to church and wash away the crimes committed during the week. But you cannot purify yourself in just one day; you need the whole week for that. You believe that it is enough if you think of God one day in the week; the rest of the week you have no time to remember him because you are too busy fighting and swindling others and sleeping with their husbands or wives. But that is grotesque. It is hypocrisy, a living lie. What is important is how you live those six days of the week.

When the new religion comes the idea of devoting a few hours or a single day of the week to praying and going to church will be thought very inadequate. We must be in God's church all day and every day, for God's church is the whole of creation. Of course, I realize that we cannot ask too much of human beings; they are still too uncouth and intractable— many think that even one day is too much. But in the new religion people will want to be mystical seven days a week; they will want to be pure seven days a week; they will want to pray and think good thoughts seven days a week, and then seven more days, and so on, for the rest of their lives. What do you do when you are here at the Bonfin? Here, every day is Sunday—or Saturday, or Friday if you prefer—and you spend every day in 'church'. 'What church?' you ask, 'I see no church.' The church can be the open-air, out of doors, for the whole of nature is a church. But first and foremost the church is an inner reality; it is within yourselves.

Remember what Jesus said to the Samaritan woman at the well. She had said, 'Our ancestors worshipped on this mountain, but you say that the place where people must worship is in Jerusalem.' And Jesus replied, 'Woman, believe me, the hour is coming when you will worship the Father neither on this mountain nor in Jerusalem... God is spirit, and those who worship him must worship in spirit and truth.' But as the time was not yet ripe for the masses to understand these things, Jesus prepared St John and instructed him in the basic philosophical, cabbalistic, esoteric knowledge, the symbolic foundation of these new concepts. This he did in secret, without the knowledge of the other disciples, and when the others found out about it they were inclined to be envious of St John; in fact, St Peter reproached Jesus for it one day. But Jesus wanted to be sure that before he left at least one of his disciples would be in possession of those parts of his teaching that had not been revealed to all. This is why he gave St John this special instruction. And St John founded a Church which was never really accepted or understood by the Church of St Peter.

Remember also what Jesus said at the very end when Peter,

referring to St John, asked, 'Lord, what about him?' Jesus replied, 'If it is my will that he remain until I come, what is that to you?' And the Gospel adds, 'So the rumour spread in the community that this disciple would not die.' What if St John were living even today in some unknown place. The Church of St John has formed an elite, an elite that has always worked in secret and been the depositary of this esoteric science throughout the ages. The religion of St John is the new religion that is to come, and however fiercely the Catholic, Orthodox, and Protestant Churches fight it—as they have always fought and tried to wipe out the Church of St John—they will be no more successful now than they have been in the past.

All the purest and most knowledgeable initiates of the past have been disciples of St John, and those who belonged to the established Churches have always rejected and persecuted them and refused to acknowledge their superiority. But even though the Church of John has always been forced to live and work in secret, it has never ceased preparing the sons and daughters of God. The time is coming now for it to manifest itself, and when it does so, its riches and its superiority will be visible to the whole world. When that day comes, the Church of Peter will be forced, whether it likes it or not, to transform itself and introduce many reforms. Of course, there are some elite beings in the Church of Peter too, but as for the majority... well, it does not bear thinking of. Instead of applying themselves to learning and trying to become better they have always been content to persecute those who were more advanced.

Do you imagine that over the centuries priests and bishops took Holy Orders for the love of God; because they had a true vocation? Not at all. They did so because it gave them a lucrative and highly respected position (an ideal position for the lazy). They did not have much to do after all—a few Masses and a few prayers to say, an occasional baptism, wedding, or funeral—and the rest of their time was their own. To be sure there were always some who had a genuine vocation and who felt called to dedicate themselves completely to the Lord, and the faithful flocked to such as these in the thousands because of the light that radiated from their souls and lit up their words, their eyes, their very presence. They were true temples of God. But for most of the clergy it was simply a very convenient profession. As a matter of fact, we see the same thing today in the medical profession. In the days of the ancient initiations, only those who had received the gift of healing from God could be doctors. They healed the sick simply by their presence, by speaking a few words or by the laying on of hands. But today people enter the medical profession because it is very lucrative and gives them considerable prestige and influence. The result is that many crooks who are interested only in making a lot of money are steadily poisoning the whole of mankind. No matter, they still pass themselves off as doctors. It is greed, the lust for money, that guides human beings. For many people the choice of a profession depends entirely on the rewards it offers in the way of money or glory. I have no desire to disparage doctors and priests or to interfere with them; I am simply telling you the truth.

The Church of St Peter has always been appallingly intolerant, chopping off heads or burning at the stake all those who refused to think or behave exactly according to the rules it laid down. The members of the Church of St John, on the other hand, have never cut off anyone's head; they have never thrown people into prison; they have always left men and women free to follow their bent while, for their part, they concentrated on trying to be closer to the Lord and to resemble him ever more perfectly. The Church of Peter has held people down in a state of mediocrity and weakness, saying that it was pride—and therefore forbidden—to aspire to resemble God. And yet did Jesus not say, 'Be perfect, therefore, as your heavenly Father is perfect?' This is the supreme ideal; and if some people choose a different ideal, that is their business.

The Catholic religion can boast of being universal if it likes. This may be how it sees itself, but it is not how initiates see it. The universal religion will be the religion of the sun, for only the sun is universal. You will say, 'But what about the Lord? Is God not universal?' Yes, of course he is. But God is so sublime, so inaccessible. People refuse to accept the religion of the sun on the pretext that only God must be adored and worshipped; but God is so far away that they are incapable of getting anywhere near him, and the result is that they are left with nothing. On the pretext that it is forbidden to adore anyone or anything but God, they have no feeling or understanding for anything at all. Is that intelligent? Why do they refuse to admit that only the sun is capable of bringing us closer to God, for only the sun can give us some idea of God's immensity, of his light, his love, and his power? By rejecting the sun, people condemn themselves to remain forever weak, forever immured in cold and darkness.

How peculiar human beings are. Theologians spend their time inventing abstract theories about the Deity. They argue and quarrel fiercely about essence, substance, transcendence, and so on, while the masses have not the least idea what any of these theories mean. But if you suggest that the sun can be an image that has the power to propel them all the way to the Deity... Oh no, that is just too much for them. Well, whether they like it or not, the religion of the future will be the religion of the sun, because it is the sun that most accurately represents the Blessed Trinity.

There is already one whole volume of my lectures about the sun,[1] and yet I have still not told you much. What horizons would be revealed to men if only they understood more about the sun. Take Jesus' command to love our enemies for example.

---

[1] See *Complete Works*, vol. 10.

The True Religion of Christ

How difficult it is to accept such an idea; to love one's friends, perhaps, but to love one's enemies? You will rarely find anyone—even a Christian—who has made up his mind to love his enemies. You cannot even be sure that he loves his friends, so how can he possibly love his enemies? Believe me, if you analyse yourselves sincerely, you will see that nothing is more difficult than to love one's enemies. One wonders where Jesus got this precept from. I will tell you: he got it from the sun. For whether you love the sun or not, it never stops sending you its light and warmth. The sun is the only being who has solved the problem; he even loves, nourishes, and vivifies unbelievers and criminals. Even if you forget all about the important role of the sun in the universe and look only at the moral aspect, the example he gives us is truly noble, truly sublime. Such a peerless example of limitless love is found only very rarely among human beings, even among those who are the most highly evolved. Jesus was one such example, of course. We know that he possessed all powers, authority over all things, for he said, 'All authority in heaven and on earth has been given to me,' but he did not use that authority against his enemies. In fact, in the most bitter moments of his agony he thought of them and prayed for them, saying, 'Father, forgive them, for they do not know what they are doing.'

If you want to know what true morality is, you must learn from the sun; no one else can teach it. Human beings are always eager to tell you what you should do, but they are incapable of putting their own advice into practice; whereas the sun says nothing, his deeds speak for him. He never says, 'You must love your enemies.' He never even says, 'I love you.' No, but he goes on loving everyone all the time. Only the sun can teach us how to discover and respect the moral laws of the cosmos. Human beings make the great mistake of seeking the principles of morality in libraries, in books written by corrupt human beings. They should go and seek instruction from the sun.

Of course we cannot force our teaching or our way of life on anyone. Only very few are ready and anxious to transform themselves and their way of life, and if they have achieved this frame of mind it is because they have already suffered a great deal and have come to realize that if they do not change they will be struck off the roll of the living. The others cannot be forced, they are still too young. They still have many lessons to learn, and they need more experience. What can I do if they do not understand the importance of our spiritual activities: our meals together, the singing, the breathing exercises, the prayers, meditations, and fasting? If they neglect all these means that are put at their disposal and fail to understand how powerful they are, what do you expect me to do about it? I cannot force them; they have to be left to go their own way and learn through suffering. But a vast field of extraordinary activities is lying open before all those who are sincerely interested in making progress. The activities of a disciple are represented symbolically by the twelve labours of Hercules, which are related to the twelve signs of the Zodiac.[2] These are the twelve activities which enable human beings to open their twelve gates and become the New Jerusalem, the city of light, where illness, death, and darkness are no more. The New Jerusalem is the human being who has attained perfection, one who possesses the twelve gates of pearl and whose ramparts are built on the foundations of twelve precious stones.

Believe me, it is the teaching of Christ that I am giving you. There is nothing, absolutely nothing in what I say that contradicts Christ's teaching. What I reveal to you may contradict some of the opinions expressed by certain writers. It may even contradict certain dogmas of the Church which are pure invention and have nothing to do with Christ's teaching, but it contains nothing that is incompatible with Christ's true philosophy. The great question now is whether you prefer the

---

[2] See *Izvor Collection*, N°. 220.

The True Religion of Christ

Scriptures, and particularly the Gospels, in which everything is so simple, or whether you prefer other sources in which that simplicity has been distorted. Until the fourth century Christians, followed the true philosophy of Christ. It was only later that all kinds of deviations appeared.

As was foretold by the Prophet Ezekiel, the changes that will take place in the future will be so great, the light and love of God will be so powerfully and so widely diffused throughout the world, that human beings will learn directly from God himself; they will understand the Scriptures and live a life of perfection; they will prophesy and see visions. When this day comes, mankind will no longer need priests or pastors—or even me. All men will be guided and enlightened directly by the divine spirit. This has been foretold, and it will come about. And all those bigots who hawk their holy medals and relics of the true cross of Jesus (after two thousand years, there must be enough of them to constitute a whole forest.)... all those bigots will be obliged to close shop because people will go directly to the source.

This was what Jesus had in mind when he told the Samaritan woman that men would worship God in spirit and in truth. In spirit and in truth: that is to say, free from matter and free from falsehood. When human beings live in spirit and truth they will no longer need all these crutches; they will be able to walk on their own strong legs. The reality that Jesus visualized was immense, grandiose. The people he saw around him were still very frail, vulnerable, and defenceless, and still dependent on material, external props, but the mankind he envisaged was strong enough to rely only on the inner power of the spirit.

The Bonfin, August 25, 1965

III

The Master reads the Meditation for the day:
Through prayer and meditation a disciple purifies his own temple and calls on the Lord to come and dwell in it. Nothing can be compared to a human body that has been purified and sanctified so that it can become a temple of the Almighty. It is when man is a temple, when he prays in his own temple, that God hears and answers his prayer.

Most human beings are extremely negligent about the purification of their physical bodies. It never occurs to them that their bodies were designed to be temples of the living God and that they should look after them and strengthen and purify them. They continually abuse their bodies by eating and drinking things that are harmful to their health, or by smoking or indulging in various other forms of foolishness. Yes, man's physical body was destined to be a temple, but there is nothing sacred about it any longer, and obviously, in these circumstances, it is not the Lord who will come to dwell in it, but entities of a lower order, all those undesirables that covet filth and feed on impurities.

As I have often said, I have learned a great deal from the world of insects, from ants and bedbugs, for instance. These little creatures possess extraordinary antennae which science has not yet studied. For example, there are not normally any ants in my cottage, but I only have to leave some crumbs of food lying about, and within a few minutes there they are. What special flair, what powers of divination tell them that there are some scraps of food waiting for them, sometimes a long way away? Then, as soon as I sweep up the crumbs, they disappear again. The same is true of flies, fleas, and mice. In fact in the cheap, dirty hotels or doss-houses in the East, for instance, swarms of bedbugs appear all over the ceiling as soon as people are asleep. But the remarkable thing is that they do not attack every sleeper in the dormitory. A bedbug will calculate its position with extraordinary accuracy and drop exactly on to the one person whose blood contains the impurities it needs to feed on. How does it know which target to choose? It examines them all and says, 'No, not that one. Not that one. Ah, there is one that has what I need,' and presto. It drops straight on to its target.

Yes, bedbugs are really very clever. It is thanks to them that I have learned the supreme laws of purity, for the laws are the same on the psychic plane. On every plane there are creatures that sense impurities from afar and flock to feed on them. In every area and on every plane there is food for one or other kind of being. All creatures, both the malignant, evil creatures of darkness and the creatures of good and of light need to eat. In fact the Christians among you were horrified one day when I explained that even God ate. 'What? God needs to eat?' 'Yes, of course, but he does not eat sausages.' 'Then what does he eat?' they ask. Ah, these Christians, when will they ever understand? Genesis tells us that man was created in the image of God, and since man eats, why should God not eat? Yes, God eats. And it is the Seraphim who nourish him with their radiance and their emanations, with substances so subtle, pure, and precious that we can barely imagine them.[3]

[3] See *Complete Works*, vol. 11, chaps. 8, 12 and 16.

As I was saying, most human beings fail to look after their temple properly. But the Scriptures tell us, 'You are the temple of the living God,' and this means that we should take great care of our temple and keep it clean. We must not do what the Jews did with the Temple in Jerusalem and allow all kinds of dirt to accumulate in it (the Jews used to take their cattle, goats, and chickens and sell them in the Temple, so it was in a state of indescribable filth). Jesus was the only one who expressed his indignation at this; everybody else took it for granted. But what is a temple? Certainly not, as some people think, a place in which to entertain all kinds of animals. Taking some rope, Jesus made a whip and drove out all those who bought and sold in the Temple, saying, 'Get rid of all this filth. Stop using my Father's house for your trafficking.'

When a clairvoyant looks at people, he can see that the physical bodies of the majority, instead of being temples of the Most High, have become the dens of wild animals. Like the Jews, human beings have forgotten what their temple is supposed to be. We need the Lord to come back to warn us, to tell us, 'Keep my temple clean, otherwise I shall be obliged to go away and abandon you. I cannot stay in such a dirty place.'

The human beings we see around us are always anxious, troubled, and unhappy, and this is a sign that they have not managed to secure the presence of the Lord in their temple; if they had, that presence would light up their lives. It is high time they asked themselves why they are in such a sorry state. It is time they understood that by feeding their bodies on all kinds of impurities they have opened their doors to the creatures of hell, and that is why God has not blessed them with his presence. Neither can they enjoy the presence of his angels, for although the Lord himself will not dwell within his creatures until they have achieved absolute purity, he may send one or more angels or great spirits to represent him. If you have forgotten about purifying your body and now find yourself in the cold and dark, you must draw the right conclusion and tell yourself, 'It is true, I have done everything I could to get myself into this state. I have opened my doors to all kinds of vile entities, and now heaven has abandoned me.' This is what you must tell yourselves, for this is the truth.

I have already given you several different methods of purification. It is not enough to be dipped into a bowl of water or immersed in a river to be pure, and yet many sects that do not possess the light of initiatic science consider this to be sufficient baptism. No, you can be immersed in physical water as often as you like without becoming any purer, because the power of purification does not belong to physical water but to another kind of water. True baptism is something that concerns all the planes of our being, not only the physical plane. True purification touches the four regions known in the Cabbalah as Assiah, Yetzirah, Briah and Atziluth, which correspond to the four elements—earth, water, air, and fire. The elements are represented in the higher world by four angels belonging to the highest ranks of the angelic hierarchy, the Seraphim—or, as the Cabbalah calls them, the Hayoth ha-Kadosh. You can work at your own purification with the help of these four angels: ask the angel of earth to cleanse your physical body, the angel of water to wash your astral body, the angel of air to purify your mental body, and the angel of fire to sanctify your spirit. A marvellous work of purification can be done in this way if you combine this practice with your breathing exercises. But I have already explained this to you at length,[4] so I shall not enlarge on it today.

If you think about your temple every day in this way, light, warmth, life, and purity will come to dwell in you, and many things will be revealed to you. It is all very simple and clear. But those who continue to soil their temple have no alternative but to find themselves sinking deeper and deeper into corruption and depravity. Look at all the contemporary artists

---

[4] See *Complete Works*, vol. 7.

whose paintings represent the new style that they call 'abstract art'. Why are they so attached to a notion of art that no one else can understand? If the meaning of their work is a secret known only to themselves—and I am by no means sure that they themselves know it—it will never serve to elevate and ennoble others or help them to find God. Would it do you any good if I began to speak a language that was incomprehensible to you? There are certain sects in which, apparently, people speak 'in tongues', but as no one understands a word, no one benefits from what they say—not even themselves. The whole thing is quite senseless. You must speak a language that can be clearly understood by all.

Suppose that you are an artist and that you have a masterpiece—a painting or sculpture—on exhibition: everyone who looks at it should be able to understand what it means. If you created it exclusively for your own satisfaction, then you should not exhibit it. To exhibit a work of art that is incomprehensible to everyone but its author is pointless. Here, too, mankind has gone astray. It has adopted means of expression that have no rhyme or reason and has reached the point where nobody dares to say that contemporary art is, in most cases, an aberration. Everybody applauds and says, 'Amen'. A few years ago in England, a painter exhibited a certain number of abstract paintings that were widely acclaimed by the critics, but when his exhibition was at the height of its success he revealed that those abstracts had been painted by his cat. He had gone out and left his cat in the studio one day, and when he returned he found that it had had great fun getting its paws and tail coated with paint which it had then smeared onto some canvases and produced these abstract 'paintings'. Of course the critics were furious. They had made fools of themselves by going into raptures over paintings produced by a cat. Can you imagine anything more idiotic? If that is art, then any fool, even a babe in arms, can produce whatever they please and exhibit it.

The truth is that if you are an artist you should accomplish something that no one else can accomplish; something so beautiful and edifying that it propels hearts and souls upwards towards perfection, towards the Lord. This is how initiates understand the mission of art: to lead human beings to heaven, not to hell, discord, and disorder. Anyone is free to present horrors to the public in the form of music, drawings, or films, but to do so is a crime against humanity, because in the long run these so-called works of art influence people's minds. If so many people are mentally and emotionally disturbed today, it is because they are imbibing more and more disorder and ugliness from their environment. Whatever one sees and hears influences the nervous system, and when one sees nothing but disorder, that disorder necessarily enters one's being; whereas when one contemplates beauty and harmony, one becomes beautiful and harmonious. This is a law of magic.

How is it possible that artists have never discovered this law? Why have they gone out of their way to find these fads and fashions, while all the time so many splendid things were waiting to be found? The reason is that they have neglected the temple we talked about a few moments ago. They have allowed it to get so dirty that it is now full of all kinds of demonic creatures, and it is these creatures that inspire them and dictate what they do. And the results are hideous. If they had always taken care to cleanse and purify and sanctify themselves and to dedicate themselves to heaven, their ideas, intuitions, and inspirations would be of a different kind. Artists need to be informed; they need to understand that the psychic world is ruled by implacable laws, and if they live a stupid, discordant life they will attract entities of a lower order that will inspire them in evil ways and end by corrupting them completely.

Be sure to purify yourselves every day, therefore (for what you did yesterday was for yesterday, and today you must begin all over again), until your whole being is renewed. The work of purification is something that continues the whole of one's life.

The fact that a baby has been immersed in water on the day of its baptism is no guarantee that it will be protected from invasion by evil spirits for the rest of its life. That kind of baptism is not going to frighten the devil away. Christians have to work every day to enhance and amplify what they received on the day of their baptism. If they make no effort in this direction, the effects of their baptism will eventually be destroyed. But try to get them to understand this! They think that the sacrifice of Jesus has saved all human beings once and for all; that they can sin as much as they like and commit every possible crime and still be saved because the Lord has shed his blood for them. But I ask them, 'If it is true that you have been redeemed, if it is true that all your debts have already been paid, how do you explain the fact that your lives are still plagued by disease, disorder, and tragedy?' And they have no answer. The answer is that it is not enough to have been saved and baptized once. You have to strive all your life long and with all your heart and soul to continue the work of salvation and purification begun at baptism. I have seen some deplorable specimens of proud, self-satisfied Christians who considered that they had been purified once and for all and had no need to do any more. The fact that they had been baptized as Catholics was enough to keep them safe for all eternity. And yet when you see these people in their daily lives you see that they are just as bad—sometimes worse—than everybody else. This is why I am obliged to tell them that they have neither learned nor understood, nor achieved anything. Will they understand us one day? I wonder. It almost looks as though everybody except Christians will understand.

I had a letter recently from some brothers and sisters in Turkey. They told me that they had been invited to a meal with some friends, and that among the guests was an old and very learned Turkish scholar who told them, 'Islam is a marvellous religion, and we are extremely fortunate to be Muslims, but how much better it would be if there were one universal

The True Religion of Christ

religion.' Obviously this learned old man realized that Islam was not the one universal religion, and he is certainly not alone in this. There must be many people throughout the world who are tuned in to the same idea and who realize that it is no longer enough to have so many different religions, each of which is suited to only one race, nation, or tribe, that it is time we found a universal religion.

Well, for my part, I have found that one religion; I belong to the universal religion. In time, when the whole of mankind discovers it, its language will be understood by all, for it is based on the essential needs of all human beings. The central symbol of this religion is the sun, for all mankind needs, understands, and loves the sun. The only universal religion is the solar religion, because behind the sun is the One who is the God of all humanity. The fact that all human beings need the sun proves this. Christians, Buddhists, Muslims, and Jews all have different, seemingly incompatible, notions of God, and in these conditions dissension, hatred, and war will never end. Do you really believe that the Catholics and Protestants in Ireland, who are continually killing each other, have found God?

There are too many religions in the world. This is the cause of all the greatest misfortunes of mankind. One religion is enough, the religion of light, warmth, and life, and this is the religion of the sun. Does the sun strike people dead if they believe in another God? No. He is far too tolerant, far too indulgent. He simply says, 'Believe what you like, but for my part I shall continue to scatter my wealth abroad,' whereas human beings are ready to exterminate anyone who refuses to accept their conception of a God that none of them has ever seen.

But I can say that I have seen the Lord. Yes, I have seen him in the sun, for it is the sun that best expresses divine perfection, that gives us the best image of the most sublime ideal. And we should be like the sun, who never stops pouring out light, warmth, and life and no questions asked. Whether we are

Catholic, Orthodox, Protestant, Jewish, Muslim, or Buddhist, the sun sees us all as children of God. I assure you, in the long run nobody will be able to ignore these great truths; the whole world will come to the one true religion of Christ. It is the spirit of the sun that is Christ. Of course, it is not a question of seeing Christ in the disc that we see shining in the sky, but of sensing that God himself, with all his love, is there behind that sun, behind that symbol. This is why my one desire is to sweep away all the narrow, limited notions that mankind has accumulated over the centuries and show you what I know, what has been revealed to me: the light of this universal religion, this religion of Christ that will be the only religion of the future.

The religion taught by Jesus was perfect; I am not denying that. But it has been so distorted in the course of the centuries that it has become a rich culture medium in which every kind of noxious germ ferments and proliferates. This is why it is time to abandon all these false ideas and rediscover the one universal religion, the religion that has existed since the beginning of the universe and that will continue to exist until the end. The sun existed long before human beings appeared on the earth, but they have never really understood the message he sends them every day: 'Be like me, shine, radiate, give, love, and pour out warmth and life.' Human beings are so wrapped up in their own prosaic, insignificant concerns that they never think of looking at the sun and trying to resemble him. They say, 'What is the use of the sun? It has not managed to make mankind any better or kinder; it has not taught or enlightened human beings.' That is true, but it is because mankind has never been allowed to see the true importance of the sun. The Church is like Mullah Nashrudin, who, in response to a student's question as to which was the more important, the sun or the moon, replied, 'The moon, of course. The sun only comes out in daylight, and what use is that? At least the moon makes the night less dark.' And the Church reasons in the same way: it says that the Mass is more important than the sun, and in saying this it teaches people to ignore the one being capable of ripening the wheat and grapes, without which there could be no Mass. Henceforth the Church must point to the sun and tell Christians: 'Behold the symbol of Christ; we must all learn to be like that.'

I beg you to take what I am saying seriously; it is very important. Also, my friends in the invisible world are watching you and sending you a word of warning: 'Your instructor has just given you a very precious key; if you fail to make good use of it you will have to answer for your neglect.' Yes, for these heavenly beings are displeased when they see that someone is unworthy of their gifts... and they will be displeased with me too. They will say, 'Why did you give these pearls to such idlers? You should have kept them to yourself.' Please have some consideration for me and do not cause heaven to punish me because of you. The trouble is that you know so little about all these laws, about the links between people and things. You think that there is no reason why I should be punished because of your transgressions. But there is a reason: we are all interconnected, all linked to each other, and if I reveal truths to you that I should have kept to myself, it is I who will be held responsible. It is I who will be blamed. Heaven chides me and tells me, 'You are far too generous. Why not let them pull themselves up? You should leave them to struggle and exhaust themselves. Why not let them exert themselves and make their own efforts? Why not make them work their way up the mountain and wear their own fingers to the bone instead of carrying them to the top yourself? They need to know how difficult it is to reach the peak.'

Anyone who wants to find a truly universal religion can do so. It has existed from all eternity. Men have still not recognized it, but it has always been there. Thousands of religions have come and gone in the world—it would be impossible to count them all—and they have all disintegrated and disappeared in the end. But there is one true religion, and that religion will never disappear. The new religion must embrace the whole universe. Look at the sun: it illuminates and warms all creatures, all plants and animals, whereas the Christian religion lights and warms barely a few million people in the world. And who can tell just how much light and warmth those millions actually get from it, or how many millions more have never even heard of it and (sad though this may be from a Christian point of view) who are better off without it.

But now the Aquarian age is coming and bringing the universal religion into the world. Aquarius is the water, the stream of life and love from which all creatures drink, and it brings with it the new religion. Any religion that is incapable of giving mankind this water is not universal. Water is universal; there is not a single creature that does not need water. Water is universal just as air is universal, just as light is universal. The new religion will be founded on universal elements capable of satisfying the hunger and thirst of all human beings. At the moment we still see Christians becoming Buddhists or Muslims; Jews and Muslims becoming Christians, and so on. This means that there is no one religion that is universal. When the universal religion comes, no one will feel the need to wander in search of something else; all will belong to the one religion.

The passage that I read to you earlier says that it is when man prays in his own temple that God hears and answers his prayer. Why does God not answer your prayers if you do not pray from within your temple? You can always go into a church to pray, of course, but a church is a temple that is foreign to you, and its vibrations will be less conducive to the kind of prayer that carries you up to the very throne of God. The fabric of a church or cathedral may be saturated with prayers and good intentions, but if your own body is not purified it will constitute an obstacle to those influences. It is useless to enter a pure and magnificent building to pray if you yourself are impure. On the other hand, if your own temple is pure there is no need for you to go into a church; wherever you are, up in the mountains or elsewhere, your prayer will immediately be heard. It is very important to know these things. Many people go to church, and that is excellent, but they forget their own inner sanctuary.

Leave churches and temples to others, and be content to work for years and years with the angels of the four elements, asking them to cleanse, wash, purify, and sanctify you. Try to create a mental picture of yourself as a sanctuary containing a stream of living water. Let this water flow into every nook and cranny of your being; let it wash and vivify all your cells. What is to prevent you from using exercises of this kind to transform your bodies into temples of great beauty? Great inner beauty, of course. I am not suggesting that you imitate those people—mostly women—who scent their baths and smother themselves in perfumes and lotions every day but whose inner beings smell foul because they never 'wash' themselves inwardly; their inner temple is always dirty. There have been saints who never washed their bodies but who had extraordinary inner purity. This does not mean that I do not recommend this either... I am simply saying that you must neglect neither aspect; neither the inner nor the outer dimension. Even though you give the priority to the inner dimension, you still have to maintain a balance between the two.

Perhaps you have the impression that I want to destroy religion. Well, if that were my intention I could safely leave it to others, for plenty of people have been trying for centuries to do just that. No, true religion is eternal; it cannot be destroyed. Even though the Bible contains elements that are no longer appropriate for our era, it still contains thousands of essential truths that will endure for all eternity. No one can destroy these, for all those great beings, all those prophets who were sent to bring these truths into the world were inspired, guided, and inhabited by the Lord. It was only later, after they had left this world, that certain distortions developed; either because they had not had time to explain everything fully or because others had misunderstood them. The further you advance, the more clearly you will see that the religion of Christ is far greater than Christians think. If Christianity were really the one, universal religion, mankind would be better off than it is today.

The Bonfin, July 30, 1972

IV

Yes, my dear brothers and sisters, you belong to this teaching, you live in the midst of spiritual truths, and in spite of that you sometimes feel as though you were in a terrible state of abandonment, as though God had deserted you. This is a state that many saints and mystics have experienced before you, and today I would like to try and throw a little light on the question. However, the first thing I must tell you before going any further is that everything depends on your perception of God.

When one studies the history of religion, one sees that in proclaiming Yahveh to be the one true God, Moses was introducing a truly revolutionary idea. But the God of Moses was a God to be feared: a consuming fire, the vengeful, implacable Lord of the universe. And his creatures, trembling, fearful human beings, owed that God only one duty: obedience. Later, when Jesus came, he spoke of the Lord as a father and said that human beings were his children. The distance between humanity and God was greatly reduced: human beings were now 'related' to God, members of the same family; everything had changed. Yes, but where had the change actually occurred? In the minds and hearts of human beings, in their inner consciousness. They now felt closer to God. Until then God had been a remote, awesome tyrant whom they had been taught to fear ('The fear of the Lord is the beginning of wisdom'); but Jesus taught that this fear could be replaced by love. Instead of being afraid of this terrible God, human beings could love him, take refuge in his arms, feel that he was their loving father or mother. This was an entirely new development in religion.

Today it is time to go even further. As long as you think of God as existing in a cloud of glory in some remote region of the universe called heaven, where he partakes of sumptuous banquets surrounded by his angels and archangels, your notion of God is an objective, external one; God is outside you. Even if you think of him as your father and feel that you are his child, he is still outside you. And this is the tragedy: you project God outside yourself; you seek him and pray to him, but always outside yourself. God may well exist outside man, but when men conceive of him as being external to themselves they become acutely aware of their own limitations and of all that separates them from him. So many worlds, so many stars, such infinite reaches of space lie between them and God that they cannot possibly hope to reach him. But as soon as you sense that God is present within you, that he is there as light, life, and intelligence, as a unique force, you can never again be separated from him. You find God within yourself.

Human beings have never really been taught to understand God in this way. From time to time they may come across a book in which a mystic, poet, or philosopher suggests some such notion, and they exclaim, 'How poetic. What a profound idea.' but it does not occur to them to ponder that idea or apply it to their own lives. They continue to think of God as existing outside themselves. If you think of God as being apart from and outside yourself, it necessarily means that you think of yourself as being apart from and outside God. And what will become of those who are apart from God? They will be nothing more than an object.

The True Religion of Christ

What is an object? Every craftsman, labourer, or farmer, for example, uses certain tools for his work. These tools are objects that are not a part of himself. When he needs them he picks them up, uses them, and then puts them aside until he needs them again—the next day or next month or next year. In the same way, if we think that we exist apart from God, it will seem to us that God picks us up or puts us aside like objects. If the pots that come from a potter's wheel or the saucepans in a housewife's kitchen were conscious, can you imagine what they would feel like when they were left unused on the shelf? They would complain bitterly that their mistress had forgotten them. 'At least we were warm when she used us,' they would moan, 'and when she scraped out our insides the spoon made a noise that was music to our ears. In those days we were happy. But now she has forgotten all about us. How cruel and wicked of her.'

What can you expect? If we behave like pots and pans it is only normal that the Lord should forget about us from time to time. Can you blame him? It is because we are like objects that we sometimes feel abandoned. At times the Lord picks us up and uses us, at other times he puts us aside, but we have no right to reproach him for it. Would one of your saucepans dare to complain because you did not use it every day? No, you are master—or mistress—in your own house, and it is normal to do as you please. So it is unfair and illogical to rebel against the Lord when you feel abandoned. When you are really within him, in his head and in his members, then you will always be with him and in him. The very worst philosophy you can have is to conceive of yourself as being apart from God, outside him.

Believe me, it will not be long before men's philosophical and religious concepts change very considerably. At the moment people think that it is normal to believe that there is a great distance between man and God. They think that this is only right and proper. But in that case, why do they complain so bitterly when they suffer the consequences of that attitude?

I have already told you that in the future there will be a third Testament that will complete the first two, and in it this truth—that man must learn to get much closer to God, must learn to sense that God is within him—will be strongly emphasized. In fact it will be presented as an absolute essential. When man makes this truth his own he will no longer have the impression of being abandoned by God.

If we feel abandoned by God today it is because we have abandoned him. Can we say that we are always with him? Perhaps we made our first Communion and prayed to him for a few minutes fifty or sixty years ago, but have we ever thought of him since? No. We have deserted him, so why should he not have the right to do the same to us? Why should he be obliged to think of us all the time? Who are we to complain? What makes us think that we are so important that the Lord should constantly be concerned about us?

The truth is, of course, that the Lord takes care of us ceaselessly but in ways that are completely different from those we imagine. Let me explain this. When a child is born, cosmic intelligence gives it everything it needs for its life on earth. It is fully equipped with a head, arms and legs, all the proper organs and faculties, just as a soldier is sent into battle fully armed and equipped with boots, a helmet, a gun, ammunition, and so on. After that it is up to him to look after himself. You are greatly mistaken if you believe that God spends his time thinking about each one of us. He has already given us health, strength, and vitality, and everything else we need. Or perhaps I should say that it is not God who takes care of these details. He leaves all that to his servants, who know exactly what they have to do, while he is concerned with things of far greater importance.

Yes, the third Testament will give men the ultimate solution. They will live constantly in the presence of the Lord.

They will no longer be able to tear themselves away from him, and as they will no longer abandon God, God will no longer abandon them. Whereas at the moment we think of God only from time to time—and from time to time God thinks of us. Even some great saints have grieved because they felt that God had abandoned them, and this shows that they did not know these truths. Does that astonish you? It simply means that a saint may have a great deal of love and great qualities and virtues but that his knowledge and understanding may not have evolved to the same degree. Then there are others for whom the situation can be quite the reverse: they understand many things but they are lacking in virtues and qualities.

You will perhaps feel like saying, 'But it seems more respectful, more fitting, to think of God as being outside ourselves. This is what we have always been taught.' Yes, but there are thousands upon thousands of degrees of truth, and the time has come to take a step forward. We must begin to think of God as being close to us, within us. At the same time, we must think of ourselves as being minute, infinitesimal particles of God. God is the Whole and each one of us is a minute particle of the Whole. If you pray to the Lord thinking that he is far, far away beyond the stars, how can you expect your prayers to reach him? Oh, of course, I once told you that prayer reaches every corner of the universe. That is true, it does, but it takes such a long time to travel through infinite space. If the Lord is right beside you, close to you, within you, the communication is direct and immediate; he can hear you, listen to your prayer, and answer you immediately.

Distance is important. Suppose you want to scatter and dissolve some clouds. You cannot make them disappear immediately; they are very slow and it all takes time. Well, if it takes so much time when the distance is barely a few hundred yards, just imagine how long it will take to reach the Lord (especially if he is asleep and you have to wake him up). But if he is right there inside you, you can simply say, 'Hello, hello.'

and you get through to him immediately. Does this strike you as disrespectful? No, I am speaking figuratively. Try to understand what I am saying.

From now on, when you are meditating, try to cultivate a sense of the Lord's presence within you and you will see how effective this can be. The impression of being abandoned will come to you less and less frequently. At the moment you fluctuate between a few good days during which you are full of joy, inspiration, and ecstasy, followed by days of terrible drought, days in which you feel as though you were dying of thirst in the desert, and it is then that you say, 'God has abandoned me.'

Let me illustrate this: you are here on earth, many millions of miles away from the sun, so far away that mountains of black clouds have slipped between you and the sun and now you are at the mercy of those clouds. You long to receive the light and warmth of the sun but it is impossible; the clouds are in the way. What can you do about it? There is nothing for it but to wait, and while you are waiting you think, 'The sun has abandoned me.' No, the sun has not abandoned you; it is just that you are too far away, below the clouds. But suppose you take an aeroplane or a balloon and fly up above the clouds? Once you are up there nothing can come between you and the sun. It is still there, still shining; it has never abandoned you. When you feel as though you had been abandoned by God it simply means that you have slipped down below the permanent screen of cloud that prevents the sun's rays from reaching you. On the other hand, if you feel full of joy and inspiration, it means that you have risen above the clouds where the sun is always shining and where you can contemplate its light and feel its warmth seeping into you. As you see, the explanation is simple.

Now, since this sensation of being abandoned depends on our attitude, what is to prevent us from changing that attitude?

Why should we be content to remain on so low a level that every minute of every day this screen cuts us off from the light and prevents the joy and revelations of the sun from reaching us? This is why initiation exists. Initiation helps us to find our 'place in the sun', as the saying goes, a very elevated, very high place, well above the clouds, a place in which we no longer depend on anyone or anything, a place in which we are unassailable, invulnerable, invincible, immortal. Believe me, you must constantly rise higher, always higher. You must raise your perception of the Lord to a higher level. You must get closer to him; so close that you succeed in finding him within you; so closely, so intimately within you that you are constantly steeped in his presence. Then you will never again be tempted to say, in the words of St Thérèse of Lisieux, 'Lord, why do you play with me as though I were a ball?' If, like most Christians, you think of yourself as a ball, as an extraneous object in relation to the Lord, then of course you will not escape the feeling of being abandoned. In spite of all their goodness, love, and selflessness, not even the greatest saints or prophets have been spared this sensation.

Now, as I very well know, this is something that happens to you too, so let me say a few more words about it. When you feel that you have been cast aside, that you have nothing to hold on to, that all your ties with the Lord are broken and the spring has dried up, then I advise you to have a conversation with the Lord. Tell him, 'Lord, you have cast me off, you have rejected and abandoned me. As you can see, I am in revolt because you have discarded me. What do you want me to do? I am stuck. I have chosen the path of light, and I cannot turn round and go back. Sometimes I wish I could; sometimes I think I should switch to another path and go and join the unbelievers, but I cannot do it. However badly you treat me I know that this path is the best. So do what you like, but I cannot change. Even if I am wounded, miserable, and ill, I must go on. Even if I am furious and in revolt, I cannot go any other way. For me there is no other way. However much it hurts, I shall just have to continue.' If you talk to the Lord in this way he will hear you—words of this kind are the only ones he hears—and he will instruct his servants to come and help you. Whenever some poor wretch on earth utters such a prayer the message reaches God's ears immediately. He always has time for messages of this nature. He declares, 'Make a note of this man's name, for he is the most intelligent of creatures. He is disgruntled and unhappy, and yet he refuses to try a different path. We must take care of him.'

Yes, you must talk like that to the Lord. Why have you never prayed like that? You prefer to threaten him instead . You say, 'If you treat me so badly I shall refuse to believe in you any longer. This is the end. I refuse to do anything more for you—not even a lighted candle.' Just imagine, what a terrible threat: 'Not even a lighted candle.' The Lord is going to be inconsolable. He will be in the dark because there will be one less candle in church.

There is nothing worse than to think or say to the Lord, 'I have had enough.' Believe me, the best remedy is to go and talk to him, to weep and gnash your teeth and tell him how unkind he is and how unhappy you are. Tell him that you had relied on him and now he has let you down. Yes, tell him all that; but when you have had your say do not forget to add, 'The only thing is that there is no other way, I know that. I cannot go back. So whatever happens, I shall continue to believe in you and to serve you.' Speak to God with great familiarity if you like; he will not take offence. But be sure to conclude your prayer in this way, for, I repeat, this is the best, the only solution.

The Bonfin, August 3, 1968

* * * *

I know, of course, that it is not easy for human beings to conceive of the Lord as being inseparable from themselves, but as long as they continue to think of him as an extraneous being, a being who is absolutely remote and inaccessible, they will continue to be subject to extremely painful states of mind. This means, therefore, that further progress has to be made. Evolution is necessary in every area, even in religion. But in religion—more perhaps than in other areas—people tend to believe that the precepts laid down thousands of years ago must hold good for all eternity. No, this is not so. Everything evolves, everything makes progress. Look at how science evolves. Only religion fails to evolve. Why does science evolve? Why do scientists continually make new discoveries? Because instead of believing, they doubt, and their doubt seems to drive them on. Whereas faith, a faith that is not alive, makes human beings stagnate. Actually in this case it is no longer faith, it is credulity.

I have often spoken to you about Jnana-yoga, the practice of self-knowledge. The purpose of a disciple who practises Jnana-yoga is to make it possible for his consciousness to break out of the narrow circle of his own personality[5] and attain the limitless consciousness of the cosmic being dwelling within him, of whom he is still not fully aware. This being, this particle of the Godhead, dwells within each one of us, and a disciple's goal is to become one with it. There are two poles therefore: the pole of your self, the consciousness of your own being, of your own lower self; and the pole of your higher, sublime self, that being of whom you have no real awareness, but who lives, works, and manifests through you. You are not yet capable of knowing how this sublime being manifests in

[5] The word 'personality' must be understood in the context of Omraam Mikhaël Aïvanhov's teaching concerning the two natures in man—the human and divine, the lower self and the higher self—which he calls the personality and the individuality. For a fuller treatment of the subject, see *Complete Works*, vol. 11, and *Izvor Collection*, N°. 213.

the higher sphere, but from where you are down below you can visualize it dwelling within you and know that it seeks to manifest through you. For as it knows itself on high, it wants also to know itself in you, in the density of your physical matter. If you work with your imagination in this way, your efforts will eventually be rewarded, and as you draw closer to your higher self you will experience an illumination so intense that your consciousness will know no bounds. You will be suffused with light and radiance, and you will sense that you have become one with that sublime being, your higher self.

This is very difficult, of course, but it is one of the most powerful and effective exercises that exists. If you persevere with it you will obtain significant results. And once you have created this link with your higher consciousness, it will always be there, whatever your activities, always ready to take part in all you do. This then is the meaning of Jnana-yoga: the realization that 'I am He,' that nothing else exists, that the Lord is the only Being. You are simply a reflection, an illusion formed by him, but your desire is to work your way back through this illusion of self until you reach that sublime consciousness and become one with it, lose yourself in it, and live for ever in its fullness. As long as you remain outside God you are depriving yourself of his riches. He cannot let you share in them, because you and he belong to two entirely different worlds that vibrate on two different frequencies, between which there can be no communication. But when you learn to synchronize your vibrations to his, the gulf between you disappears and you begin to sense that you have become a different being, that God manifests himself within you. This is death in the initiatic sense of the word: you exist no longer as an independent entity face to face with God; God dwells within you. This is what Jesus meant when he said, 'Except you die you shall not live,' and, 'The Father and I are one.'

Of course, it is not given to everyone to reach this level, but all human beings can free themselves from certain limitations

The True Religion of Christ

if they make the effort. The trouble is that they do not know how to use the means that God has put at their disposal. God has given us the power to become like him. All human beings have this power but, because of what they are at the moment, they are unable to make use of it. Most of them remain on too low a level and have no knowledge, no sense of it. Yet no one is totally bound; even the most limited people have the means to reach beyond their limitations. If only they would raise their eyes and their thoughts to the regions in which God dwells they would discover their innate possibilities. But how many people are willing to try to change anything in themselves? Of course, as I have always said, the reason is very simple: it all depends on what counts most for them. If money or pleasure is so important to them that there is no room in their minds for anything spiritual, how can we expect them to advance? But show me someone who gives precedence to light, love, beauty, and the spirit, someone who does not worry about whether he will be rich or poor, whether he will always have enough to eat or not, whether he will be well dressed or in rags, honoured or ridiculed, and I will tell you that to such a being everything is possible.

It is the importance you attach to things that determines all the rest. I know that the vast majority of human beings are not attached exclusively to material possessions, but their interest in the spiritual life is incidental, no more than an ornament to their lives. Every now and then, when they have a little spare time or when they are bored, they will read a few pages of a good book, go and listen to something vaguely elevating, meditate or pray a little, but what they really consider to be essential are the material things: physical comfort and a peaceful, untroubled life. This is why they will never bring down the blessings of the divine world on themselves. They will continue to live and take advantage of all the things of earth but they will never be blessed with spiritual riches; they will never feel or experience the riches of the divine world in their lives. Only when they depart for the next world will they realize that they have made absolutely no progress, that they have been wasting their time.

If you sincerely want to evolve you must give first place to the impulse of your spirit, to light. But you cannot do this unless you have the desire, the need to do so, and unfortunately you cannot manufacture this need for yourselves. You either have it or not when you come into the world; it depends on the kind of life you led in other incarnations.

For those who come into the world with a taste for spirituality, it takes very little—a book or a few spoken words—to light a fire within them and launch them on a path from which nothing can make them deviate. Whereas others can listen to the sermons of every preacher on earth and remain entirely unchanged. The recommendations and advice of all the saints and all the prophets would fall on deaf ears, because their innate tendencies lead them in a different direction. But if you want to come to earth in your next incarnation with the desire to transform yourself, you must begin now, immediately, even if you do not feel the need to do so, because the efforts you make today lay the groundwork for your next incarnation. Next time you come to earth you will already have a taste for this work because you will have sown the seeds in a previous incarnation. Now you can see how useful the work we do in the Brotherhood is. It is perfectly true that some temperaments have absolutely no use for spirituality. And yet all those who come here—even if their only motivation is curiosity—are unwittingly infected with germs that will manifest themselves at some future date.

But let us get back to the exercise of identification that I was speaking about earlier. You will see, if you do it, that it is extremely effective. However I must warn you that it can also be dangerous, because you can begin to believe that you are already God and allow pride to take over, and pride always leads to disaster. Even if you attain divine superconsciousness

The True Religion of Christ

you must still be humble; in fact you must become even more humble and unpretentious, and be even more careful not to offend others or use your superiority as a weapon against them. There are people who, having learned the formula, 'I am He,' start quarrelling with their family and friends and become absolutely intolerable. Their lives are one long series of conflicts and disputes because they want the whole world to acknowledge them as divinities. But if you want to become more and more like God you must have more and more love and generosity. Because God is love. If you have to massacre and ride roughshod over others in order to prove that you are a divinity, it shows that you have not understood the first thing about it.

I warn you, therefore, that from a psychological point of view this exercise of identification can be dangerous. You must be very vigilant, and in order to avoid any possibility of pride rearing its head, you must begin by recognizing that you are not unique, that other people are also part of God. Yes, if you want to practise this exercise as perfectly as possible you must begin by thinking and feeling that not only the Lord but all human beings are also within you, that they are you. This whole collectivity, the whole of mankind is you; it lives in you and you in it. You are apart and separate from others only in appearance. In this way, instead of opposing and tormenting others, you will sense their needs, their cares, and their sufferings and be obliged to help them. This is how you can truly become a divinity and not a monster for whom others are vermin to be crushed underfoot. Remember that if you fail to take appropriate precautions, methods such as this can be detrimental to you. And then of course it will be my fault once again.

Always remember that all the creatures that you see around you are really part of you. Yes, when you tread the path of true initiatic philosophy you begin to realize that all creatures are one. In reality there is only one being: the Creator. All creatures are simply the cells of his immense body, cells that are one in everything but their consciousness. Imagine what it would be like if every cell in your body had an individual consciousness. Naturally, the cells of the feet, the liver, the spleen, and so on would feel different and apart from each other because their functions are different (the heart has one function, the liver another, and so on), and they would either collaborate or conflict with each other. Yes, but if they reached a higher degree of consciousness they would realize that they are all an integral part of one person, of one being who embraces and nourishes them all.

Well, we must follow the same reasoning. We must remind ourselves that all the individuals on earth—be they Japanese, Chinese, Turkish, Russian, French, or German—are the cells of a single collective being. If their attitude and behaviour do not seem to conform to this reality it is because their consciousness has sunk so low that they are not capable of seeing themselves as the cells of a whole. But once one becomes conscious of being a single cell and feels oneself bound to all the other cells that go to make up the supreme being—God himself—one sees that the whole of humanity is one single being. Once you reach this point you will feel so much love, pity, and consideration for others that you will really and truly fulfil the formula, 'I am That.' As long as human beings have not reached this degree of consciousness they will always want to annihilate others; there can be no real change, only a constant inflation of their personality.

I assure you, true change will only come about through this consciousness of unity. We do not exist as separate individuals; each one of us is a cell in an immense organism, and our consciousness must melt into the universal consciousness that embraces the totality of man, cosmic man. This alone represents true progress, true evolution.

Tangible proof of this bond between individuals can be seen in the fact that, however ignorant and illiterate mediums may be, when they are in a state of trance they can feel within themselves the suffering of the person beside them. And initiates, whose sensitivity is even more highly developed than that of mediums, can also feel the physical and psychic state of others. If they do not usually show it, it is because they have achieved true mastery and to do so would hinder their work. If they were in a continual state of pain or anxiety, how could they help others? It is precisely because they have gone beyond this stage that they are masters and are capable of helping others. I have often experienced this myself: I suddenly feel a pain in one part of my body, and knowing that it comes from someone else, I concentrate on helping that person. Then a few days later I hear from someone who tells me that they had had a terrible pain in that same part of their body, so then they thought of me and now they feel well again. Yes, but it was I who had to bear that pain. It is true that I am capable of overcoming it, but it still involves a great deal of work. This is why it is said that Jesus bore the sufferings of mankind—I can well believe it.

Some people might think that in these conditions it would be better not to be a master or an initiate. Yes, but then they would be deprived of all the rest, too. The suffering that you bear for other people is only temporary, after all; and it is so wonderful to be useful. An initiate is happy to be able to help others and alleviate their suffering. At other moments he feels inspired and elevated because he is in constant communion with a very different order of creatures, creatures that dwell in a permanent state of happiness and bliss. There are so many creatures, both visible and invisible, who live in peace and joy, and you too can experience this marvellous state. So there is nothing to worry about.

Yes, life on earth is an illusion, a dream; reality is something quite different. What is the point of losing eternal life for the sake of an illusion that will soon disappear without a trace? True, you have to eat, clothe yourself, have a roof over your head, and so on, but the intelligent way to behave is to do no more than necessary in this area and leave yourself free to acquire the riches that will be yours for all eternity. Otherwise everything will be taken from you, and you will end by being naked and destitute. Even the books you have read and the knowledge you acquired at the university will be taken away and wiped from your mind. Next time you come to earth you will have to begin to read and study all over again, because the wealth you possess today is not really yours; it has been given to you by others. If something does not rightfully belong to you, you are going to have to give it back. You will be allowed to keep and bring back with you in your next incarnation only the gifts and qualities that you have explored, experienced, and absorbed for yourself. All talents, all gifts of genius can be explained in this way. A philosopher or musician of genius is someone who comes into the world with knowledge acquired through profound personal experience in a previous incarnation.

Each human being is in this world in order to proclaim the glory of God and help others. But instead of doing this, the great majority bury themselves away and become like brute beasts, because they are always afraid of what the neighbours or their family might think. Of course if everyone is always ruled by fear, nothing new will ever happen in the world. Where will you find anybody today who is ready to endure privations, anybody who says, 'That is not important; I have everything I need within myself. My inner life is so intense and rich that I need nothing else'?

Are you beginning to understand me? Perhaps you think that those who are not very rich or comfortable in life will certainly understand me. Not a bit of it. On the contrary, they are in a continual state of fury at not being as rich or as socially prominent as others; they think of nothing else day and night. Their thoughts are so occupied by envy of others that they fail to take advantage of the good situation in which heaven has placed them; they consider it an injustice. Do you really believe that the poor see the tremendous advantages of their poverty and know how to use it as a stepping stone to perfection? No, they are constantly in revolt against it. Why? Because they want to be like the rich. Outwardly they profess to be scandalized by wealth, but deep in their hearts they long for it with all their might. If the rich had a better understanding of their own situation, they would be distressed to be rich and would distribute all their wealth to the poor. And the poor would refuse that wealth, saying, 'No, no, we do not want any of it. We are very well off as we are.' If the rich were enlightened, they would be anxious to rid themselves of their wealth, and the poor would want no more than they have. Is this not the most monstrous, incredible nonsense you have ever heard? Yes, and yet it is absolutely true. The only salvation for the rich is to go to the poor and beg them to take their wealth. And the poor should refuse categorically. Of course, you will say that I am turning everything upside down. Yes, because this is the only way to set everything straight.

One day when I was talking to you about the sun,[6] I described an exercise that you could do when you are up on the Rock for the sunrise.[7] It is very similar to the one I gave you a few moments ago: you can try to picture your higher self up there in the sun, and imagine that it is looking down at your puny, imperfect little self sitting here meditating. In this way you create a current between your higher and your lower selves, and this current is the beginning of a new life. Of course you may not feel the effect at once, because it takes time for the current to become stronger and more intense, but before long you will have no more doubts, for you will sense

---

[6] See *Complete Works*, vol. 10, chap. 3, and vol. 17, chap 8.

[7] The Rock is a platform at the top of a hill near the Bonfin where Omraam Mikhaël Aïvanhov gathered with his disciples every morning in spring and summer to meditate and watch the sun rise.

that something extraordinary is beginning to take place within you, bringing you a sense of absolute certainty. There is nothing more marvellous than this certainty. It is only when you are certain of what you say, of what you have experienced, that you can be strong and powerful, capable of convincing others. As long as you are not quite sure of things you will never convince others, because they will always sense your hesitancy. Of course, you cannot know certainty until you have experienced certain manifestations. Certainty cannot be manufactured. Those who possess it possess unequalled powers of persuasion.

Sèvres, April 4, 1970

V

You have all seen the two triangles in the lecture hall at the Bonfin: the red one with the apex pointing up and the blue one pointing down. I have often talked to you about the symbolism of these two triangles, but today I want to speak about them again, for I want you to understand the extraordinary depth and wealth of meaning in them.

As I have already told you, these two triangles symbolize the masculine and feminine principles, spirit and matter. For this is what the universe is: spirit and matter, the work of spirit and matter. Or—for the sake of materialists who do not like us to talk about the spirit—energy and matter. For the spirit is energy. The only trouble is that by speaking of 'energy' rather than 'spirit' we are failing to attribute to energy all the other properties of the spirit: intelligence, consciousness, and love. Energy is a force that is blind and without consciousness. But however you look at it, no one can deny that the universe is held together by these two realities; spirit and matter, energy and matter, the masculine and feminine principles.

Science has focused principally on the evolutionary process that has led forms and species to become progressively more highly organized, subtler, and more intelligent. In other words it has restricted itself to a study of the red triangle which points upwards. And as scientists are not instructed in initiatic science they have failed to see that the evolutionary movement was preceded by a movement of involution. They have not seen this because involution takes place in the subtle world, but it is this gap in their knowledge that falsifies their whole philosophy. Initiatic science teaches that every evolution is preceded by an involution, the involution of spirit descending into matter. Once the spirit has reached a certain degree of materialization, it endeavours to return to its source, and this is evolution: the return journey, the striving for perfection, the ascent through the denser layers of matter toward the highest point of development. And evolution cannot occur without the participation of the spirit. Only the spirit can raise matter, forms, and creatures to perfection, because only the spirit possesses life, consciousness, and intelligence. It is important to understand, therefore, that there can be no evolution without involution. Nothing can take place here on earth unless something has first descended from above. To imagine that forms have been capable of evolving, while denying that this evolution had to be preceded by the involution of a divine form, a descent of the spirit, is to reveal an abysmal ignorance. So there you have it, the two triangles represent involution and evolution. The triangle pointing downwards represents the spirit that descends into matter in order to animate and breathe life into it, and the triangle pointing upwards represents matter as it evolves toward reunion with the spirit. When these two triangles are combined they form the Seal of Solomon.

Esoteric books have much to say about the Seal of Solomon, but very few show any real understanding of the profundity and the magical power of this symbol that comes from the meeting and interpenetration of the two triangles, the two principles. An initiate in whom the two principles are united is called an androgyne. Whereas most human beings, those who represent only one of the two triangles—that of man or of woman—are maimed, mutilated beings, and this is why they continually seek their missing half, the other triangle, so as to form the Seal of Solomon. All human beings have only one desire, to be a Seal of Solomon. This is why men and women need each other. Men need women and women need men, because they have this unconscious desire to become Seals of Solomon.

These two triangles exist in many different forms. In the temples of India, for instance, we frequently see a symbol that is known as the Lingam, consisting of a horizontal base (representing the feminine principle) surmounted by a vertical element (representing the masculine principle). When I was in India I talked to many priests and gurus, and I would often tell them that they did not understand the meaning of this symbol. 'How can you say we do not understand it?' they would protest, 'It is an integral part of our tradition.' 'That is true, but I still say that you do not understand it. If you did you would not have married. The feminine principle should be within you, but as it is not, you have to find it elsewhere.' Of course, they were not exactly overjoyed to hear this, particularly as it came from such an unexpected quarter, from a Westerner who was a Christian into the bargain. If a man, who represents the masculine qualities of energy, strength, and will-power, also possesses the feminine qualities of delicacy, tenderness, purity, and love, he is a complete being and has no need of a wife. Equally, if a woman possesses both the feminine and the masculine qualities, she does not need to look for a husband. As long as you are still looking for a husband or wife, it means that you do not yet possess these two tendencies that alone can bring you fulfilment.

You will say, 'But men have always looked for wives, and women for husbands.' I know, and that simply proves that human beings have always been dominated by separateness, weakness, and divisiveness. The philosophy of the initiates is perhaps difficult to accept, but it is the truth. The things I say in my talks to you are not intended to please the masses. If I were obliged to say only what would please human beings, I should have to accept all their weaknesses and vices; they would even expect me to encourage them in those vices. Ordinary people might do this, but a master, whose only desire is to lead his disciples towards perfection, is obliged to tell people the truth, even if it is not pleasant to hear.

And now let us look at what these two triangles mean in the spiritual life. In the past, religions such as Buddhism and even Christianity urged human beings to detach themselves from the physical world and seek to approach God and become one with him. The earth was nothing but a 'vale of tears' and life an illusion from which man was advised to detach himself as quickly as possible so as to return to heaven or nirvana. Each individual was encouraged to think only about saving his own soul so as to enjoy the splendours of heaven. Now I am not saying that this point of view is bad, but it is imperfect. It is a point of view that has enabled men to discover a great deal about the inner life, but it is no longer appropriate to our times.

To adopt the philosophy of the feminine triangle is to reject matter and all the activities and duties attached to it, and this leads to certain anomalies. Today we must work with the triangle of the spirit, which is the triangle of realization, of manifestation in the world, in our physical bodies, in matter. We must no longer concentrate on elevating ourselves above the world; on the contrary, we need to descend. I am sure that there will be a few 'mystics' who will object in horror: 'But that is terrible. That is the way of perdition. Religion has never taught us to descend; on the contrary, we must elevate ourselves and rise above the world.' Well, have it your own way, but such an attitude will never bring about the kingdom of God and his righteousness on earth. The few who seek to save their own souls will simply leave the rest of mankind sunk in disorder and misery, because this philosophy of flight is incapable of transforming the world. We need another philosophy today, the new philosophy that is coming with the Aquarian age. This new philosophy is water from above, a fountain of life flowing from the heavenly regions, and it will transform the earth and cause the seeds of the kingdom of God to germinate with new life. Heaven, of course, is a perfect world, a world of blessings and splendour in which we may find freedom and happiness, but if everyone abandons the earth for heaven, the earth will continue to be a wilderness.

In the Lord's Prayer Jesus said, 'Thy kingdom come, Thy will be done on earth as it is in heaven,' but men have never understood that Jesus wanted to transform, perfect, and embellish the earth so that it would resemble heaven. Everybody flees the world, because flight suits those timid souls that are so anxious to save themselves. But today, instead of trying to save our souls, we must throw ourselves wholeheartedly into the glorious work of bringing heaven down to earth. You will protest, 'But how could we ever do that? It is quite impossible.' Not at all, the triangle of the spirit shows us how to do it. A disciple must still seek heaven, that is true, but once he has found it he must bring down to earth all the light of heaven, all the love, all the power, and all the purity of heaven, and introduce them into his own physical body, into his brain, his lungs, his stomach, his whole being. In this way, after years of striving, he brings spirit and matter together again within himself and attains the fullness of perfection symbolized by the Seal of Solomon.

Many extreme tendencies are surfacing in the world today. There are countries that are technically, economically, and socially advanced; they have done everything possible to improve their material conditions, but they have done away with religion. And then there are others such as India (although, even in India, things have changed to a certain extent) that have such a strong spiritual tradition that the material dimension is almost totally neglected, and millions and millions of their people live in filth, poverty, and disease. Naturally, I cannot say that either solution by itself is the right one; both are necessary. We must always be linked to heaven, but we must also work on earth.

This then is what the new religion teaches: we must work to bring something of the divine into the world. You will protest, 'But what about heaven? We want to work for heaven.' Yes, but heaven does not need you; it already has everything. What could you possibly add to all the wealth that heaven possesses? It is here on earth that you are needed, and this means that you must revise your tactics. I am not saying that you should turn your backs on heaven. On the contrary, you must continue to maintain close ties with heaven so as to be in a position to give to others. For after all, if you cut yourself off from heaven you will never be rich and never have anything to give to others.

Remember the advice I have already given you in this respect. Just as in some of the poorer countries the fathers of families have to go and look for work abroad, so you too must go 'abroad' to earn the money you need to feed your family. I am speaking symbolically of course. By 'abroad' I mean heaven, for it is to heaven that you must go every day through prayer, meditation, and contemplation. This is what I do: every day I leave you and go abroad to look for gold so that I can bring it back and give it to you. Why do you have to stay glued to your family and friends all the time? Because you love them? No, you do not love them, or rather you love them in the wrong way. You allow them to starve to death because you are incapable of giving their hearts and souls the food they need. And that is not a proof of love.

Let me illustrate what I am saying. Suppose you have a wonderful idea; you feel that it is really good, and the thought of it makes you happy. This means that your idea has moved down from your intellect and reached the level of your feelings. Yes, but it is still incomplete; it is only when you

The True Religion of Christ

express it in words and actions that the normal process will be complete. Are painters, musicians, or poets content to keep their creations in their heads? No, they give them concrete expression. Then why should we be content to leave spiritual things on the level of thought or feeling? Why should we not give them concrete expression also? Yes, spiritual and religious ideas must also be implemented. The religion of many people never gets any further than their hearts or minds, and their behaviour contradicts everything they think and believe. This is all wrong, and it means that they do not understand the point of view of cosmic intelligence. First we think of something, then we wish for it to happen, and finally we have to work to implement it.

When a boy falls in love with a girl, what does he do? It is not long before he tries to kiss her. Why is he not satisfied to keep his relationship on the level of thought and feeling? Ah, in this area men and women behave just as cosmic intelligence planned that they should. But we must remember that the things of the spirit also have to be given concrete expression in our actions, our attitude, and our work. Otherwise they are as worthless as a letter or an official document without a signature. The signature represents the concrete expression, the realization. Or take another example: a general prepares a brilliant plan of attack that he is sure will bring him victory, and he has set his heart on that victory. But what use will his battle plan be if he never gives the order to attack? The 'signature' that validates his plan is the order to attack, which implements it on the physical plane.

Some of you will probably think that I am contradicting myself. You will say, 'You are always criticizing materialists for being concerned only about their worldly interests. You say that they are working for the benefit of thieves, because they will not be allowed to take any of their acquired wealth with them. They will arrive in the next world naked and destitute, and no one will welcome them.' But there is no contradiction here, for it is one thing to care about nothing but money and possessions, and quite another to strive to manifest heaven, goodness, and light on the physical plane. When what you achieve here on earth is true, luminous, and divine, you will be allowed to take it with you, and in this way you create your own future. But if you are content to think and wish and never actually achieve anything, you will be naked when you leave this world because you will not have left your signature on anything.

Yes, I am bringing you a new philosophy, a new way of behaving, a new way of thinking, acting, and manifesting. This new way is very different from all that other people have taught about religion, but I cannot help that. I have been given the task of bringing you these new notions. The old notions were valid for the individual but useless for the collectivity. The time has come to stop working only for our own individual salvation. Today we must work for the whole world, for the whole of mankind, and the only way we can do so is by putting this new philosophy into effect and rising mentally to heaven so as to bring the light, love, peace, and eternity of heaven down to the physical plane. This process of bringing heaven down to earth has to begin with our own physical bodies; the life of heaven must impregnate and radiate from our physical bodies. When human beings achieve this, the kingdom of God will truly come about, and each individual will be a light, a sun, a living spring. The great thing is to accept the teaching of the triangle that points downwards, the triangle of the spirit, and no longer cling exclusively to the philosophy of the triangle of matter.

The tendency of matter is to ascend; that of the spirit to descend. This same pattern is reproduced by a man and woman who unite in the act of love: the man faces down and the woman up. In this, human beings are simply behaving in conformity with principles established from all eternity by cosmic intelligence, according to which matter—which needs

The True Religion of Christ

to be spiritualized—and the spirit—which needs to be materialized—meet and are joined in space. And it is in this union that the spirit fertilizes matter. As you see, there is symbolism, eloquence, and philosophy in every human action, but human beings themselves see and understand none of it. Our task is to bring the spirit down to earth. This is why you must use your meditations and prayers to beg for this light and visualize it, visualize this spirit, this divine force, descending into you and impregnating every cell of your being. One day, when you have worked at this for years and years, you will sense that heaven is within you, that light is within you, that love is within you. When this day comes you will find that it is much easier to help other people and awaken them to this reality. But if, through a false understanding of spirituality, you remain barren—a blank page—you will be no good to anyone. The spirit must be allowed to descend.

It is when the spirit descends into matter that the child—that is to say, the kingdom of God and all the beauty of God—will be born in the world. This is the new dawn, the new work that is before us: to bring all the splendour, all the blessings, all the light and peace of heaven down to earth—down, first and foremost, to our own earth, our own physical bodies, and then to the whole world, to all human beings. We must tread a new path, for it is sheer selfishness to want to flee the earth on the pretext of spirituality or religion. Blessed are those who are capable of understanding me.

If anything is sacred to me, it is what I have been saying today. I must admit that I hesitated before deciding to talk about it, for it is too sacred. In talking about it I feel as though I were tearing something from my heart in order to give it to you. I finally decided to do so in the hope that you would understand and make up your minds to follow this path.

There, I hope that this is quite clear now: instead of losing yourselves in nirvana, instead of wishing to eat and drink and rejoice forever in the company of the elect, think that you are bringing heaven down to earth; that its light shines through you to the world; that you are a light in the world. What glorious work lies ahead of you.

The Bonfin, September 9, 1977

* * * *

Involution is the sacrifice of the spirit that makes it possible for matter to evolve and enrich itself. The twin processes of evolution and involution are at work throughout creation, but as human beings are not particularly inclined to consider the philosophical aspect of things, they never see the laws and principles that account for every phenomenon or event in life.

Nothing can exist unless something first sacrifices itself in order to make that existence possible. Thus evolution can exist only if it is preceded by involution. If human beings are to pursue their upward path they must know this. Everything falls apart if life is not based on an awareness of sacrifice, selflessness, and love. Take the example of a family: the parents spend all their energy and make innumerable sacrifices so that their children may grow and develop. In fact, one sees parents who have become weak and shrunken, while their children, who are strong and vigorous, do not always realize that they have developed at the expense of their parents.

Spiritual masters, and even professors and schoolteachers represent the triangle of the spirit. When they instruct their disciples or students they are 'involving'; whereas those who listen and learn from them are 'evolving'. Here too we see the manifestation of the two triangles. But this situation cannot last for ever, either for the teacher or for the students. Eventually students and disciples have to pass on what they have learned to others. Similarly, a child cannot remain a child for ever; one day he is going to have to work, marry, and have children of his own to feed and educate.

The symbolism of the two triangles can be seen in every activity of our daily lives. You pour yourself a glass of water, and the water in the glass increases while that in the bottle decreases. Then you drink, and the glass is emptied but your stomach is filled. Every time you eat or drink, the food you eat and the liquid you drink represent the triangle of the spirit, which sacrifices itself in order to make you stronger. You go into a shop to buy something, but if you have nothing to offer in exchange for what you need, no one will give you anything. Your purse has to 'involve' so that the goods you need may 'evolve' in your direction. All the actions of our daily lives should help us to understand that the same processes exist on a cosmic scale, and without the initial involution of the spirit there can be no evolution of matter.

As you can see, the symbolism of the two triangles is truly immense; it embraces and sums up the whole of the science of life. Take, for example, the way in which cosmic intelligence has designed the solar plexus and the brain. The materials of these two organs are identical—grey matter and white matter—but their relative position is reversed. The grey matter of the brain is on the outside and the white matter inside; whereas the grey matter of the solar plexus is inside and the white matter on the outside. And this opposition is reflected in the way in which the two organs manifest themselves: the solar plexus is hidden and its action invisible, whereas the brain talks, pontificates, pronounces anathema. But the brain could not manifest with such brilliance, could not reason, explain, or give orders—it could not function at all, in fact—if there were not something that spent and sacrificed itself in order to subsidize it and supply it with the energies it needs. And that something is the solar plexus. The solar plexus nourishes and sustains the brain, because its role is to give. The solar plexus corresponds to the triangle of involution therefore, and the brain, which receives, corresponds to the triangle of evolution. The role of the solar plexus is to sacrifice itself in order to ensure the proper functioning of the brain, and not only of the brain, but of all the other organs as well. This means that the role of the solar plexus is more spiritual than that of the brain, and, knowing this, we should do all we can to ensure that it has the conditions it needs to work and fulfil its mission.

The essential thing to remember is that man cannot lock himself into a one-sided attitude. Once the cup is full it has to be emptied again. This is true in the life of every single individual, for we all begin life as children, who only know how to take, before becoming adults and learning to give. It is also true in the life of humanity as a whole. For a very long time humanity has been in the selfish state of childhood, in which it has thought only of taking everything for itself, and the result has been war and devastation. It is time now for humanity to learn to give. This is why I say that the religions that urge men to concentrate on saving their souls and seeking eternal bliss for themselves are no longer valid. It is time to give something to the earth, to make the earth beautiful so that it may vibrate in harmony with heaven.

In the past, individuals were concerned only about their own development. This was perfectly normal; in fact it was a necessary phase of human evolution and as such was planned by cosmic intelligence. Just as a child has to begin by growing and becoming strong, humanity—which was still a child—had to grow and build up its strength, and it was helped in this by its 'elder brothers', those highly evolved souls and spirits who incarnated in order to help it. And now mankind has reached adulthood. Ah, but I can see that you are wondering what I mean when I say that mankind has become adult. Well, think of how children develop: to begin with it is their physical life that manifests itself and grows strong as they eat and drink and exercise their limbs. Then, little by little, the spirit begins to descend into them, awakening first their astral body and then their mental body, and by the time they are twenty-one we can say that all their essential faculties are developed. Emotionally and intellectually they possess all the tools they need and can begin to use them to their fullest extent.

The process by which the spirit gradually descends to the physical plane has also taken place in mankind as a whole. This is why we can say that mankind has now reached adulthood. If modern man possesses such extraordinary powers in the realms of thought and feeling, it is because the spirit has taken possession of his astral and mental bodies, and in so doing it has penetrated so deeply into matter that it is almost buried. Thanks to the spirit, human beings have become more and more capable of handling matter, but at the same time they have lost touch with the subtle worlds. In the remote past, when the spirit had not penetrated their physical body to any great extent, human beings were in closer touch with the spirits, the entities of the invisible world, the souls of the dead. Of course, these human beings were not very clever when it came to handling matter, and if they now have such great skill on that level it is because they have gradually cut themselves off from all the other forms of life that inhabit the universe— so much so, in fact, that, because these forms of life are invisible, they no longer believe in their existence.

What is needed now is a return to the spiritual world. It was necessary for mankind to attain its present intellectual development, but to continue in the same direction without a simultaneous development of its spiritual faculties would spell its ultimate destruction. In fact this has already occurred more than once. The annals of spiritual science—which will soon be discovered—contain records of several human races that have disappeared from the face of the earth.

We might wonder why the spirit, having penetrated so deeply into matter, has not succeeded in rendering it nobler and subtler. The truth is that the spirit cannot manifest itself on the lower planes, in the opaque density of matter, with the same omnipotence and omniscience that characterize its manifestations on the higher planes. The more deeply it penetrates matter the more it is restricted and prevented from manifesting its true qualities.

In reality the descent of the spirit into matter has been going on for millions of years, and although it has not yet achieved the true spiritualization of matter, it has already brought about a tremendous flowering of human intellectual and emotional faculties. Yes, matter has reached the stage of intellectual development, but that is not enough. This is why the time is now ripe for the cosmic spirit—not just the spirit of each individual being—to descend into humanity and spiritualize it. Until now it has been the task of the individual spirit to descend and make its dwelling in each individual physical body, and in the struggle to animate and refine the matter of that body, it has lost many of its qualities. But now there is to be a collective, cosmic descent of the divine spirit, which is coming to vivify and resuscitate all creatures.

People are always astonished at the extent to which the all-powerful spirit can be subjugated and paralysed by matter. Yes, the spirit is all-powerful in the world above, but it is not all-powerful in the world below unless it is set free. It is exactly the same as atomic energy: as long as that energy is imprisoned in matter it is powerless, but liberate it and you will see what it is capable of. The spirit can be virtually paralysed by matter, but once it is set free it shows itself to be so powerful that it can pulverize the matter that held it prisoner.

And now, my dear brothers and sisters, make up your minds to become triangles of the spirit and to do something for others instead of being content to be miserable little non-entities who want the whole world to revolve around themselves. Those who think of nobody but themselves retard their own development, but those who work for others become stronger in themselves. When you are always trying to help and encourage others it may seem as though you lose something (and it is quite possible, in fact, that your physical strength will diminish), but you will become spiritually stronger and more powerful. Of course, as this spiritual strengthening is not visible, everybody thinks that the spirit, like the physical body, declines with age, whereas the truth is exactly the reverse. The trouble is that human beings get everything mixed up and identify with their physical bodies. The physical body works, uses up its energies, and becomes weaker with age, that is true, but the spirit becomes stronger. One triangle diminishes while the other increases. That is life. The French saying, 'You cannot make an omelette without breaking eggs,' is very apt.

In point of fact, this is not always true. I have my own formula, which says, 'Your guests have eaten their fill but your cake is still whole.' Yes, but there is a secret here that only the great masters have discovered, and it is this: when they help and enlighten human beings, they spend a great deal of energy, but at the same time the divine world gives them far more strength and energy than they give to others. It is when you give to others that you receive, that you are filled to the brim. So there you have the two triangles: you give below and you receive from above. When you are the triangle of the spirit in relation to human beings you give, and in this way you become the triangle of matter in relation to heaven. You give and receive, give and receive. If you have never learned to do this you will soon be drained and empty and begin to regret having worked for others. You have to learn, therefore, to be the triangle that gives to the earth and at the same time the triangle that receives from heaven. In other words you must be emissive in relation to the world below and receptive to the world above.

It was in this sense that I once explained Jesus' words: 'Unless you change and become like children, you will never enter the kingdom of heaven.' For two thousand years Christians have failed to understand what it means to be 'like children'. The weakness and frailty of children arouse a protective instinct in adults. A child who has someone to look after it has nothing to worry about; it is the adults, the parents, who do all the worrying. Jesus was telling us that we must be as children in relation to those who are more advanced and who are able, therefore, to take care of us, to guide and instruct and protect us. Just because you have come of age it does not mean—as so many people think—that you can sever your ties with all those more advanced beings and never obey anyone again. It is precisely when you do this that trouble really begins to rain down on you. No, the only way to enter the kingdom of God, to enter that realm of joy, happiness, and hope, is to be as children in relation to those who are more advanced. Even if we are obliged to become adults here on earth, we must still be as children in relation to our parents in the higher world.

Why are human beings incapable of discovering these great truths for themselves? Because they are not free. Yes, for there is a connection between freedom and knowledge. It is true that people are always ready to fight for freedom, to fight for the liberty to behave according to their own tastes and desires (which means, often enough, the liberty to commit every conceivable folly). But the freedom they seek is not the freedom that would give them the power to see, explore, and understand the divine world. On the contrary, they get involved in all kinds of activities which blindfold and shackle them. If you walk through a beautiful garden while you are totally absorbed in your own worry or distress, you will not see the beauty surrounding you. But it never occurs to human beings that when they devote themselves to banal, mundane occupations they become incapable of seeing and rejoicing in the splendour of the universe and the creatures that inhabit it. It is only when you are free that you can begin to see reality. Until then, a great many things can happen, even within yourself, without your being aware of them, simply because you are otherwise engaged.

What extraordinary things you will start to discover once you have succeeded in freeing yourselves! You will acquire the ability to read what is written, first within yourselves and then in others, thus gradually attaining true clairvoyance. All the wonders of heaven and earth are there, around you and in you, but you have to be free in order to see them. For an initiate this is the only true freedom. The very least you can do while you are here is to begin to acquire a taste for these truths, and when you do so you will see that everything becomes so much lighter and easier. Do you think that I waste my time and energy in useless activities? No, if this question were not of vital importance I should never have talked to you about it. Why should I be too to know as well as anyone what is important and what is not?

All around us in the world today, in every aspect of life, are the manifestations of the triangle of matter, the triangle that does nothing but take—even in the intellectual sphere. This is why so many ideas stagnate in people's minds without ever being expressed in their actions, gestures, or general behaviour. But in the teaching of the Great Universal White Brotherhood we learn to put the most sublime ideas into effect, to bring them down into the material dimension. All that we learn, all that we receive, all that we have understood must be expressed and implemented in our actions. This is perfection. This is how the kingdom of God and his righteousness will be established on earth.

Videlinata (Switzerland), February 15, 1978

Chapter Three

The Concept of a Pan-World

I

One of the things I find reassuring today is the fact that one meets more and more people who have achieved a certain degree of wisdom. Yes, even scientists and materialists are beginning to be a little more prudent, a little more reasonable. They no longer presume to lay down the law with such self-assurance or to greet every hypothesis that does not conform exactly to their own view with derision and scepticism. Only a few years ago the word most often on their lips when they were faced with something new was 'Impossible!' But now they are beginning to acknowledge that nature may still have some surprises up her sleeve—even for them—and as they do not want to appear ridiculous to future generations, they are more cautious. They say, 'Well, it is possible... We do not know... We must wait and see.' At last they are acquiring a little wisdom; at last there is some hope. Yes, and I can go even further and say that only a few years hence they will all adopt our ideas and speak our language. Well, perhaps not all, but many of them will share our ideas, and once they have chewed and digested them thoroughly, they in turn will propagate them. A few years from now we shall see some tremendous changes.

The other day I even heard the idea of universal brotherhood—an idea that hardly ever occurred to anyone before—

being discussed on television. I do not know who was talking because I was late for the beginning of the programme, but someone was saying that with things as they were in the world today, with the proliferation of nuclear weapons, the only solution was universal brotherhood; the only hope for mankind was for all men and women to unite and extend the hand of friendship to each other. I was astounded and above all delighted to hear this, for it proves that the idea is beginning to spread. Yes, one day human beings everywhere will be obliged to make their voices heard to force the issue; there is no other solution.

The Universal White Brotherhood ceaselessly emits currents of unity and brotherhood, and one day those whose receivers are already tuned in to these currents are finally going to make up their minds to do something about it. This will be the brightest day in the history of mankind. Think of the tremendous changes that will be possible once the whole world becomes a single family. All those billions that are being wasted on arms and espionage will be used to transform the earth into a Garden of Eden. At the moment such a thing still seems impossible and unrealistic, a Utopia. Yes, but one fine day it will not only be possible, it will happen, and everyone will be astounded. The idea is going to take hold and dig itself in, and little by little everyone will accept it. If human beings refuse to accept it they will be condemning themselves to annihilation—and events will prove this. All around us we hear talk of plans for a Pan-Europe, Pan-Asia, Pan-America, or Pan-Africa. Such schemes represent immense progress, but they are not the ultimate solution. The only solution to all the world's problems is a 'Pan-World', the whole world gathered into one single family. Otherwise, instead of an individual country going to war with another country, we shall have a whole continent declaring war on another continent: Asia at war with Europe, for instance. Will that be any better?

Yes, I believe in all these unrealistic achievements. I

The Concept of a Pan-World

believe in all that is unattainable and impossible. I have no faith in the rest. I throw myself heart and soul into such impossible achievements because they are the best, the most grandiose, the most solemn and glorious, and you cannot tell me that I am not right to do so. In fact I say to every head of State, 'Do you really want to be great and glorious? If so, be the first to propagate this idea of a Pan-World, and you will be immortal.'

I assure you, the realization of universal brotherhood is possible today because human beings have reached a stage of technical evolution that makes it possible. All the modern means of communication, which enable people on opposite sides of the globe to talk to each other, have made unity possible by reducing the distance between countries and continents to an astonishing extent. You will say, 'Yes, but there are still so many things that we cannot agree about. Look at the European Common Market or the division of Germany into East and West[1]. And there are so many other examples; how can we possibly hope for universal brotherhood?' Of course these little problems exist, and it is precisely the little problems that are always the most difficult to solve. A problem caused by nationalism and chauvinism (by petty individual interests) is always more difficult to solve than one that concerns the world as a whole, because everyone wants the biggest slice of the cake; everyone puts his own interests first. But all human beings throughout the world have a common interest in being free to live in peace and plenty, and if they all put this interest first, the whole situation would change and everything would be possible. If you object to my idea of a Pan-World on the grounds of a comparison with the Common Market, your objection is not valid, for they are not at all the same thing. It is obvious that when the negotiators in Brussels have to calculate the price of wheat, butter, and eggs, they can

---

[1] As can be seen from the date, this lecture was given at the height of the Cold War.

never agree or understand each other. But in the case of the Pan-World there are no longer any little details to quarrel about. The only thing that matters is the well-being of all human beings, freedom and peace for all, and this is something that all human beings can agree on.

Sèvres, November 28, 1966

II

The people you meet in life are like shops. You visit them in the expectation of finding a little hope or consolation, a little love or faith. Sometimes you are disappointed because you are greeted with a metaphorical kick on the shins, and this means that the 'shop' in question does not have what you were looking for. This is why our work here in the Brotherhood is to encourage human beings to become 'shops' that are so civilized and spiritually cultured that whenever you visit one of them you can be sure of finding the Godhead. This is the kind of humanity that we are working to create, and once we succeed, no one will want to hide away in his own little corner, because everyone will know that if they visit others they will be able to find what they need and go home happy, their problems solved.

Yes, this is the new humanity that we are preparing here in the Brotherhood. The brothers and sisters who are here are all 'shops', and each one offers his or her own particular brand of energies, fluids and qualities. One is working to cultivate purity, and when you are with him you feel yourself becoming pure. Another is full of love, and with her you are influenced by love. With yet another you find yourself becoming wiser or stronger. In this way you are nourished by all the qualities and virtues you need and can continue to grow towards perfection. Nature has designed us in such a way that if we lack something we need we can look for it in others. Why do men look for wives? Because a man lacks certain elements that he can find only in a woman. And the same is true of women: they look for husbands in order to find something that they lack. But marriage is an inadequate solution—very inadequate. The only way to find everything you need is to maintain fraternal relations with a whole collectivity.

To be sure, you cannot cease to exist as an individual in order to melt into the collectivity. You will always be an individual, but that individual must learn to vibrate in unison with others and share fully in the life of the collectivity. It is possible to become a collective being while remaining an individual. A man and his wife, for instance, will always be separate individuals; in spite of the love that unites them they will always be two separate, different beings. When they get on a bus, go to the theatre, or eat in a restaurant, they will always have to pay for two tickets, two seats, two meals. In fact if they tried to object, claiming that they were one, not two, they would never convince anyone else of that unity; they would be more likely to end up in a lunatic asylum. When I talk about being part of a collectivity, therefore, you must understand what I am saying. It is not a question of cutting yourself up in little bits and scattering yourself throughout the collectivity. No, you must always be an individual, with your own name and your own body, but inwardly you can live a collective, cosmic, universal life. It is only in your thoughts that you can become one.

I have studied many spiritual movements, and I have seen that they all stick to their antiquated ideas. They do not seem to realize that we need something new today, because life is new, life has changed. The forms and rhythms of life today are so different that the methods of the past can no longer help people to become better. It is because human beings themselves are not the same that the old forms and old explanations offered by the Church no longer satisfy them. Young people especially need something new, something that the Church is incapable of giving them, because it has no real will to change. All the established Churches and doctrines try to nourish people with 'tinned food', spiritual nourishment that was dried or salted or bottled thousands of years ago. But there are no tinned foods on the menu in the Universal White Brotherhood; on the contrary, in this restaurant all the fruit and vegetables are freshly harvested and the bread is just out of the oven.

Archaeology is very fashionable today. In fact it sets the tone in every area, and people are being fed on archaeological remains—tinned foods. If someone tells me that he is a painter, a musician, or a philosopher, I know that this means that he is an archaeologist; he is only interested in old ideas. But here in the Brotherhood we breathe and eat the sun; we contemplate living nature; we are in communion with the divine forces of today. What is the point of cutting oneself off from the living reality of today in order to go and look for what has been extinct for ten thousand years? All that is dead and gone. What is it that makes people want to poke about among the rotting remains of the past? Of course, you must not misunderstand me. Archaeology is a legitimate science, and there have been archaeologists who have made some extraordinary discoveries. What I have said about archaeology must be understood symbolically.

I can see that this point of view is new and rather surprising to you. Yes, because we are talking about what is new. Everything I tell you is new and will always be new—one day you will find this out for yourselves. Do you know why it is all new? Because I am not an archaeologist; because the water I give you to drink is always fresh, newly drawn from the source. Everybody chases off nowadays to study the ancient Egyptians and Persians, the Druids, Bogomils, or Cathars, and never thinks of studying the realities of today. They are proud to be seen as people of the past. They have no interest in learning about what is new, about the new life springing from the fountainhead about the new message that God is sending humanity today. They cannot see that God is still with us, that the same truths are still with us today; and the reason why they cannot see this is that they are archaeologists. In fact, if an initiate came with even more to offer than the Bogomils, Cathars, and Albigensians, they still would not recognize him, simply because he was alive.

Everybody is eager to seek out the dead; the living are of no interest to anyone. People glorify those who are dead and gone and despise the living. They wait until they are dead before building temples in their honour. Yes, this mentality is truly amazing. Of course, when I was young I was an archaeologist like everybody else, but the truths taught by the initiates of the past are accessible to me today because I am open to what is new. And this can be true for all those who open themselves to what is new. The truths that I see all around me will become visible to them too. Why have they never been able to see them before?

You will say, 'But this new life that you are talking about, the collective, fraternal life, is still a long way off. It is still too difficult to understand.' Difficult to understand? How can it be difficult to understand? A hundred people all looking at you with such love that you feel so happy you would like to die— is that so difficult to understand? To die and be buried... Yes, but you will have died of love and that is far better than dying of anger or hatred. We still do not know all the divine treasures human beings contain and what they will one day be capable of producing. Do you not think that every pretty girl you see in the street is burning to let others see all the charming and adorable treasures of her heart? She is, but the trouble is that she is not allowed to; she is obliged to hide all these treasures and keep them locked up inside, because she has to obey those idiotic archaeologists, whose narrow archaeological wisdom teaches that she must always distrust everybody and never smile at a stranger. This is why I say that mankind in its true form still does not exist. An evil mankind exists, yes, and that is why, in spite of all his culture and civilization, man is still a troglodyte, a caveman.

When the new era comes, human beings will allow all that is good in them to manifest itself without fear of danger or harm, and it will be the kingdom of heaven on earth. The world will be filled with love, joy, and song. You will say, 'But that is bound to degenerate into debauchery.' No, just the opposite; debauchery exists today because people do not know the true meaning of love. In a world in which all human beings love each other, men and women will no longer feel the need to pounce on each other simply to gratify their lust. A true understanding of love prevents man from behaving like an animal. Look for true love and you will no longer feel the need for such things. You will feel fulfilled, you will be bathed in splendour.

You will never achieve very much all by yourself; you can accomplish much more when you are part of a collectivity. Have you not already experienced this for yourselves? You are feeling discouraged, tired, or let down, and then you come to the Brotherhood and the sight of all those friendly smiles, all those faces shining with ardour and enthusiasm, soon restores your courage. Whereas you can curl up and bemoan your fate all alone in a corner for years, and nothing will ever change; no one will come and console you. Why are people so stupid that they fail to understand this? They say, 'I do not want anything to do with a collectivity, thank you. I'm perfectly happy by myself.' All right, if you insist, but you will see what is in store for you. So many men and women, even when they are still very young, have their own ideas and plans and systems, and they are absolutely convinced that everything will work out exactly as they planned. But later in life they see things differently. Even distinguished philosophers are forced to change their philosophy and admit that they were mistaken.

Of course some people are quite happy to be alone. But suppose a young man who was once content with his solitude meets a ravishingly beautiful young girl. As soon as he compares this new sensation of well-being to the satisfaction that he experienced in his solitude, he will find that he much prefers his present state. Ah yes, he is much better off with his beloved in his arms than when he was all alone. And to have his beloved in his arms is already the beginning of the collectivity, for it is not long before a whole brood of little ones arrives. Of course there are people who do not want to get married because they are too selfish and do not want to work to support a family; but they do not know that selfishness does not give them the right to remain single and that they will be punished for it. It is sometimes legitimate to remain single, but only if your motivation is divine. Otherwise it is much better to marry and have children, for then you are obliged to do something for others instead of shutting yourself away in selfish isolation.

We must make it quite clear to human beings that the collectivity is in their best interest, for the only thing they understand is what concerns their interest. You can reveal all kinds of truths to them, but you can never be sure that they will allow themselves to be convinced. Except in a few rare instances, the fact that something is true does not carry much weight. If you can show people where their interest lies, then the battle is won, they will be convinced for ever after; whereas if you only show them that something is true...

Years ago I used to meet people at receptions, and many of them were magnificent, highly educated, cultured people. But let me give you an example of the kind of conversation I would sometimes have with them. I am talking to an elderly man who tells me that he is seeking truth. I immediately look suitably impressed, ecstatic even, for as you well understand, it is a very honourable occupation to seek truth; it is greatly to his

The Concept of a Pan-World

credit. Then I ask him, 'And have you not found it yet?' 'No, alas.' 'But you are still seeking?' 'Yes.' 'Ah, that is wonderful. But is it so difficult to find truth? How old are you, sir?' 'Seventy-five.' 'Seventy-five, and you still have not found truth?' 'No.'

Well, at this point my expression begins to change and I say, 'My dear sir, let me tell you that you have found truth several times in the course of your life but you have never accepted it. I can also tell you why you have never accepted it.' At that he looks at me with astonishment. 'Yes,' I go on, 'it is very easy to find truth, for it is everywhere. You have certainly met it and seen and heard it, but you have never accepted it because you have had too many others things in mind. You have been looking for your own brand of truth, and when you met the truth and it failed to match what you had in mind, you said, "No, no, I am looking for a different truth, one that will give me money and pleasure, one that will be my servant and allow me to be the master." But truth, my dear sir, is not a servant; it is a princess, and it is we who must be at her service. The trouble is that you do not want to serve; you want to be served. I can only conclude, therefore, that you have never really sought truth; you have only sought a servant to gratify all your whims. If you had really wanted to find truth you would have found it a long time ago, for it is always there. Even now, today, it is there if you want it, but you do not really want it.' Well, I will not tell you how such a conversation ended.

So, as I was saying, we have to show human beings where their interest lies. We have to show them that a collective way of life is wealth, that it is a blessing. The face, the eyes, the voice, the thoughts of each individual emanate something and contribute something to the whole. For my part, I have been nourished by this life for years and years; my brothers and sisters give me so much love. You will say, 'Yes, but for you it is different. What about us?' You too. If you know how to behave, you too will receive so much love from all the others that by the time you leave you will be filled to overflowing. What is stopping you? Your wife? Do you think she would not let you love or be loved by someone else? Do you think she would be jealous? No, you do not understand. It is not a question of being loved by another woman but by all the brothers and sisters of the Brotherhood. Your wife cannot possibly hold that against you. She could not be jealous, because she too would receive the same love.

The trouble is that people just do not know how to live. They think that if they had just a little niche of their own, all their problems would be solved. No, they do not know how to live. Just think. If all men and women lived in brotherhood and love, you could move freely about the world and be welcomed with open arms in every country as members of the same family; whereas, as things are today, you are a stranger in every country but your own. Foreigners find all doors closed to them.

Let me give you the example of an experience I had one winter night during the war. One evening I took a late train from St Lazare station in Paris, intending to go back to Sèvres. I do not quite know what happened, because I took the train from the same platform as usual, but I soon realized that it was not going the right way. I got out at the first stop only to find that there were no more trains to Sèvres that night. I thought that if I told the man who was selling tickets what had happened, he would tell me if there was a nearby hotel where I could spend the night, but he refused to listen to me or answer my questions and shut the window in my face. He must have been frightened because of my foreign accent (after all it was wartime, the country was occupied, and nobody felt safe). I went out to the street hoping to find somebody who could tell me where to go, but everything was closed; people had barricaded themselves indoors. What could I do? I walked about for a while wondering where to go. It was no great hardship to spend a night out of doors—I could always meditate. The only trouble was that this particular night was very cold and my overcoat was not very warm.

Finally I sat down on a bench and began to pray, asking the invisible world to come to the rescue. Within a few minutes I heard footsteps coming closer, and I could tell from the way they rang out on the cobbles that it was a German patrol. I thought to myself, 'If I start to walk away they will see me and it will look suspicious,' so I got up and walked briskly towards them. When I found that they understood French, I explained what had happened to me, and they must have sensed that I was telling the truth, because they took me to a house that they seemed to know and knocked on the door. When an upstairs window was opened, they explained my problem to whoever was inside, but without a word the person slammed it shut again at once. 'It doesn't matter,' the Germans said; 'Come with us.'

They then took me to a mansion where there were a lot of people, mostly German officers, I believe, and gave me a bed. On another bed in the same room was a German, who woke up from time to time in the night and spoke to me, but not knowing German I did not understand a word he said. As for me, I lay there unable to sleep very much, thinking how strange it was for me to be there in the middle of the war, benefiting from the hospitality of the Germans. The next morning I was invited to join them for breakfast, and once again I was astonished to find that nobody questioned me. I had expected at the very least to be asked why I was there having breakfast with them, but not a word; and after breakfast one of them walked to the station with me. Why had they treated me so kindly when not a single Frenchman had even listened to me?

If human beings persist in their refusal to understand that their best interest lies in brotherly relations between all peoples, life itself will intervene to teach them a lesson. And life is relentless. Why do people still cling to notions that date back to the Stone Age when their only concern was to survive, when their only task was to find food and protect themselves against the weather, wild animals, and their own kind? Today, in view of the extraordinary development of human culture and civilization, things must change. All the elements necessary for a world-order of universal brotherhood are now in place. The only obstacle is the ill-will of human beings who refuse to let go of their atavistic tendencies. Universal brotherhood is just around the corner, but they will not consent to it. They refuse to participate in this work, because they are always busy with other things. Each individual is absorbed in his own affairs, and the rest does not interest him. How can universal brotherhood ever be achieved in such conditions? And yet, if all human beings gave their consent, it would happen very quickly.

Yes, the key to the whole thing is consent. Take the example of what happened with Hitler: do you think Hitler had any really outstanding qualities? No, and not only was he quite unexceptional, but he was sick and deranged into the bargain. The one thing he had in his favour, the thing that made him so powerful, was the consent of millions of Germans. He himself was not a powerful man, but for a few years the consent of others made him almost the ruler of the world. If this could be repeated, if this massive consent could be given not to a Hitler but to an initiate, in order to put the idea of a Pan-World into effect, you would soon see the results. Unfortunately, when it comes to plundering, sacking, and burning, there are always plenty of volunteers willing to participate; but for an idea, especially for a divine idea, no one is willing to lift a finger. If you stop on a street corner and start to make a speech against the government or against the rich, you will soon have a crowd round you ready to lend a hand and demolish everything. But try talking about Christ or the kingdom of God and no one will bother to stop and listen, except perhaps two or three old ladies who have nothing else to do. And if I started a club for all those who had lost their teeth or their hair or their waistline, I would have millions of members; but for this idea of the kingdom of God I have had no success at all.

You must not think that I am so naïve that I do not know how difficult it is to convince and stimulate people to work for good. I do know it, but should I stop trying just because it is difficult? The greatest difficulty lies in getting human beings to give up certain pastimes, certain pleasures that are a waste of time, and persuade them to commit themselves to this gigantic, useful work. Yes, but the fact that it is difficult is no reason why I should stop trying, stop talking about it. No, I am not so naïve—a little, no doubt, but not so much as all that. I know that what I am calling for is almost impossible to achieve, but we must achieve it. When will it be achieved? Before very long: when life's difficulties are even greater; when people see that it has become truly impossible to live together and start seriously looking for solutions. When this day comes they will find the solution in the teaching of the Universal White Brotherhood. There is no other way. And when they find this, the only solution, they will have all the methods they need to start making things better.

Lyon, March 6, 1966

III

The Master reads the Meditation for the day:

Mankind is like a body in which each country is an organ made up of living, working cells. But the organs of mankind are not animated by the same intelligence, the same disinterestedness[2] as the organs of our physical bodies, because each country works for its own interests to the detriment of its neighbour. The way in which the human body functions was decreed by a sublime intelligence, whereas the functioning of human society is the work of human intelligence, and this is why things do not work; the body of mankind is ill and in danger of death. This is why we should study the structure of human beings and take it as a model. We must know how nature designed them, how they function, what is good for their health and what makes them ill; and then we must understand that all the same rules apply to mankind as a whole.

When your brain and your heart are in good condition, even your feet feel well; you can feel that your feet, and even

---

[2] Disinterestedness, meaning altruism, the absence of bias motivated by personal interest or advantage, is a key word in Omraam Mikhaël Aïvanhov's philosophy.

The Concept of a Pan-World

your toes, rejoice. And then if your feet are cold, your nose starts sneezing; it is your feet that are cold but the nose that sneezes. Do I need to give you any more examples? When one organ is well, all the other organs feel it and rejoice; and when one organ is in distress, all the other organs feel the same distress. Only human beings rejoice when another country is in distress, because human beings are bad cells, bad organs.

Why have politicians, economists, and philosophers never taken the human organism as a basis for their studies? The human organism embraces everything: you can study it for thousands of years without coming to the end of the immensity it contains. As I have told you time and again, our physical body is a summary of the entire universe.

One of the first things one sees when studying the human body is that when the organs fail to work together disinterestedly for the good of the whole, all kinds of deficiencies and diseases appear. Just as human beings try to grab everything for themselves and give nothing to others, there are cells in our bodies that are unwilling to collaborate and work for others. These are the anarchic, egotistical cells that keep all the food and energy for themselves and produce tumours and cancerous growths. And who teaches a man's cells to behave like that? He does. His cells are simply following the example of their master; it is he who introduces the disorder in his cells by setting them a bad example.

Cosmic intelligence has decreed that all our organs—the stomach, heart, lungs, and so on—must work unselfishly together for the good of the whole being. How can men fail to see that it is thanks to this unselfish attitude, this self-abnegation and spirit of sacrifice, that they are alive and healthy? It is because disinterestedness is thousands of times more beneficial to us than egoism that the initiates attach so much importance to these qualities. We may think that we are gaining something by being selfish, but in fact we are sowing the seeds of disease in ourselves. Human beings are always looking for a chance to take advantage of their neighbour—in fact they pride themselves on this attitude. For my part, I read what the human organism tells me and I foresee that those who behave like this will perish, for they are sowing the seeds of their own destruction. You will say, 'That is all very well, but you cannot survive in this world with a spirit of self-abnegation and sacrifice. You will die.' On the contrary, it is this selfless attitude that plants within you the seeds of health, harmony, resurrection, and eternal life.

The trouble is that human beings have sunk so low that they can no longer see what is staring them in the face. If they were willing to study the laws of nature they would reach the same conclusions. Believe me, these laws exist, and it is high time you knew and respected them. It is also because of these laws that we work without payment. I have been working for an idea for years without payment. Occasionally, if some money falls into my lap I will accept it (usually, but not always), but I have never asked or demanded to be paid. Human beings do not know how to work for nothing; they always want to be paid. This is why they are ill and unhappy, because they have swallowed the germ that disrupts and destroys their cells. You will object, 'But it is not possible to work for nothing; we have our families and our children to look after.' Of course, I understand, but I have solved the problem for myself. Just think of how much a doctor asks for a consultation that takes five minutes. My advice is far more useful than that of any doctor, and yet I never take any money. I would be a multimillionaire by now if I did.

You too must learn to work without payment. When all those for whom you have worked so generously see how radiant and luminous you have become because of your idealism and your disinterestedness, they will not leave you in poverty; they will give you more than you would ever have asked for. Not all at once, perhaps, but in time they will come to recognize your good qualities, and even those who begin by exploiting and taking advantage of you will end by regretting it and paying you a debt of gratitude.

Knowing how greedy and unjust human beings are, disciples are aware in advance that, however hard they work and however devoted and unselfish they are, none of it will ever be properly appreciated. And this means that they expect no reward from their own kind. They know that their only reward will come from heaven—and the rewards we receive from heaven are far more precious than money. What is money, after all? It cannot give you happiness, peace, or light. But if you work for a divine idea, your name will be recorded in heaven; and unlike human beings, heaven will never let you down. It will send you all its most precious gifts of joy, inspiration, and bliss. Are these not worth a thousand times more than a few coins?

People pay others for their services, and then they do not have to love them. They say, 'I have paid them, haven't I? Why should I love them as well?' Sometimes, in fact, they dislike those they pay and want nothing to do with them any more. And those who are paid often sense this. They receive money but they are unhappy, for they receive no love, and nothing is worse than to be deprived of love. If you want to be loved you must learn to do something for nothing; then you will be paid with love. In the future the currency of love will be valued more highly than any other.

As you see, human beings never really think; they never learn what they must do to be happy, how to bask continuously in the light of heaven. They say, 'I really could not care less about loving other people. What I am interested in is having enough money to eat and drink as I please, to go wherever I like, and to make love with any woman that takes my fancy.' Yes, these are the things they want. And the love of others? Well, that is another matter. Those who want a lot of money are neither sensitive nor spiritual. They have many crude needs, and it costs money to provide for them. If they were interested in serving heaven they would have fewer claims on them from all sides and would not need so much money.

I am not against money. It is perfectly legitimate for people to be paid for the work they do, I have no objection. But for my part, I work without payment because I know the immense happiness that comes from working day and night without expecting anything in return from human beings. And you can have no notion of what I receive. It is nothing material or visible, but it is worth far more than money, and it can only be bought with disinterestedness. Yes, with disinterestedness you can buy both heaven and earth. All you have to do is give your heart and soul, your thoughts, your will, your health, and your whole life to the heavenly spirits, saying, 'All I have is at your service; my life is yours.' And since nothing is more precious than life, your sacrifice surpasses everything else, and the heavenly spirits are obliged by the law of divine justice to give you a particle of their celestial bliss. But if you are not ready to give anything, you cannot hope to receive anything; they will give you nothing. Here on earth it is possible to cheat and swindle others, but you cannot do that with the sublime entities; if you give nothing, you will receive nothing. If you want to hoard your wheat and refuse to sow it, it will either go mouldy or be eaten by rats.

A disciple must learn to give his life to heaven. He must say, 'Here is my life; it is yours for the service of the kingdom of God, for the light of the world, for the happiness of all humanity.' The sublime spirits on high are so astonished when they hear a human being—one among the four billions that inhabit the earth—saying such a thing, that they come from all directions to look and listen. The event is so rare that they gather together to marvel and rejoice to see an earthling offer them his heart and soul, and promise to serve them with his whole life.

Yes, this is all too rare. Everybody keeps everything for themselves. A young girl says, 'I intend to live my own life.' Yes, she will live her own life, but how? With great 'weeping and gnashing of teeth'. Why does she not decide to give her life to the Lord? He would know how to make so much better use of it than she ever could. He would send her intelligent beings to teach her what she should do to gain eternal life; whereas, by wanting to live her life in her own way, she will not have the guidance and enlightenment she needs and will live a life of sensuality and stupidity. By wanting to live her life in her own way she is preparing to do herself an injury that she will never be able to repair. So many young boys and girls talk about living their own lives, and those who hear them expressing this wish think that it is perfectly legitimate. But when an initiate hears these words he knows that those who say them belong to the category of ignorant and unhappy human beings who have no idea of what is in store for them.

Dear Lord. How are my brothers and sisters ever going to understand me? Give me the most overwhelming arguments and the most striking images so that at last, for the first time in their lives, they may be convinced. Yes, I pray to heaven to help me make you understand where your happiness and your interest lie. Your interest lies in disinterestedness.

Of course, there are always some who give a few minutes of their time without payment, but they keep all the rest for themselves; they still cling to their personal joys and pleasures. Those who have really solved the problem are not very numerous. Many people are ready to make an occasional effort, to sacrifice and renounce something every now and then, but I am obliged to say that there are not many who dedicate themselves totally to the service of light. Human consciousness is still too limited to grasp the splendour of this work. Most people are still trapped in their ancient conceptions, still ruled by the traditional fears and stratagems of the family and of society.

However, although I talk like this, I fully realize how difficult it is to dedicate oneself to the Lord. For a disciple to dedicate himself to God from an early age he must have already done a great deal of work in this direction in previous incarnations; otherwise it is impossible. With the best will in the world he could not do it; his whole being vibrates on a different frequency. He would find no joy, no inspiration, nothing that appeals to him in the idea of dedication; on the contrary, it would terrify him. It is not possible for everybody to understand this idea. Some may understand it theoretically, philosophically, but they still cannot put it into practice, because all the tendencies of their being lead them in another direction; they have other needs, other desires, other pleasures.

It is extremely difficult for most human beings to achieve this kind of spiritual dedication, therefore; but there are some, a few rare beings, who come into the world with this idea. From a very early age they feel that they are already dedicated. Nobody forces them; it is just that it gives them great joy to dedicate themselves. And as soon as they do so, they are under the protection of heaven. They receive all the light and guidance they need to see where they are going, and whatever their circumstances, however great their trials and tribulations, they are always protected, always safe. The sufferings they endure are not sent in order to destroy or annihilate them but to strengthen them, to incite them to conquer and prevail, to lead them to the highest peaks.

This does not mean that those who dedicate themselves to the Lord from an early age can expect to live in comfort without many hard lessons and trials in life. Far from it. Heaven takes care of them, but it does not let them stagnate in an effortless, uneventful, insignificant life. He who dedicates himself must realize that he will be tested. Not because he has to be punished or destroyed, but because he has to move on and reach other levels where he can develop and blossom, where he can awaken other possibilities within himself that could never be awakened if he were left to a life of tranquillity and ease. If you read the biographies of great initiates who dedicated themselves to heaven, you will see what they went through. Some of them knew that their trials were for their own good and neither kicked against the traces nor allowed themselves to be defeated. They knew that those trials could transform them into divinities. But there were others who were not so enlightened: their suffering was too much for them, and sometimes they rebelled. They could not understand why heaven continued to treat them so cruelly, even though their whole life was dedicated to God and they were filled with love and selflessness.

The one thing that spiritualists[3] stand most in need of, therefore, is knowledge, true knowledge. They think that once they dedicate themselves to God, milk and honey will flow for them; they will walk on rose petals and be welcomed with garlands. Of course it is true that we find promises of this kind in the Bible, and it is also true that they will one day be fulfilled, but only when we have come through all our trials with success. Many spiritualists have no idea why God seems to ill-treat them although they do nothing wrong, and they rebel against this seeming injustice that they cannot understand. Here you are being given the light you need to understand that if these things happen to you it is for your own good. Even the purest, most upright, noble, and luminous of beings, even those who are overflowing with love must endure certain trials, and this does not mean that God has abandoned them.

Apparently even Jesus experienced this terrible sense of solitude, for when he was on the cross he cried out, 'My God, my God, why have you forsaken me?' How could he, who was

---

[3] The word 'spiritualist' in the language of Omraam Mikhaël Aïvanhov means one who looks at things from a spiritual point of view, whose philosophy of life is based on belief in a spiritual reality.

so exalted, so luminous, utter such words? God never really abandoned him; he was always with him. Yes, but in spite of what Christians believe, Jesus was not God, and in the Garden of Gethsemane he prayed, 'Father, if it be your will, remove this cup from me,' because although he knew that his death was decreed, he still wanted to avoid it. And when the Gospel tells us that while he was praying his sweat became 'like great drops of blood,' it reveals the almost unimaginable state of tension he must have been in at the thought of the death that awaited him.

I am not saying this in order to belittle Jesus in any way; on the contrary, no one is more aware of his greatness. But Jesus was a man, and at the bottom of every man's heart lurks a trace of fear and anguish in the face of suffering and death. But a heavenly messenger was sent to comfort him and tell him, 'Your prayer has been heard. The Lord knows how great your suffering is, but it has been decreed. There is a reason for your torment. You know this reason, and you know that it will reverberate through the centuries so that all mankind may benefit from your sacrifice.' Then Jesus accepted what was asked of him, saying, 'Lord, not my will but yours be done.' It is not easy, when our trials are upon us, to say, 'Lord, may your will be done. I know that it is for my own good and for the good of humanity.' You have to be very highly evolved to be able to say such a thing.

You must make sure that what I am revealing to you today is indelibly imprinted in your minds. If you are not working for good, if you have not dedicated yourself to the Lord, the trials you have to endure will be of a different kind. They will be a punishment for the faults you have committed, and if you do not know how to overcome them, you will descend into hell; you will become a demon. Yes, there are different kinds of trials. When someone works for the glory of God, the purpose of his trials is his ultimate transformation into a divinity. But if he works against the light, against good, the trials he

The Concept of a Pan-World

experiences are stumbling blocks and punishments. True, they are also designed to help him and to prevent him from sinking even lower, but they are still a punishment. It is important to understand, therefore, that these two kinds of trial are quite distinct. Many people—even many spiritualists—get them mixed up. They are incapable of seeing the difference because they do not possess the criteria they need.

This you must know, therefore: if you persist in an attitude of cupidity, egoism, and animosity, you will be introducing the seeds of disintegration into yourself. This is an absolute law. Analyse yourselves, and if it gives you pleasure to imitate the lowest beings because they seem at first sight to enjoy some success, then by all means do so. But I warn you, you will never know peace. Why not? Because this truth that I have explained to you will never leave you in peace. Never. You will never feel safe; you will always be saying to yourself, 'What is in store for me?' Even if you do not believe what I have been saying, some of it will have filtered in and registered within you. Without your realizing it, all my words are etched into your being. One day in fact, when they rise to the surface and manifest themselves, you will be astonished to see how much of what I have said has been recorded within you. So much the better. Believe me, when I say something, it is never in vain. From now on you will not know a day of peace. You will say, 'But that is terrible; you are our sworn enemy.' No, I am not your enemy, but I still say that you will never know peace again because of this truth. It will continue to tighten its grip on you, and sooner or later you will be obliged to restore order to your lives and get back on to the right path. Only then will you know peace and tranquillity. 'And in the meantime,' you say, 'it is your fault if we know no peace.' No, do not blame me, blame heaven; I am only the servant of heaven.

The human organism is a book, and in this book I find all the essential truths. But most educated people never attach any importance to what God has placed in man. All their research is limited to what so-and-so said or wrote, and they take pride in quoting their favourite author, however nonsensical. They never have any opinions of their own. For my part, I never quote anyone.

Human beings have never observed what goes on in their own bodies. They have no idea that when they are well it means that their organs are functioning harmoniously. They do not know that the foundation of their health is the law of sacrifice and self-abnegation. Mankind as a whole is also a body, and the different countries are its organs, but instead of working harmoniously together, these organs are devoured by cancer, and the world is doomed to perish because egoism and self-interest are the order of the day.

The Bonfin, August 8, 1975

Chapter Four

The Cosmic Body

I

Mankind needs a new religion. New, not in its essence or its principles, but in its applications. I have already talked about this a good deal and given you innumerable explanations concerning the more obscure passages in the Bible—particularly in the New Testament. Have I succeeded in making myself understood? Only time will tell. I am not at all sure that I have, for the minds of human beings are so deformed that it is almost impossible to get them to understand that their conception of religion is wholly inadequate. If it were adequate, would they always feel as though they were in a void? Would they always be so ill, distraught, and disorientated? If their conception of religion were adequate, they would all be immersed in peace and light—and this is very far from being the case.

Of course, every now and then one meets people who are content with life, but when I talk about happiness, I am talking about a stable, lasting condition, not a fleeting, ephemeral happiness. Everybody experiences happiness at some time or another, but only briefly. A man is happy because he has just got married; but before long his wife leaves him and he is unhappy. Or he has a child and that makes him happy; but his child turns out badly and he tears his hair in grief. Or he is happy because he has come into a fortune; but as he squanders his fortune, he soon begins to worry about where his next meal will come from. True happiness can endure, but it can only endure if it is based on a proper understanding of its nature. As I have so often said, happiness is a state of consciousness that is the result of how one understands and feels things. Human beings cannot be happy if their minds and hearts are continually pervaded by bizarre, dark thoughts and destructive feelings and emotions. This is why the work of initiates from time immemorial has been to teach men love and wisdom, for the light of the mind and the warmth of the heart give birth to harmonious movement, to a constructive, well-balanced activity.

As long as men and women have not attained this light and warmth, their actions will always contain certain negative elements that are liable to distort or even destroy their own happiness and that of others. And this is what hell is. Hell is not a place that exists in some distant corner of the universe; it exists here on earth, in the hearts and souls of those who delight in disorder and anarchy. And there are a great many such people in the world today, people who have embraced the philosophy of anarchy, without realizing the dangers lying in wait for them. Sooner or later, such people will be destroyed. If they had studied the laws of nature and seen how the universe was created, if they had learned about all the different regions of which it is composed, and all the different creatures that inhabit those regions, they would have understood that they, too, were an integral part of this living body of nature and that their behaviour must harmonize with the whole. If their anarchical attitude becomes too troublesome, nature will simply take a purge and expel them. Anarchists are never tolerated for very long. If other human beings do not exterminate them, nature intervenes and does it herself, for she cannot allow disharmony to prevail. Disharmony is a tumour, a cancerous growth in her body, and she takes the necessary steps to get rid of it.

The Cosmic Body

   This is what initiatic science tells us. And once initiates understand this truth, their one great fear is to become a tumour in the cosmic body by failing to vibrate in unison with it. Initiates fear only one thing, and that is to find that their psychic state is such that their vibrations are at variance with universal harmony, for they know what is in store for them if this happens. This is why they always strive to conform to, and vibrate in unison with, the great body of the cosmos. If singers in a choir or musicians in an orchestra refuse to sing or play according to the score, they will be dismissed immediately, for they destroy the harmony of the whole. This is why I say that anarchists are very stupid, because this is exactly what will happen to them. If they were intelligent, they would understand that they cannot prevail for long, for they are always liable to meet and be annihilated by those who are even more anarchical than themselves. In any case, if they are not destroyed by other human beings, they will be destroyed by the laws of nature, for these laws are terrible and implacable.

   The teaching of the Great Universal White Brotherhood is the teaching of hierarchy; and hierarchy supposes a synarchy. Synarchy is government by an elite, by the head; but government today is in the hands of the lower organs—stomach, belly, and genitals—in the hands, that is, of the ignorant masses. It is the masses that rule, the masses that make the decisions and give orders, and as long as it is the masses—the cells of the stomach—that govern, mankind will not make much progress, for the cells of the stomach are only interested in money, pleasure, and food, and the freedom to do whatever they please. They are not capable of interesting themselves in anything more elevated. The function of these cells is to digest; that is all they know how to do. It is not their business to make decisions or give orders; that is the function of the cells of the brain, which, thanks to the faculties of sight, hearing, speech, and so on are in a position to lead and govern. For the time being, the cells of the brain—the initiates—are silent; they have disappeared, hidden themselves. When they saw how human beings behaved, how violence was becoming more and more prevalent, how brute force, ambition, and the lower appetites were gaining the upper hand, they went away and left mankind to its own resources.

This state of affairs will last until such time as human beings, ill, exhausted, and on the verge of extinction, finally realize that they are incapable of finding the solutions they need by themselves, because they are too degenerate, their desires are too material, and they know nothing either of the spiritual world or of the methods they should be working with. The day they understand this, they will begin to call on this elite, on the initiates who still exist and are still at work, but who have left mankind to learn what can only be learned from harsh experience. It is not that these beings are cruel; it is just that they keep an eye on mankind and wait for the right moment to act. They have no desire to meddle in the affairs of the world for the moment, for human beings are incapable of producing anything but war and tragedy. You will object that this is not true; that there are a great many people who long for peace. True, but those who long for peace are weaklings, incapable of doing anything to bring it about. Nobody listens to them; they have no part in making the decisions that count. The decision to make war, for instance, is in the hands of those who have money, prestige, and power. It is they who prepare wars and decide when and where they will take place.

What did Jesus mean by the words, 'Thy kingdom come'? The notion of the kingdom of God is not very clear to Christians. Many of them see the kingdom of God as somewhat like an earthly kingdom, with a monarch, Cabinet ministers, a police force, and so on. But it is not that. The kingdom of God is an order that is far beyond the grasp of human beings, and no amount of explanations can convey an idea of it. The only way to understand this state is to live it, and in order to live it, we have to uproot ourselves, that is, we have

The Cosmic Body

to discard our old, mistaken notions and embrace new, true ones. It is as though we had to leave the dusty, crowded roads of the plains and climb to the top of a mountain, where the air is pure and the view immense.

If human beings want to understand the kingdom of God, the first thing they must do is stop living in the midst of anarchy. Yes, there is still a great deal that needs to be said on this subject. For one thing, an attitude that would generally be termed anarchical is not always and necessarily bad. It is the state of mind of someone who intends to live his life in his own way and refuses to be subject to the established order. Whether that order be good or bad, he wants to live according to his own ideas, and, in fact, it can happen that his ideas are superior to those of the established order. In this case, society would consider him an anarchist, but in the eyes of heaven he is no anarchist, for he aspires to more love, more fraternity, and greater justice. From the point of view of the initiates, an anarchist is one who refuses to recognize the divine order, who denies the existence of a Lord of the universe and of higher entities and forces, who refuses to acknowledge that there are higher laws to which he must submit. Such a man may be in perfect accord with a society composed of millions of his fellow men who have no spiritual life, but he is an anarchist in relation to the sublime intelligence of the universe, because he transgresses its laws.

Actually, most human beings are anarchists without realizing it. Outwardly they may be thoroughly decorous and law-abiding—so much so that some of them are awarded with medals by a grateful society—but although they have never transgressed a human law in their lives, they are ready to transgress every inner law. They respect the laws of society only because they are afraid of being found out and punished if they break them; but even though the divine laws are far more to be feared than the laws of society, people do not seem to be afraid to break them. If people are reasonably intelligent—or simply lucky—they can always side-step the laws of earth, but no one, however astute or intelligent, has ever been able to evade the divine laws, because another, higher intelligence is always there, watching and recording everything they do. Evil-doers are always found out and punished because, without their realizing it, their misdeeds always leave a trace on the invisible plane. Even a thought or a feeling leaves a trace. Even though you may not actually commit a crime, if you entertain evil thoughts, these thoughts leave their trace, not only on you but on your surroundings. This is why the law—divine law, that is—is able to track you down, and before long you yourself begin to feel the effects of those evil thoughts.

The main reason why human beings make no attempt to control their thoughts and feelings is that they simply do not believe that divine justice exists. They confuse divine justice with human justice, and as so many of them manage, in spite of their crimes, to elude human justice, they imagine that they will also be able to elude divine justice. They have never studied the question sufficiently to realize how different the two are: divine justice may not lay its hand on you outwardly, but it will certainly reach you inwardly. If you examined the state of health of criminals who have supposedly eluded justice, you would see that they are inwardly in ruins, their physical and psychic health devastated. Outwardly, there is still something that holds them together, but one day even that will collapse, for it is the inner dimension that sustains and nourishes the whole, that serves as the foundation of the whole structure. If the inner dimension collapses, sooner or later the outer dimension will also collapse. Divine justice is instantaneous. At the precise moment of breaking a law, something within you crumbles. It often takes years, however, for this inner decay to show itself outwardly. This is why, for example, one sometimes meets women who are veritable demons inwardly but who are still outwardly beautiful. And the reverse can also be true. But I have already talked to you at length about this,[1] and I do not wish to talk about it again today. Today I prefer to stick to the question of anarchy.

According to initiatic science, an anarchist is someone who refuses to submit to the divine order of creation, and this means that nine-tenths of all human beings should be classed as anarchists. People's understanding of anarchy is usually based on political or social criteria, but these are inadequate; the only true anarchy is anarchy in relation to heaven. Of course, in actual fact, many people are doubly anarchical, being anarchical in their attitude both towards earth and towards heaven.

Think of the parable of the prodigal son, who left his father's house because he was bored and went out into the world in search of freedom and adventure. To begin with, he enjoyed the novelty of it all, but his enjoyment did not last long and his fortunes gradually deteriorated. Wherever he went he was a foreigner, and people distrusted him and refused to give him work. So the poor young man began to suffer from hunger, thirst, and bitter cold; he had nothing to eat and nowhere to live, and he began to regret having left his father's house. He remembered that there he had had everything he needed; everybody knew who he was, and his father and mother and the whole family loved him. He knew now from his own experience that neither love nor pity ruled the world, and so, a wiser and a humbler man, he decided to go back home. And his father recognized his son in the miserable, half-starved creature who appeared before him dressed in rags and covered with dust. The Gospel adds that he welcomed him with open arms and ordered the fatted calf to be killed to celebrate his return. Of course, his brother was rather angry at all this and grumbled a bit, but the father soothed his feelings and reminded him that he should be generous to someone who was destitute.

---

[1] See *Creation: Artistic and Spiritual*, chap. 9. Izvor Collection, N°. 223.

The story of the prodigal son is the story of all those who, instead of living in harmony with divine law, want to do exactly as they like and take pleasure in being anarchical. And, as I have said, the worst form of anarchy is that which reigns within man. This is why the goal of all initiatic schools is to induce human beings to return to their Father's house, to the safety of that 'secret place' of which Psalm 91 speaks ('He who dwells in the secret place of the Most High shall abide under the shadow of the Almighty... He is my refuge and my fortress; my God, in him I will trust'), and which the forces of evil cannot enter. Human beings always seem to be glad to get away from this secret place in which they are under the protection of the Lord. They are eager to live their lives in their own way by breaking God's laws and getting as far away from him as possible. Well, let me tell you that people like that have a great deal of suffering in store for them. Their constant tendency to be out of step and to disobey means that their destiny requires them to suffer. But those who have already suffered a great deal, and whose sufferings have brought them understanding, are ready to return to their Father, to that 'secret place'. This is why they join a spiritual brotherhood, an initiatic school, for to do so symbolizes a return to the divine order.

Many years ago I talked to you about this 'secret place' in which man is invulnerable. It is a world of such harmony, a world in which the vibrations are so intense and so pure, that the slightest negative element is immediately rejected and cast out. Jesus said: 'I am the vine, you are the branches. Those who abide in me and I in them bear much fruit, because apart from me you can do nothing. Whoever does not abide in me is thrown away like a branch and withers; such branches are gathered, thrown into the fire, and burned.' This expresses exactly the same idea. Find and take refuge in this fortress, therefore, so that you may be protected and nourished. How can anyone fail to understand this? Human beings are all

The Cosmic Body

anarchists, they all want to break away from the Lord in the hope of getting something more, something which, in fact, they can never get. Before launching out blindly like that, they would do much better to study the laws and understand how things are likely to turn out. But they are like the prodigal son: he too should have seen what life was like in his father's house and compared it with the life he would find in the outside world, where men claw, bite, and hack their way to success. But he did not study anything, the poor wretch; he just imagined what he would find. And this is what all anarchists do, they imagine. This is why I advise you all to examine the whole question very thoroughly to see what is in store for you if you continue on the path of anarchy.

This question of laws is so easy to understand. Suppose you overeat: you will not be prosecuted in the name of any human law—no policeman will come and arrest you—but you will suffer from acute indigestion. In the name of what law are you laid low and put to bed? The laws of nature are not those of human beings. Human beings will come and see you and commiserate with you in bed, but however much they sympathize, they will not be able to cure you; only nature can cure you. If you start to obey the laws of nature again you will be cured. You must learn these laws of nature, the divine laws that rule the intellect, the heart, and the physical body. You should know exactly what everything you say and do represents in the way of energy, see where these energies go, and make sure that they do not disturb or harm anyone. In the Tales from the Arabian Nights there is a story about a merchant who sat down to rest from his travels and eat some dates, and as he ate he threw the stones carelessly in different directions. Suddenly, a monstrous genie appeared and declared that he would kill him. 'But why?' stammered the unfortunate merchant; 'What have I done?' 'When you were throwing those stones away,' replied the genie, 'my son was passing by, and you threw one into his eye and killed him. Therefore I must kill you.' Of course this is only a legend, but there is great meaning in it.

There is also a popular tradition that when one goes out at night one must carry a light. This external light symbolizes the inner lamp that you must keep burning in order to protect yourself against evil spirits. For just as wild beasts hunt their prey at night, so do many evil spirits roam freely at night, seeking to harm human beings, until at cock-crow they are obliged to disappear. But human beings are so ignorant; they leave their doors wide open night and day for any entity to enter and lay waste their inner world.

So there you are, my dear brothers and sisters, do as you please; cut yourselves off from the Lord and maintain your independence if you like, and you will see what your destiny will be. For my part, I do not need to wait and see; I already know what it will be. How do I know that? I only have to see a person's attitude and I can immediately sense what he wants from life. The goals of those who cut themselves off from God and from the fellowship of initiates, who turn their back on the light, are necessarily extremely banal and mundane. They want wealth, power, and glory; they want to be able to gratify their appetite for food and drink and sexual pleasure. In other words, their ideal is not very lofty; on the contrary, they spend their time in the filth and slime of the lowest regions, and the only possible outcome is misfortune and suffering. As you see, I only need to know a person's ideal and I can immediately tell you what his final destination will be; he will end up exactly where his ideal has led him. When you possess initiatic science, nothing is easier than to prophesy. When you know which track a train is running on, you know exactly which towns it will go through and where it will end up. Every station-master is a prophet. And astronomers are prophets too, because they can tell you the exactly where the planets will be years in advance. All those who are really proficient in any

The Cosmic Body

science are prophets. Predictions for the future are based on an occult science.

There, this is what I wanted to say about anarchy. All these intellectuals who think they are God's gift to mankind must learn that their philosophy of breaking away from the centre can only lead to enslavement and total restriction, for there can be no freedom far from the centre. What is in store for you if you withdraw from the light and warmth of the sun? Darkness, cold, and death. And the sun symbolizes the initiatic confraternity. The Psalmist says, 'I walk before the Lord in the land of the living,' and this 'land of the living' is the true confraternity, the sun, for in the sun dwell the noblest, most luminous of beings. That which we call sunlight is the vibrations, emanations, and radiations of these incandescent beings. The light that illuminates the planets comes not from the sun itself but from the sun's inhabitants. The sun is a richly fertile, cultivated land, a very advanced civilization, and it is the inhabitants of this land that project light out into space. All this will one day be discovered by scientists, but initiates have known it for ages, for they have travelled in their etheric bodies into every region of space and visited the sun and the other planets. Believe me or not, as you please, but I am telling you the truth.

It is a great mistake to think that to belong to an initiatic confraternity implies that you have to restrict yourself and forfeit your freedom; on the contrary, only in such a confraternity will man find freedom and happiness. True self-realization can be achieved only in the one true brotherhood, the Great Universal White Brotherhood which exists in the higher world and of which our own Brotherhood here on earth is no more than a reflection. Also, if you think that it depends on your decision to belong or not to belong to that great Brotherhood, that too is an illusion. Some people may say that they do not want to belong, but the truth is that they would not be accepted. If they were worthy to join it, they would be eager to do so, but it is not all comers who can be accepted just as they are. Each one has to work for years and years and prove that they are worthy before being allowed to join this confraternity. Perhaps you will say, 'But I have never done anything to earn it, and yet I have been accepted as a member of the Universal White Brotherhood.' Yes, but the Brotherhood here on earth is no more than a vestibule; it is not yet the Holy of Holies. It is much more difficult to be accepted into the Brotherhood on high, but once you are accepted your name is inscribed in heaven and you receive all the gifts and all the help you need every day; just as the employees of a company here on earth receive a salary, family allowances, and so on.

Perhaps you are thinking, 'Where on earth does he get all that?' Well, you have read the Gospels: surely you remember that Jesus said, 'See, I have given you authority to tread on snakes and scorpions, and over all the power of the enemy; and nothing will hurt you. Nevertheless, do not rejoice at this, that the spirits submit to you, but rejoice that your names are written in heaven.' Once your name is written in the book of life you will not be forgotten. You will be given strength, health, and joy. You will feel that support, advice, and guidance are bestowed on you, and even if you do have to endure trials and difficulties, you will find either that they will not last so long as they used to or that you are stronger and more able to deal with them. This is the Gospel, the living Gospel; and it is up to you now to make the necessary effort to enter this fortress, this secret place, for once you are there you will be safe. There is a Sanskrit text that says, 'A pilgrim has reached the far bank of the river, an *arhat* is born, a new *dvija*, a saviour of the world,' and in Christianity this idea is expressed by the quest for the Holy Grail. In one form or another, all religions speak of this confraternity under the rulership of Christ.

Human beings look for a confraternity to join, of course, but never this one. They prefer to join a political confraternity and are ready to be massacred for an ideology that will soon be

The Cosmic Body

out of fashion and replaced by another one. They are not interested in putting themselves at the service of an ideal that would make them immortal and invincible. But for heaven's sake, if they really want to shed their blood, why cannot they at least choose a cause that is eternal? They just do not use their brains; they sell their freedom for too little. All their brave words about the price of freedom are just that, words. The truth is that they do not care two hoots for their freedom, their life, their blood. Someone who really wants to save his life entrusts it to a bank that will never become insolvent; to the bank of the sun, not to a ship that is sinking because it has a hole in its hull. I was still very young when I realized that I should never achieve very much if I relied on my own freedom, my own will, and my own intelligence. This is why I did everything possible to enter the divine order of the Universal White Brotherhood. And if you, for your part, continue to believe that you will achieve great things on your own without this confraternity, I can prophesy that what you gain in this way will be far less than what you would gain by joining it.

To possess your own house and have money in the bank—is that your idea of success? If so, when it is time to depart for the next world you will see that you have worked in vain—or, rather, you have been working for the benefit of thieves. So acquire all the material possessions you want, but know that you will be obliged to leave them all behind; whereas the things you acquire through your spiritual work will always be yours, and you will take them with you into the next world. Wherever you go, your capital, your wealth, all your precious stones will go with you and will benefit the whole world. You will probably think that what I am saying is very difficult to understand; it is as though I were speaking an unknown language. You would all understand me if I talked about higher mathematics, but people no longer understand the language I speak, although it seems to me that nothing could be clearer.

It is not a sign of intelligence and freedom to refuse to

submit to the great laws of the Universal White Brotherhood. The Gospels tell us that we are all obliged to serve a master. If we refuse to serve Christ and the light, we shall be obliged to serve the devil and the powers of darkness. This is a law. People say, 'Oh, you know, this thing about Christ and the light is not for me. I cannot accept that.' Well, if that is your attitude, you too will be unable to avoid falling into the power of dark forces. Those who seek to be free in their own way cannot find true freedom; they will find only slavery. They are influenced and controlled by other entities. Their ignorance is such that they are easily hoodwinked into thinking that they are following their own wishes and making their own decisions, while in fact they are working for others. Human beings are like children; they just do not understand. When small children want to be free, they are liable to do all kinds of stupid and dangerous things that will restrict their freedom even more. Young people—and adults, too, for that matter—have no more understanding of freedom than a baby. Only the wise know that if you want to be free you have to impose limitations on yourself. Others, on the pretext that they want to be free, let their wild beasts out of their cages, and then they are torn apart and devoured by them.

I happened to switch on the television yesterday, and what did I see? Four hairy ruffians who looked like animals, screaming and gesticulating incoherently. This, apparently, was a concert. Never have I heard anything so repulsive and discordant. But the audience—mostly young boys and girls—were wildly enthusiastic, clapping and jumping up and down and twisting about in hideous contortions. I could not help feeling sad at the sight. I thought to myself, 'My God, how can anyone understand human nature today? What is it in man's soul that has the power to estrange him from beauty to such an extent? How can four such villainous creatures be such a popular success?' I am not so strict and narrow-minded as to condemn young people for wanting to express their vitality and joy, but there was no joy here at all; the movements which should have been an expression of vitality were no more than horrible, unsightly contortions. Wild animals! Yes, the doors of their cages had been flung wide open, and they were prowling about, devouring whatever good there was in those so-called musicians while the crowd looked on and applauded.

Seeing this, I almost lost hope of ever leading human beings to something beautiful and meaningful. They are going to have to go all the way; they are going to have to touch bottom. How can people like that understand the magnificent laws of nature? They have never done any work on themselves; they do not even know that there is work to be done. The only thing they know is how to open the cages of their own wild animals. And they call that freedom, liberation. Yes, they are liberated, independent—unleashed.

The Bonfin, July 25, 1965

II

What a magnificent sunrise we had today, and how privileged we are to witness such splendour.

I am well aware that the sun does not mean anything to some of you; it does not arouse any special feeling or vibration in you; you feel no particular attachment to it. It is as though, as far as you are concerned, the sun were dead. Yes, the living, vibrant sun rises every morning and distributes its treasures to the world, but some of you are entirely untouched and unmoved by it, as though there were a screen between you and the sun. And indeed there is. That screen is the way you have lived the day before... or for many days before that. You have never realized that your thoughts and feelings could make any difference—for good or for ill—to the way you react in front of the rising sun. This is why the sun means nothing to you.

If you were inwardly organized and prepared to meet the sun every day, you would understand that it is a living being, a brilliant, dazzling world inhabited by the most highly evolved beings, and that it can give you the solution to all your problems. It never occurs to people that the sun can do more than give them light and heat. They only scoff if you tell them that it can also instruct them and teach them a great deal. For most people, the sun is just a ball of fire, and nobody knows

The Cosmic Body

quite why it is there. So they stick to what they do know and interest themselves in everything except trying to understand the wealth and splendour of the sun.

I have just used the word 'organized', saying that you must be inwardly organized and prepared. We often hear this word these days: people say that they have to organize this or that, that such and such an organization is good or bad, and so on, but they do not always understand the real meaning of the word.

The word organization comes from organ. And what is an organ? You could say that an organ is an instrument whose function is to form a relationship, a link between objects, forces, beings, or other instruments of the same kind. In the absence of an appropriate organ, there can be no exchange between two beings. Our skin, our ears and eyes, and so on, are the organs by which we perceive and are in touch with the world around us. If one of your essential organs is missing—an arm, a leg, or your tongue—you cannot do your work properly, for you cannot move about, hold things, or speak. And this is just as true on the spiritual as on the physical plane: if the appropriate organs are missing, you will not have the instruments you need in order to know the subtle world. This is why the invisible world is incomprehensible to most human beings: they have not yet formed the organs that would enable them to make contact with it.

Human beings do not know how to reason correctly, so they arrive at the stupid conclusion that since they cannot see or feel the invisible world, therefore it does not exist. They forget that scientific instruments have been showing us for a very long time now that both sound and light exist on vibrational frequencies that are beyond our powers of perception. Man's powers of perception are limited, but his reasoning powers are even more limited, for, rather than acknowledge that there are things that cannot be perceived by his sense organs, he prefers to deny the existence of anything he cannot actually see or touch. Nothing could be more stupid. From the beginning of time, there have always been people gifted with highly developed organs that enabled them to see things in the invisible world. Such organs go by different names—a sixth sense, the pineal gland, intuition, the eye of the spirit—but it makes no difference what you call them, the important thing is that they are as real as our physical organs. In the distant past, all human beings had these subtle organs in perfect working order, and it was only gradually, as they became increasingly materialized, that they ceased to function. It is time now to restore these faculties to their original state, and this can be achieved by means of spiritual work and a suitable way of life.

As I say, we hear a great deal about organization today, but it is always a question of material organization. As a matter of fact, although things are still not perfect in the social and political spheres, men have already achieved a fairly good degree of external organization. But what chaos in their inner lives. It never occurs to them that they need to organize things on that level too; all their efforts are focused on the external world. Where the inner, philosophical, metaphysical realm is concerned they are content to invent all kinds of complicated, incomprehensible terms and notions, which often have no relation to fact, but they never attempt to develop the organs that would enable them to make direct contact with the spiritual world. And yet that world does, after all, exist; it is a reality. As long as human beings are not actually in touch with this world, anything they say about it will be hollow and meaningless. It is important, therefore, to begin to organize your spiritual life and to live and work in a way that enables your spiritual organs to unfold and develop so that you can make contact with invisible, celestial realities. As long as you are too absorbed in your ordinary, mundane activities you will not be free to develop that inner organization and to discover the reality of this unknown world, which is so much vaster, richer, and more beautiful than the everyday world we know.

The fact that you come to the sunrise in the morning without having prepared yourselves proves that you have not understood. This is why there is no communication between you and the sun, why you do not receive the waves he sends you. Every sunrise should make you richer. All that abundance, all that untold, incalculable wealth is there for you to draw on so that you may then distribute it to others. Go to this inexhaustible source every morning with all the receptacles you possess, for it is capable of quenching the thirst of all creatures.

It is true that scientists, who love to calculate everything, have interested themselves in the sun to the extent of trying to determine how long it will live. Instead of going to the sunrise to draw light, warmth, and life from it, they compute the hour of its death. But their calculations will always be wide of the mark. The sun can prolong his own life for just as long as he pleases, for he has drunk the elixir of everlasting life. I assure you, I saw him drinking it, and I know that he will live as long as he wants to. You do not believe me? All right, go and check it for yourselves. Why is it that when you do not believe something I say you never go and find out the truth for yourselves? If you did, you would see that it is true that the sun has drunk the elixir of everlasting life. You are perhaps wondering who gave it to him. The elixir of everlasting life is what alchemists call the Magistery of the Sun, which is simply a condensation of the sun's rays. So the sun does not need anyone to give it to him; he gives it to himself without ceasing. The sun is the true phoenix, that fabulous bird that is portrayed as rising constantly from its own ashes. But there are no ashes in the sun.

The phoenix is the symbol of all highly evolved beings who, knowing the laws of life and immortality, are capable of constantly renewing themselves. The sun is their model. Those who aspire to everlasting life must take their lesson from the sun, because only the sun can teach us what elements we need in order to win immortality and how to go about obtaining them. These elements are three in number: the light, the warmth, and the life that the sun pours out unceasingly into space. And the only way a disciple can benefit from all this wealth distributed by the sun is to keep a close watch on himself and not lose himself in activities that restrict him and tie him down. Otherwise, even if he is brought face to face with the fountainhead of life, with the Almighty himself, even if a myriad of shining, sparkling beings reveal their splendour to him, he will be so engrossed in his inner state of dissatisfaction and gloom that he will neither see them nor receive anything from them.

As long as your spiritual organs are not in good working order, there is nothing you can do about it; the sun will still be there before your eyes but you will not feel it. Even the power of the sun is not enough to give you physical eyes; that is up to you. And this is equally true in the spiritual life. The sun exists within every human being, but they neither see nor feel its presence because their spiritual organs are not yet formed. The first thing they have to do, therefore, is to start forming these inner organs—or awakening them, rather, for centuries of disuse have left them in a state of atrophy. So as I say, it is possible to attend the sunrise for years and years without learning anything. But the day you understand what I am saying, the day you prepare yourselves for the sunrise as though it were more important than any other event in life, you will begin to drink the sun, to be nourished by the sun, and to do some intelligent and useful work.

However much you explain things to human beings, however many mysteries of creation or of the kingdom of God you reveal to them, they will not yet be able to understand or use those revelations, because the necessary organs are missing. No doubt you will be wondering why, although well aware of this, I go on with my work. First of all because there is always a chance that things will improve if I persevere. I continue to explain and work for the few whose organs are already in working order. Then, too, I know that there is a law of magic that decrees that if you enlighten others in order to help them to evolve, even if your efforts fail to bear fruit, you will have given an outlet to the forces of love within you, and it is you who will benefit from that love, you who will be happy, who will develop and grow and be enriched. Others can stay as they are if they want to, but you at least will prosper and grow.

Yes, I know the reality, but it does not discourage me. Whatever comes, I persevere with my work, if only for my own sake. Even if you were not there, I would still go to the sunrise—in fact I would sometimes feel much freer alone—but I still prefer to be at the sunrise with you, for when we are together, there is an added dimension, an atmosphere of warmth and love, and I prefer that. No doubt I am biased, but I prefer to attend the sunrise with all my 'family' around me.

So, as I have said, we need to reach a deeper understanding of the word 'organization'. Scientists speak of organic and inorganic chemistry. Organic chemistry studies substances produced by living organisms; whereas inorganic or mineral chemistry studies elements that are considered to be lifeless. In fact, everything is organic, but not everything is organized. The brain, for instance, exists organically, but that does not mean that the brain of every human being is really organized. An organized brain is one in which the psychic activity of thought and feeling is free from all friction or disorder. And what about human society? Is it organized? Outwardly, at least, it seems to be: trade and commerce, the police, postal services, hospitals, and so on, are all highly organized; but it is an organization that is purely mechanical, for the harmony that is part and parcel of the notion of organization does not yet exist. The truth is that the word organization can be applied rightfully only to the divine world, in which everything functions smoothly and without conflict. When we talk about perfect organization on earth, about the organization of a brain or of society, we can do no more than mouth the words: the reality is still unorganized.

Humanity needs a model of perfect organization in which everything functions as it should, but you will not find such a model on earth. You must look for it in the region in which it can be seen in action, and this region is the sun. Of course, when I speak of the sun, I am not speaking of the visible, physical sun but of the world of harmony and peace that the physical sun symbolizes. Perhaps some of you will say, 'It is not the sun that is the most highly organized, it is the Church.' Oh dear, if you knew what went on in the Church. Outwardly, it is true, it is hierarchically organized, but inwardly it is not so very different from any of the other so-called organizations we see in the world. Organization in the true sense of the word is not only external. External organization is necessary of course, I do not deny it, but it is not the be-all and end-all. In fact it is useless if it is not accompanied by something else, something higher that animates and vivifies it. That is the kind of organization I want.

Look at yourselves. All your functions are organized, your respiratory, digestive, and circulatory systems are all in working order, and yet you are always unhappy, discouraged, weak, and lack-lustre. Why? If physical organization were enough you would have everything you need. So we have to conclude that it is not enough. This physical organization needs to be infused by another, inner organization. Let me take another example: you have installed a complete electrical system in your house with all the necessary wires, cables, and meters, but nothing works. Why? Because there is no power coming into your house from the mains. Everything is in place but this one connection. Plug it in or switch it on and there you are, the lights come on, the heaters start to warm up, and you can begin to cook your dinner. 'But I have tried and it still does

The Cosmic Body

not work,' you complain. Well, you are going to have to find out why. What is missing? Perhaps something is broken or one of the poles of your plug is not in place; and there can be no contact unless both poles are in place. You see, we always come back to the two principles.

There, I hope that these few words will be helpful to you in preparing for the events of the next few days. As I have already told you in past years, the date of Easter was not determined by chance; it was calculated in accordance with an astronomical and astrological science that can be traced back to earliest antiquity. At this time of year, certain phenomena occur in the heavens, and human beings can benefit from these phenomena if their consciousness is sufficiently developed and they prepare themselves to receive the influx of celestial currents. Otherwise, these currents will simply pass them by and flow into other regions, and human beings will still be the same in spite of Easter. Easter has come and gone thousands of times already, but human beings have still not been transformed, because their consciousness was busy with other things. Until they succeed in organizing their lives in such a way as to have time for spiritual activities, they will never make any progress.

Neither science, nor religion, nor art has yet succeeded in improving human beings, because they are always focused on what is peripheral and inessential. Look at the way they behave with regard to the sun, for instance. Scientists are beginning to understand that even the energy contained in an atomic bomb is nothing compared to that emitted by the sun, and they are building more and more instruments to make use of solar energy. The only trouble is, of course, that they always work for a material, utilitarian purpose; they never do anything to help people to expand their consciousness or improve themselves. They would bottle the sun and sell it for a profit if they could, but they are not interested in finding out how the sun can be a means of perfecting the human race and bringing about the kingdom of God on earth. Their goal is always profit, wealth, commerce. They are even ready to sell the Lord himself. Go to Lourdes, or Lisieux, or any other place of pilgrimage in the world, and you will see endless rows of shops in which the Lord is bought and sold.

Human beings have been brought up in this materialistic, utilitarian attitude for centuries. Today, no technical achievement seems to be beyond their reach. They will soon be setting off for other planets, but they themselves are no better than they ever were. You will say, 'But culture and civilization have made tremendous progress.' Yes, on the surface, but inwardly the situation is worse than before. People are more grasping and acquisitive, crueller and more sensual than they used to be because they are more 'intelligent'. No, humanity has not improved. True improvement does not consist exclusively in better buildings, clothes, food, or means of transport. Improvement in these areas is technical, mechanical, or whatever else you like to call it, but it is not true improvement, for true improvement consists in spiritualization. Moreover, the most flagrant proof that man is not very highly evolved is that he attaches no spiritual significance to the sun.

The one thing I am really concerned about is the value of things, and I am sorry to say that my research has led me to the conclusion that human beings attach no value to essentials, while attaching great value to incidentals, to things that are worthless. They spend their time chasing after shadows while, for my part, I have discovered that the only thing that matters, the only essential, is light. Even nature gives priority to light. The fact that the speed of light cannot be matched by anything else means that light is superior to everything. The fastest runner always wins the race, and light is the fastest because it has stripped itself of everything that could burden it or slow it down. It is free to race ahead; whereas all others are so burdened that they crawl along at a snail's pace. Yes, speed is a measure of perfection. When your mental activity slows down you can no longer rely on it, for if it cannot give you a rapid

The Cosmic Body

and accurate view of a situation and its possible dangers, you will have an accident or find yourself trapped. Similarly, when your psychic life slows down, everything becomes much more laborious.

Light is a yardstick, a criterion. There is no evil, no self-seeking in the mind of light, and this is why it is always first, because it is utterly detached and without greed. If you want to explore the human heart and the universe, if you want to study all the treasures of the universal soul, you too must have the intensity and the speed of light. If you do not understand the language of the light that comes from the sun, if you still do not understand that this light is the only school in which you may learn true norms and measures, then you have not understood anything at all. Yes, as long as human beings have still not understood that the sun can give them the most effective means of attaining knowledge and of learning to reason and to evaluate reality, to my mind they have understood nothing; they are living in error. This is why I urge them to enrol in the school of the sun, for it is from him that they will get the best advice. He will tell them, for instance, 'Never follow those who possess neither warmth nor light, for they will lead you to the abyss.'

Human beings imagine that they will find truth in books, but all books are meaningless nonsense compared to the sun. No book can give you absolute truth. That is the way of earth reality: we have to make do with relative truths, for everything on earth is relative. If you want absolute truth, you will have to go to the source, the centre. Here on earth, we are at the periphery, and we can glimpse only a few aspects of truth. As soon as you speak and try to explain things to someone, you are at the periphery. It is when you say nothing that you are at the centre. As soon as you try to talk, you descend into the physical body, and that is already the periphery.

Henceforth, therefore, forget about what the various philosophies, the Church, and all kinds of other people tell you, and ask the sun for his opinion. The authors of all those books you read had a great many limitations—not to mention the fact that they are now dead. But the sun is not only still alive, he is in excellent health. Is it not much better to sign up with someone who possesses the secret of immortality rather than with someone who is already dead? This has always been my way: if someone tries to sell me a bottle of patent hair tonic, I look at his bald head and tell him, 'No thanks, I do not want any.' And if he says that there is no better remedy for baldness, I tell him, 'If that were true you should have a noble crop of hair, but I see that you are as bald as an egg.' Yes, this is why I turn to the sun, because everything he tells us is true. Of course, there is no reason why, having listened to the sun, you should not also leaf through a few books. I am not so fanatical as to say that you should never read a single book, but what I do say—and this is the absolute truth—is that you cannot learn everything nor can you become truly free thanks to the writings of human beings.

You will ask, 'What about the Gospels? Doesn't Christ himself speak in the Gospels?' No, Christ never wrote anything. Other people wrote the Gospels, and it is quite possible that they did not always write the exact truth. I know that no one will agree with me, but even here there are certain criteria we can apply. All the books that human beings write have to be compared with the one book that is indestructible: the great book of living nature. If what you find in books can also be found in the book of living nature, then you can believe it because it is true. Otherwise, it is untrue. There are passages that are not completely true even in the Gospels. Yes, even in the Gospels. Do you want me to prove it to you? Very well, take the passage that says, 'If your eye causes you to sin, pluck it out and cast it from you.' Is it really the eye that causes a man to sin, or is it some other organ? In this case, we should cut that organ off too. But even if we did, would that rid us of all our inner greed and lusts?

No, it is not a question of mutilating oneself and removing one's eyes, one's genitals, or any other part of one's body. If your hands are too fond of finding their way into the pockets or the cash box of your neighbour, it is not by amputating them that you would lose the desire to steal. Even if you had no hands, the desire would still need to be amputated. The desire not the physical organ. It is the force, the impulse behind an organ, that drives people to crime. This passage of the Gospels is not very accurate, therefore, for I do not believe that Jesus ever said anything like that. You will say that I am contradicting the Gospels. I am ready to contradict anything that is not true. I am very bold. Yes, when it comes to defending the truth, I am bold. I put my explanations alongside those of others and call on nature to be the judge. It is not for human beings to pronounce judgement, but for the whole of nature.

Even if someone mutilated himself in the hope of finding salvation, he would still go to hell if his desires were infernal, because it is his desires that bind him to the regions, substances, and entities to which they correspond. This means that it is his desires that he must cast from him, or, rather, that he must transform. Yes, he must transform not kill them. The divine world does not kill, it only transforms, educates, and enlightens. 'Kill', 'destroy', 'uproot', and 'massacre' are words for the weak and ignorant, for those who are incapable of grasping the notions of transformation and sublimation. Human beings need words that mean something to them, and at a time when they were too ignorant for anything else they were given these words, which they could understand because they had been making war and putting their enemies to the sword for centuries. But one day men will have to begin to understand things differently, for it is useless to kill. You cannot rid yourself of an enemy, even by killing him. History shows this very clearly. Look at how many revolutionaries have had their heads chopped off because of their ideas; but although their heads were chopped off, their ideas lived on. In fact, their death only served to reinforce their ideas and propagate them all the more rapidly.

It is not by killing people that you can get rid of their ideas; nor is it by cutting off a limb that you can get rid of your desires. Leave your limbs alone and concentrate on your thoughts and feelings, and on your soul. Your limbs and organs do no more than carry out the orders that come to them from above. An arm can strike or caress, slay or save. Why blame the arm? The arm is not the culprit; it has no responsibility in the matter. It receives an order, which may be either good or bad, and carries it out. It is exactly the same with a tap: do you destroy a tap if the water that comes from it one day is dirty? No, because the water will probably run clean the next day.

Human beings always think that if they have a problem with something, the solution is to destroy it. They do not recognize the true, remote cause of the problem. They have always demolished all that was good and useful without looking for the underlying problem. If you remove a man's sexual organs, he will no longer be able to gratify his appetites and desires, but that does not mean that they will have ceased to exist. There have been people whose faith was so ardent that they mutilated themselves in order, as they thought, to avoid going to hell; only to find themselves in another hell where the flames were even fiercer. Heavens above. How can people be so ignorant in certain areas? Aberrations of this kind will never convince others that they should seek purity, that they should seek God. On the contrary, they will only turn people away from belief in God, and that is very grave. You might have been able to convince people with such absurd ideas in the Middle Ages, but not today. Today, human beings need other notions, other precepts. This is why the day will come, I assure you, when even the truths of the Gospel will be presented differently.

For the moment, I have a different programme for you. I

cannot give you more than this because there are certain elementary concepts that you have not yet digested or understood. Even the question of the sun is not clear to many. They attend the sunrise but they get no benefit from it. Afterwards, they are as prosaic as ever, ready at once to start arguing and quarrelling with everybody. As I have already explained, it is because they have never prepared themselves to attend the sunrise. If you want to understand the sun, you have to be detached and free. Yes, if you can achieve this, you will understand what the sun is. I cannot tell you... no words are adequate to express what the sun is. And if, in spite of all that I have explained to you so far, you still cannot understand or appreciate it, it is no use hoping that anyone else will be able to make you understand.

It is true that some concepts are so far beyond the comprehension of human beings that even when they are explained by an initiate or a great master, they will still not be understood. Some people may be capable of an intellectual understanding, but there are things that cannot wholly be grasped by the intellect, and this means that until human beings acquire spiritual comprehension, many notions will remain beyond their reach. Even if I give you such clear, simple examples as that of the spring, the spring that is indispensable to life, you will not understand them beyond a certain point; you will fail to grasp their spiritual content.

We shall always need our intellect in order to understand and get along in the concrete physical world, but it is not enough. There is another kind of intelligence whose role is to prepare us for heaven, to prepare us to sense, and savour, and imbibe heaven. And both forms of intelligence are necessary to us, for neither can take the place of the other. Both are necessary, because each one corresponds to a particular region. I know that I shall not be understood, because I am leading you into realms that you no one has ever talked to you about before. It is only normal that you cannot understand me. But that is no excuse for me to talk of something else, because my aim, the task that has been entrusted to me, is precisely to prepare you for this other world that you do not yet know. Others can be trusted to explain politics, the sciences, literature, economics, and so on. Dozens of people know far more than I do about such things, and I am filled with admiration when I read their books, but it is not these books that enable me to drink from the fountain of life. The trouble is that everything is mixed up in your heads because you do not possess the criteria you need to discern whether something belongs to heaven or to earth.

When God created the world, he gave the blueprint, the overall design, to his servants, the angels and archangels, and it was they who carried it out. And this pattern is repeated in every area of life: there is one who draws up the plans and others who carry them out. Workers are always needed, and I am glad to see that there are some workers, some brothers and sisters in my Brotherhood, who are capable of working hard. But if you did not have what I give you, you would not get very far with your work. Each of us has our appointed task. What I give you belongs to another dimension, another world, and it is not very clear to you; it seems to be formless. Yes, and it is precisely your task to give it form. It is like life: life has no form.

I give you the contents and it is up to you to find the various vessels, vases, or pitchers to contain it. I cannot give you everything. I already give you the liquid, the fluidic aspect; the least you can do is to bring your own jugs and bottles. Of course, I could also give you all the containers you need—the very best that exist—but if you had no fluid to put into them, what use would they be? What use is all your wiring if there is no electric current flowing through it? My task is to connect you to the sun, to the current of divine life. If you have other ambitions that need to be satisfied, go and satisfy them elsewhere, but try at least to understand what this element is that I give you. Try to understand its nature and its essence, why it is necessary, and how to use it. Do not confuse it with all kinds of other things, which, however useful and magnificent they may be, belong to a different realm.

What I need now are some able workers, and with those workers I shall shake up the whole world; it is only a question of time. The events taking place in the world today are going to force human beings to change their philosophy and lead them to the Great Universal White Brotherhood. It is impossible for them to end up anywhere else, for everywhere else there are only fragments, parts of the whole. Political parties, philosophical movements, sects, and associations of all kinds are all parts of the whole; only the Universal White Brotherhood embraces the whole. I know that, at the moment, you do not believe me. You are so fascinated by the little innovations that can be seen here and there in every domain that you forget what is essential. Human beings need to have something to marvel at—that is only normal—but I advise you to marvel only at what is essential, that is, at light, love, goodness, the sun, and the stars—at the whole of creation. And if, in second place, you want to marvel at certain human beings, do so by all means, but only to the extent to which they express and reveal the Source of all life.

If you do not possess these criteria, sooner or later you will be let down. You will attach yourself to those who tempt and seduce you, and they will disrupt your psychic life and bring you nothing but darkness and final ruin. And once they have destroyed you, they will abandon you and go in search of another gullible victim to destroy. This is how it goes in the world, and, naturally, regrets always follow, but by then it is too late. Everybody regrets their mistakes eventually, and it is always too late, because they have never managed to attach themselves to the essentials. There is nothing worse than to be incapable of discerning what is essential.

Sèvres, April 14, 1965

Chapter Five

The Kingdom of God and His Righteousness

I

There is one thing you have to learn, my dear brothers and sisters, and that is not to be in a hurry. Instead of waiting impatiently for these few minutes of meditation to end, you must learn to remain in silence for longer and longer. I have often told you that the thing that causes your brain to seize up and prevents the full flowering of your spiritual faculties is this deplorable habit you have of always being in a hurry. Of course, I do not deny that rapidity, activity, and dynamic energy are very desirable qualities, but you must not concentrate on them to the exclusion of others which, on the contrary, have to be developed through patience and greater inwardness and receptivity. When you achieve this inner state of peace and harmony, you will sense that forces, powers, and entities are beginning to work within you, and what they accomplish is so prodigious that most of it cannot be seen or understood; it surpasses all imagination. Of course, this reality has many different degrees, but even if what you experience is no more than the first, the lowest degree, you can already sense that an unknown, inner force is beginning to forge something within you, and if only for a few minutes, you rise above the commotion and worries that restrict you and enter into that 'secret place' that Jesus talks about.

It is important to understand these two aspects within every human being: the mortal being, who is subject to so many limitations, and the immortal, eternal being, who is free of all limitations. One of these aspects has to retreat and diminish so that the other may grow and flourish. This is exactly what St. John the Baptist said with reference to Jesus: 'He must increase but I must decrease.' Yes, these words are symbolic. When you are here in the Brotherhood, you must detach yourselves from the habits of your everyday life. What is all the hurry about? You have not got to go and type letters in an office, or collect taxes, or plead a case in court, so why not tell yourselves that for a little while at least you are finally going to come face to face with eternity, with the sun, with nature, with a multitude of luminous beings—face to face with yourself. Those who manage to change their attitude will, at last, feel divine forces awakening and dwelling within them in order to transform them.

Many people have told me, 'I want to concentrate, I want to pray, but I can never do it.' They do not see that they fail because they set about it the wrong way; they are too tense. They keep thinking that they have not got much time because they have so many other things to do. In these conditions concentration is impossible. There is an obstacle in their unconscious or subconscious mind, some element in their habits, that prevents them from meditating, and it is worth looking into this and trying to analyse it. I know that they will object that it is life that dictates the situation, that when you have to work and provide for others you cannot waste time. Yet if they could get into the habit of not being in a hurry—if only for half an hour or an hour a day—they would soon see that everything would go ten times, a hundred times better once they got back to work.

There is a time and a place for everything. While you meditate you must not think of anything else; there will always be time to take care of other things afterwards. But what usually happens is this: while you are here listening to a lecture or praying and meditating, in reality you are somewhere else. And when you are somewhere else, instead of concentrating on what you are doing you think, 'I should be meditating or praying.' This is why nothing really works. It is not while you are preparing a meal, washing the dishes, or driving the car that you should be thinking about meditating. You must be present at what you are doing at each moment, for there is a right time for everything. Otherwise, there will never be time for anything; your mind will always be somewhere else. How true this is. When you are here you are still at home—or goodness knows where—and when you are somewhere else, you are here. Finally, you are never wholly anywhere, and that is very bad.

How many bad habits still need to be corrected. Yes, very, very bad habits. The first thing you have to learn in our teaching is just this, to correct your bad habits. Once you have done this you can go much further and much faster. You will say that now that I have explained it, you understand. Perhaps, but I think that without any explanations at all, simply by sitting in silence, you would have understood better still. Believe me, if you were not always so engrossed elsewhere, you would understand a million times more from that silence than from my explanations.

Words are not really so important. It is because you have not managed to establish close contact with heaven that you need words. The day you truly know how to meditate and contemplate the splendours of heaven, I shall continue to speak to you, but in silence. Already, during our moments of silence, I continually talk to you, but what I tell you is of a different nature; it belongs to a different dimension. Does this astonish you? Even during the night I continue to speak to you. In fact, this is why you sometimes experience a sudden illumination; it comes from something you have heard during the night several months or even years before, and it is beginning at last to filter through into your brain.

You will perhaps ask, 'But why does it all take so long? It is very discouraging.' It does take a long time, that is true. It is the same for everybody. A great deal of patient, persevering work is necessary before human beings finally begin to understand. But think how many billions of years it takes for stones to become plants; how many millions of years it takes for plants to become animals; and how many millions more for animals to become human beings. Of course, as you go up the scale from one kingdom of nature to the next, the tempo increases. Stones need a stupendous amount of time; plants need a little less; animals need less still—and even less time is needed for human beings to become superhumans or angels. This is because, with each step upwards, the potential is greater. But even so, even if human beings evolve more rapidly, it still takes them hundreds of thousands of years to reach the level of evolution of the angels.

There, that was just a few remarks about the attitude you should have while you are here. It is always one's attitude that needs to be improved. A few minutes ago I mentioned the 'secret place' that Jesus spoke about. This is a magnificent and very profound symbol, and it was certainly known long before Jesus. Every initiate knows that one has to enter this place in order to pray, for if your prayer does not come from there, heaven cannot hear it. Why not? Well, it is as though you were out in the street and you wanted to talk to a friend in another town: you can only do so by going into a telephone booth and dialling his number, and then the telephone will put you in touch with your friend. If you like, you can stay in the street and shout and scream for all you are worth, but your friend will not hear you. Similarly, if you want heaven to hear you, you must go into that secret place that Jesus talked about, for it is equipped with a 'telephone' by means of which you can communicate with the higher worlds. Then there is another similarity: when you go into a telephone booth in a busy street, you close the door because you need silence in order to hear

The Kingdom of God...

and be heard. This secret place must also be quiet; no inner work can take place in the midst of noise.

It is important to understand that you have this secret, silent place within you and that you must go in and shut the door firmly behind you. To shut the door means to shut out all other thoughts and desires, otherwise they will interfere with your communication with heaven and you will not get an answer. It is only if you are in this secret chamber that your call can go through correctly, that you can hear and be heard, that you can ask heaven for something and get an answer. If heaven's answer does not come through clearly, it is because you have forgotten to close the door. The secret place, therefore, is linked to the idea of silence, of secrecy. You must not let anyone else hear what you say, how you say it, or to whom you say it. Naturally, you cannot always be sure that someone will not see that you are praying, but the less obvious it is the better. The Gospels speak of the Pharisee who prayed ostentatiously in the Temple, and this is a good example of the exact opposite of the secret place.

You could say that this secret place is the heart, the silence of the heart. If you are still unable to attain true silence it means that you have not succeeded in reaching this room. There are so many 'rooms' in man, and very few human beings have ever discovered which of them is the one that loves silence. Most people stray into other rooms and try to pray in them, but as those rooms are not equipped with the proper instruments, heaven cannot hear their thoughts and prayers. If you want your prayer to be heard, you have to respect certain conditions.

Why, for example, did the initiates of the past teach people to join their hands when they prayed? The gesture is symbolic. True prayer is a joining of the two principles, heart and intellect. If your heart is alone in what it asks for and your intellect refuses to join in, your prayer will not be heard. If you want your prayer to be heard, it must come from both heart and intellect, from both thought and feelings; that is, from the masculine and feminine principles. We have all seen innumerable paintings that show people—even children—with their hands joined in prayer, but people have never understood the profound significance of this gesture. I am not saying that you must necessarily join your hands physically when you pray, for it is not the physical gesture that counts; it is the inner attitude that is important. It is the soul and the spirit, the heart and the intellect that have to be joined, for this is the union that gives prayer its power and enables you to project something truly potent. You give and receive at the same time; you are both active and receptive.

Christians still have a great many misconceptions about prayer. They imagine that what counts are the words they use. No, words often fall short of the mark; they never manage to get up to heaven. A person may recite words, but he is not really praying if nothing vibrates within him. Of course, as I have often told you, it is important for the realization of your prayer to put it into words. Yes, but your words will be effective only if your desire and your thought are already powerful on the spiritual plane. Then your words will act as a signature which releases the higher forces and sets them in motion.

If you want to awaken sentiments of love for God in yourself, for instance, you can do so simply through the strength of your desire. In this case words are unnecessary, because feelings are a purely psychic reality. If you want to obtain something on the physical, material plane, on the other hand, the spoken word is necessary, but even so, it is the intensity of your thoughts and feelings that is the essence of prayer. Without that intensity, you could recite words for hours on end, but you would not get any results; your prayer would not be answered. As a matter of fact, it is possible to feel whether a prayer has been heard or not. There are days when you experience such a sense of strength and fulfilment that you

The Kingdom of God...

know that heaven has heard you at last. This does not mean that you will see immediate results on the physical plane. No, the realization will not be immediate, but your prayer has been heard, your request has been noted. And that is what counts: to know that your prayer has been heard.

Everything depends on the intensity of your prayer, therefore, and this intensity is linked to the ability to disengage your thoughts and feelings from every preoccupation that is foreign to your prayer. This is why you have to learn to leave everything else to one side and immerse yourself in intense spiritual work. Only on this condition will heaven answer your prayer.

But I know what you are thinking. You are wondering whether I, who teach you these things, receive what I ask for in my prayers. Yes, I get what I ask for because my requests are more unlike yours than you could possibly imagine. My requests are always granted. Perhaps you are also wondering why, since heaven always gives me what I ask for, I do not ask for a lot of money, for instance. I will tell you: because it is not worth asking for. What are a few billion dollars? If I shared them out among you, none of you would get very much. No, no, you cannot begin to imagine what I ask for. And, as I say, my requests are always granted. I am always astonished to see the kind of requests human beings pester heaven with. How can they waste their time on such nonsense? I assure you, it really is a waste of time—and all for what? The day I saw that there was only one booth in heaven without a queue of people waiting in front of it, I decided that that was the place for me. Nobody else wants to hand in their requests at that booth, so that is where you will find me every day. More and more often, in fact.

Now it is up to you to discover what I ask for. In any case, I can tell you that it is neither houses, nor money, nor worldly glory, nor a wife and children. This is why my prayer is always heard. Yes, always, without exception. Since what I ask for is not for myself, I receive it at once. If you ask for something for yourself, you will be told, 'You will have to wait. We have to study your file. Where are you from? What is your father's name? Do you think you deserve what you are asking for?' and so on and so forth; there is no end to the questions. Whereas I am given what I ask for immediately. You will say, 'But you possess no more now than you have ever had.' Exactly, because possessions are not what I ask for. And I am not going to tell you what I do ask for; all that takes place in my 'secret chamber'. It is none of your business. It is my secret.

You must never tell anyone what you ask for, but if your request is the same as mine, it too will be granted immediately, because it is no longer a question of knowing whether you deserve it or not; it is not a question of merit or superiority. The only consideration is the nature of your request. Even if it were made by a child or a drunkard, it would be granted. You will say, 'But does this mean that all our prayers are granted?' Yes, if your prayer is sincere, intense, and disinterested, it will be granted, but it will be granted progressively. It is an ongoing process which expands and develops with time, for you are asking for something that cannot be achieved in a day. So the seed is sown and begins to grow; the ultimate fulfilment of your prayer is already assured, but it takes time for it to be complete. It takes time for a seed to reach the stature of a tree, but as soon as it germinates and begins to grow, it means that your prayer is answered. If you ask for the kingdom of God and his righteousness, you cannot expect it to materialize the same day. The kingdom of God is a gigantic tree; it is impossible for it to reach its full stature all at once. But it is planted. The seed is planted, and the tree is growing. 'But I cannot see it.' you complain. No, if you are short-sighted, of course you cannot expect to see it. But I can see it, and I assure you, it is growing.

When I say that my prayers are always answered, it is not because I think that I am such an exalted being that the whole of heaven is at my elbow, ready and waiting to serve me. Not at all. As I have already said, if your prayer is the same as mine, whoever you may be, it will be granted immediately, because there is a special reception desk, a special department in heaven, to deal with requests of this kind. And as God himself has decreed that those who ask for such things shall be given what they ask for, nobody questions you about who you are or where you come from. They do not even ask the permission of the Twenty-four Elders before granting your request, for this kind of thing is no longer within the jurisdiction of the Twenty-four Elders. It has to be referred to a higher authority, one that is very close to God; and this authority is love. The Twenty-four Elders are the Lords of destiny, and their mission is to apply the laws of justice. But a prayer for the establishment of the kingdom of God does not come within their jurisdiction; it is beyond the reach of the laws of karma, the laws of justice. There is no cause for astonishment in this. If you are capable of making such a request, it means that you have risen above the regions ruled by the laws of karma and that they have no more power over you.

There you are then, the one prayer that is so sublime that heaven is always ready to grant it is the prayer for the establishment of the kingdom of God. 'Seek first the kingdom of God and his righteousness,' said Jesus, and not only will the kingdom of God come, but in addition, 'all these things shall be added to you.' Yes, if you are generous enough to ask for nothing for yourself, you will be given something more; you will be given all you need. Since you are not thinking of your own interest, others will think of it for you. Not only will your prayer for the collectivity, for the whole of humanity be granted, but you yourself will not be forgotten. This is the law decreed by God himself. The more people there are in the world who ask for this, the better it will be; the kingdom of God will come all the sooner and all the more effectively. What else can I say? Ask for the coming of the kingdom of God and his righteousness.

You will say, 'All right, so this is what you ask for, the kingdom of God, and you say that your prayer is always granted, but there is no sign of it.' Well, that is where you are wrong. I think that my prayer is answered, and if you do not think so too, it is because you do not know how these things work. The kingdom of God cannot be established on the physical plane until it exists on the intellectual plane, on the plane of thought. From there it has to descend to the heart, the level of feelings, and finally to the level of actions. This is the path that has to be followed before the kingdom of God can become a tangible reality. First and foremost, it has to reign in our ideas, our thoughts, and it is on that level that I can already see it. It is beginning. We are not the only ones who think and feel as we do; thousands of people in the world—many more than you imagine—share our ideas and desires. The kingdom of God is already finding its way into the minds and hearts, and even into the behaviour, the way of life, of many; for the kingdom of God is an attitude, a state of consciousness, and a way of living and working.

Of course, the kingdom of God has not yet come for the whole of humanity, but it will, for it is contagious. This is what Jesus was saying in the parable about the leaven in the dough. Alchemists say that if all the oceans of the world were molten metal they would need only a few grams of the powder they call the philosophers' stone to turn it all into gold. Yes, because there are rules, apparently, for increasing the power of that powder. But human beings too can be a leaven in the mass. If we are truly a spiritual leaven, the whole of humanity will be influenced simply by our presence, by contact with us. It depends on the intensity of our light, the intensity of our love, and the strength of the life we live. But in order to achieve this, of course, we need a teaching, a system, and methods. This is the crux of the matter: we must learn to live a new life with a new understanding based on and nourished by a new, intense love. In this new life everything becomes easier; everything can be brought into harmony, and we can become a beneficial, constructive factor for the whole of humanity.

There, I shall now wish you all a very good morning... and remember, never be in a hurry when you are here. It is not worth coming here if you are always tense and restless. Before coming here, organize your affairs so as not to be in a hurry. In this way you will get a great deal more out of your stay and will be the happiest of men and women.

Sèvres, April 24, 1963

II

The most important aspect of all your activities is your motive, your goal, the reason why you do things. So much the better if what you do makes you rich and respectable, but that is not what really matters. You may not seem to be doing anything very significant by coming to the Brotherhood, for instance, but every time you come here with the desire to reinforce and spread the ideal of the Universal White Brotherhood, you gain elements that will enhance your future, your evolution, your body of glory. So this is an activity that changes your whole destiny. Blessed are those who understand this truth. You may go for years without seeing the results, but one fine day you will sense that blessings are pouring in on you from all directions.

Human beings treat you according to what they see, but heaven sees your motives, and it rewards or punishes you accordingly. You must look to heaven, therefore, to reward you for coming here to promote the idea of brotherhood. What do you think my reasons are for giving these lectures and meetings? Money? Prestige? Anyone else in my position would have given up in despair a long time ago when he saw the negligible results. Human beings are so fascinated by spectacular achievements in the material dimension that any attempt to get them to dedicate themselves to an idea is bound

The Kingdom of God...

to fail. They say: 'An idea? What is the good of an idea? That is idiotic. Stupid. I cannot waste time on ideas. I know that some poor wretches in the past lived for an idea, an illusion, but I also know how they ended up, and I have no intention of imitating them.'

Everybody wants a solid, reputable occupation, but there is no divine idea behind that occupation; only money, the belly, sex. Of course, they may be successful, but one day they will see how little all that is worth. When they get to the other side they will be shown their brilliant 'successes'. For my part, I shall continue to repeat the same things, to tell you over and over again that you must come here for the sake of an idea and, like the vestal virgins, tend the sacred flame so that it may never be extinguished in the world; so that the Universal White Brotherhood may be established in the hearts and souls of all men; so that this new understanding may prevail. True, this will not swell your bank accounts, but it will fill you with something called hope and enthusiasm, something called love and light.

Make the effort to look into the depths of your own being and you will see what great riches exist there. Every time you come here to sing and pray and meditate, your wealth increases. And for my part, I go home after every meeting full of happiness and gratitude towards heaven, thinking to myself, 'Ah, they were all there again today, as faithful as ever. Yet another beautiful day for the glory of God. The fire is still burning; we must continue to sustain, guard, and feed it.' As I have so often told you, we must never forget that we are not alone. Thousands and thousands of invisible beings are with us, taking part in our work and sending waves and currents into the minds of all the men and women who are capable of receiving them. And what fantastic power these waves have. They form a tremendous whirlwind that rises over our heads and streams out in all directions. We are working to awaken the consciousness of untold numbers of people we have never even heard of. Whether you believe it or not, I know that we have already influenced thousands of beings whom we shall never know and who, in turn, will never know where these currents came from. And we must persevere. One day, thousands of people will come and join us and find in this work the reason for their existence on earth. For it is this work that is our true nourishment; no other activity can give us the same fulfilment. So go ahead. Never give up. Other activities will captivate you and make you happy for a brief moment, and then the very next moment you will feel that something is missing. You will find true fulfilment only in this work with love and light, only in the work of spreading love and light throughout the world.

Yes, that is what is important: an idea, to work for an idea. Many young people are idealistic, but they do not know what direction to give to their lives because adults have never shown them the way. On the contrary, they tell them, 'You have to look out for yourself in this world.' by which they mean, 'You must be what the world calls "a success" You must make money.' You will never hear them advising a young person to work for an idea, a divine idea.

An idea... Yes, meditate on this question. You will say, 'Oh, I see that I shall have to read Plato.' No, that is not necessary; you can understand what an idea is without reading Plato. An idea is a creature, a living being from a very high plane, from the higher world of thought, that comes to work in you and on you. If you sustain and nourish an idea, it will gradually fashion and form you until, one day, you yourself reflect the world of ideas, which is the world of archetypes, the divine world. The great advantage of working for a divine idea is that it contains in itself the power to model and perfect you so that, one day, you become a citizen of its world, of that world in which the inhabitants are called ideas. So we must work for an idea, because it links us to the world above. If there are no ideas working within you like a swarm of bees to bring you their blessings, it means that you are deprived of all that is best.

Of course, as long as you consider ideas to be unproductive, inert abstractions, they will do you no good. This is why it is so important to know what an idea is and how to work for one. Each idea is a living creature, a being of great intelligence and beauty, endowed with clearly defined properties. When you work for a particular idea, it exerts an influence on you and shares all it possesses with you. This is the magical aspect of it, and it means that in spite of your ignorance, in spite of all your weaknesses and imperfections, if you cling to just one idea that belongs to the higher world of light, it will introduce you to all its friends and put you in touch with other beings and other regions. It will bring you heaven itself. This one idea of the kingdom of God puts you in touch with all the kindred ideas that vibrate in harmony with it, so that you end by having everything else as well. This is why Jesus said, 'Seek first the kingdom of God and his righteousness and all these things shall be added to you.' Between the beginning and the end of this sentence is a vast area that needs to be explored.

This, then, is one of the most important truths of initiatic science: a single, limited idea can bring you wealth greater than that which it possesses in itself, because it is connected and in harmony with a whole network of kindred ideas. Little by little, these other ideas get to know you, as it were, and as each one possesses some land here or a house there, symbolically speaking, all their treasures become yours— thanks to just one idea. In the higher world, everything is connected, nothing exists in isolation, and you only have to be in touch with one idea from that world to be in touch immediately with all the others. As long as you make friends with one idea, as long as you love and nurture that one and try to draw it to you, it will be your link to all the others, and they too will give you their treasures. As I say, there is a vast empty space between the beginning of this sentence: 'Seek first the kingdom of God and his righteousness,' and the end: 'and all these things shall be added to you.' And today I can fill this empty space for you.

What I am explaining to you today is not spelled out explicitly in the Gospels. They say that 'all these things shall be added to you,' but they do not explain that this promise will be fulfilled, not only because there is a special affinity, a magical, magnetic bond between one sublime idea and all other similar ideas, but also because every idea has its representatives here on earth who know you. This is why you will be given all the rest. There would be no sense in it otherwise. Why, when you ask for one thing, should you be given everything else? If people do not understand this truth, it is because they have asked for money, for instance, and that is all they have been given. And how paltry that is. They have not been given intelligence, health, happiness, beauty, or goodness. You will say that if you are rich you can buy anything you want, but I do not agree. True, your wealth can bring you many things, but they will be things such as anxiety and distress. Above all it will attract thieves who will come and rob and even murder you to get their hands on that wealth. Even if you ask for knowledge or beauty, they will not bring you all the rest. In fact if you are very beautiful, your beauty can well lead to tragedy, of which you will be the principal victim. 'Seek first the kingdom of God and his righteousness and all these things shall be added to you.' This promise is so vast, so sweeping, that at first sight it seemed to you that it could not be true, but now you understand it.

Now let us stay together in silence for a few minutes while we thank heaven for the gift of this Christmas Day spent in the midst of harmony, music, and an ambience of brotherhood. So many terrible things could happen to us, but we are allowed to be here, safe and well, to rejoice with all the brothers and sisters. How wonderful to be all together. When I get home, I shall continue to thank heaven, to say, 'Thank you Lord for another splendid day recorded in the book of life, another day

The Kingdom of God...

that has brought us closer to you, for we have been gathered together for the sake of your name and your glory, to feed the flame and bring light to the hearts and souls of all our brothers and sisters.' What could be more marvellous than to live one's life in a spirit of gratitude with a song of praise on one's lips? But even when I say this, you do not believe me. You are so used to the burden of all your cares that if the weight is removed from your shoulders for just one day, you say that something must be wrong, that it is not normal.

This reminds me of a friend I had when I was young, in Bulgaria. He belonged to a group of anarchists, and all his comrades had been shot. He himself was being hunted and was obliged to go into hiding. At the time, I was living near Ternovo with some friends who were also disciples of the Master Peter Deunov. Our house was some distance from the town and was surrounded by vineyards, and we spent our days working and meditating. One day we saw this young boy coming towards us, obviously hungry and very frightened. We gave him something to eat, and little by little, seeing that he could trust us, he began to tell us about himself. He stayed with us for several days, and we had some long conversations together. He found our philosophy astonishing and deeply moving, and he soon began to understand that the state of the world could not be improved by anarchy. Before long he was in a much better frame of mind, for in his heart he was not a bad man; on the contrary, he had great integrity. It was just that he was revolted by injustice, and circumstances had made an anarchist of him. Deep down he was full of love, and this showed in his later behaviour.

So this young man decided to change his way of life and join the Brotherhood. I told him, 'If you really try, if you form a bond with this Brotherhood, the authorities will forget about you; you will be the only one of your group to escape death, and everything will change for you.' He believed me; his whole life was transformed and he became one of the best brothers in the Bulgarian Brotherhood. His name was Dimitri Zvesdinsky. He was extraordinarily kind, generous, humble, and loyal, and we had great affection for each other. But Dimitri was so used to going in fear and trembling for his life, he was so used to being in hiding, to never having enough sleep or enough to eat, that when he first knew what it was to be safe from pursuit and torment, when he began to see that people liked him and smiled at him, it was almost worse than before. He could not get over it, could not understand what was happening to him; it was as though he missed his past distress. And you are the same; you are all a little like Dimitri in this: you are not accustomed to living in peace. If your cares leave you, you call them back: 'My dear old cares and worries, please come back to me; I feel even worse without you.' And back they come.

So, as I say, let us stay together for a few minutes in silence and peace while we thank heaven because we are well and happy and surrounded by friends, and above all, because we have this teaching, this magnificent ideal.

A few minutes of silent meditation.

And now let me say again that what matters most is the ambience: the warm, fraternal, vital climate of harmony that reigns here. Whether or not you acquire anything significant here in the way of knowledge is secondary; it is the ambience that really matters. This is why all my science consists in seeking ways of creating this indispensable ambience of harmony which is so nourishing. Well, I do not know whether you manage to nourish yourselves on it or not, but I can assure you that I do. Henceforth, you must pay much more attention to creating this ambience, for it is this that gives us joy, prolongs our life, and makes us happy.

Sèvres, December 25, 1964

III

Every day, two, three, four times a day, we gather to meditate, pray, and sing together. How wonderful these moments are; they are the most wonderful moments in our lives. There is just one thing that prevents them from being perfect, and that is that all these vital energies and impulses lack a specific destination; there is no address on them. How can a letter reach the person you are writing to if you forget to address the envelope? You have to write the address, and then, if you lose your letter on the way to the post, someone will find it and post it for you, and it will reach its destination. Similarly, the spiritual energies emanating from the Brotherhood must be addressed. They must be given a specific destination, otherwise they will lose themselves in the great cosmic reservoir and fail to produce any significant results. You have to give a specific orientation to your activities, work towards a specific goal, and this is something that very few people manage to do.

Everybody is active on the intellectual, emotional, or physical plane, but their activity is dissipated and incoherent; it is not directed towards a single goal, and this is why it is not very effective. There is only one way to achieve results, and that is by concentration. Take a sheet of paper and a magnifying glass and concentrate the sun's rays through the glass on to one spot on the paper, and within seconds it will burst into flames. Without the magnifying glass you can leave your sheet of paper in the sun for years, and it will never burst into flames. The great secret is concentration. This is why, when we are meditating together, we must concentrate our thoughts and all our energies on one point, one centre, one goal. A goal can be either individual or collective, but ideally it should be both at the same time. If the two are combined wisely and in the right proportions, they will be congenial, necessary, and indispensable to each other.

You have to take care of your own problems and those of the collectivity at the same time. If you think only of the collectivity and neglect your own problems, you yourself will suffer and deteriorate; and if you think of nobody but yourself, you will be in direct conflict with the collectivity. When you forget that you are a tiny part of a whole, with which you must maintain a reasonable and harmonious balance of give and take, everything begins to go wrong; you feel hemmed in on all sides and you wonder why. Why? Simply because you have forgotten that you are an integral part of the cosmos and should vibrate in unison with it. True wisdom counsels us, therefore, to reconcile the two; oneself and others. The problem is to find the right proportions: how much should be given to Caesar and how much to God. Actually, as I have already explained to you, the answer is clear. If you burn a log of wood, you will see that three-quarters of its substance disappears into the world above, while one-quarter remains on the ground[1]. So, three-quarters should be for the collectivity, for immensity, and one-quarter for self. If you do the opposite and take three-quarters for yourself and give only a quarter to the Lord, you will be in direct conflict with the calculations of heavenly mathematics.

---

[1] See *Complete Works,* vol. 11, chap. 14.

But this is not really what I wanted to talk about today. I just wanted to throw a little light on the question of what you should be doing when we gather to meditate together for the good of this great collectivity, for the whole of mankind. If you study yourselves and do some experiments of your own, you will realize that nothing can compare with the beauty and splendour of the activity in which the Universal White Brotherhood invites you to participate: the concentration of all your thoughts on the kingdom of God and his righteousness. Everything else pales beside this.

This ideal, this fundamental thought which should be at the heart of our preoccupations, is capable of producing phenomena of indescribable power, particularly if there are a great many of us and we all direct our thoughts toward the same goal. Today, we see more and more evidence of men's bloated personalities manifesting themselves in ambition, pride, and vanity. Where can we find the reason and intelligence needed to restore the balance? The world today needs order and harmony. That is what the kingdom of God is. The kingdom of God embodies all the essential qualities: light, intelligence, wisdom, gentleness, humility, kindness, and, above all, harmony. In other words the kingdom of God means a way of life that is extremely beneficial to all, and we should wish with all our strength for it to come.

Compared to all those who wish for disorder and chaos, there are very few who wish for the coming of the kingdom of God. If we want to counterbalance all these unrestrained passions effectively, we must bear with sufficient weight on the other side of the scales. This is why the most glorious activity, the most glorious and most worthwhile work a disciple can do is to dedicate all his time and energy to asking for the kingdom of God and his righteousness. And, as the Gospels tell us, 'all the rest shall be added to you.' All the rest—yes, but what else is there once you have the kingdom of God?

The kingdom of God includes and embraces everything

anyone could wish for, and I sometimes wonder why Jesus said, 'All the rest shall be added to you.' He was probably speaking to all those ignorant people who know nothing of the glory and wealth implied by the words 'the kingdom of God'. When people do not understand that when you have the kingdom of God you have everything you need, they have to be encouraged with promises of all the rest—a shack, blankets, shoes, and socks. It was for the sake of such people that Jesus said this, but in the higher world the precept is rather different. It says, 'Seek first the kingdom of God and his righteousness and you will not need anything else.' Yes, to my mind, this is the authentic version. If you do not believe me, you can go and find out for yourselves, and you will see how the Gospels were first conceived and how they were given to men.

The most necessary and most glorious work heaven asks of us is our participation in the realization of the kingdom of God. When we are here together, instead of being distracted and letting your minds wander everywhere and nowhere, keep bringing them back to this one goal: the kingdom of God and his righteousness. As we are very numerous and we meet frequently, the forces and energies that we emanate are recorded and registered on high and collected in the divine reservoirs—and we can be sure of getting results. When? Ah, that is not our business. The kingdom of God will come, that I can assure you; the golden age will come. In fact astrologers have calculated these things and are now saying what I already said years ago: that the golden age will be here by the end of the century.

Yes, my dear brothers and sisters, we gather together not to ask for money, a man or a woman, a house or a car; we gather together in order to bring about the kingdom of God on earth. And if our thoughts and prayers fail to bring it about, they will return to us, and the kingdom of God will be established within us. If it is not realized on earth, it will at least be realized within us, because we shall have worked for it. So we never stand to lose anything by wishing and praying for such a magnificent realization, for even if others refuse it, it will be given to us.

The important thing, therefore, is always to direct your spiritual work to a specific goal, to tell yourself, 'My meditation, or prayer, or reflection is for such and such a reason.' Yes, be sure to indicate a reason, a purpose, so that all those forces will not drift away and be lost. In this way your thoughts will become obedient; they will be really and truly at your service. It is difficult to tame the faculty of thought and make it obey you; it is like an unbroken horse. In Hindu literature one often reads the lament of yogis: 'Oh Indra, how difficult it is to subdue thought. As soon try to make a rope of sand or to capture the wind.' But if you persevere and practise every day, you will end by making your thoughts docile, obedient, and compliant.

This is the significance of our daily exercises of meditation, and it is a magnificent work. You must never think that we spend too much time on it; on the contrary, those who become accustomed to meditation never want it to end. They feel so much at ease that they would like it to go on indefinitely. So now let us try all together, for just a few minutes, to concentrate on the kingdom of God. We want the kingdom of God and his righteousness. We ask, and clamour, and pray for the coming of the kingdom of God and his righteousness. Together we shall send out a prodigious, collective force which will do its work in the world.

A few minutes of silent meditation.

That was magnificent. We were surrounded by entities of the invisible world; I could hear them saying, 'Ah, if only there were servants of light in every corner of the world who could project their thoughts in the same direction, the face of the earth would be changed.' I assure you, that is what they were saying.

At the moment, of course, there are only a few scattered handfuls of men and women doing this work, so it cannot achieve very much. But that will not prevent us from persevering in the hope that many other minds will respond to our call and begin to vibrate on the same wavelength, for true evolution leads to the collectivity. Those who flourish in the collectivity evolve wonderfully. The others, those who feel unhappy and oppressed in the collectivity and want to evolve alone on the intellectual level, through reading and scholarship, show that they are governed only by their personality. But this is not the right kind of evolution. We have to love the collectivity, love to feel ourselves immersed in it as in an ocean in which every soul vibrates as one. Yes, you still need to evolve a good deal. Sooner or later you are going to have to overcome and subordinate certain personal tendencies. You are going to have to strip yourselves so as to be capable, at last, of saying, 'I am a collective being: I am no longer a caterpillar; I have become a butterfly.' Then you will be free to leave the earth and travel to other planets, to other stars.

This is the evolution to which I invite you. Human beings have already developed the individual and personal dimensions sufficiently; they feel more at ease when they are absorbed in their own affairs. Many people have confessed to me that they avoid the company of others because they are unable to put up with their own weaknesses when they are with others; whereas when they are alone, it is not so difficult.

Of course, I also know that many people like working with the collectivity because they want to command, judge, and criticize others without abandoning their own personal tendencies—on the contrary, they seek to impose them on others. There are very few who are ready to immerse themselves in the collectivity and make sacrifices for it in a spirit of true selflessness. Some people like to work with the collectivity in order to play at being the boss, but that does not mean that they are capable of living in a collectivity. On the contrary, although they want to impose their own views, they are often incapable of doing so. For example, a young man may want to dominate the world, but then he has a child that is unruly and disobedient, and he is quite incapable of controlling it. Or he wants to have a love affair with every girl he meets, and yet he is already tearing his hair out in frustration over just one.

If you analyse yourselves, can you honestly say that you would be satisfied if you got what you asked for? You would not. This is why you should embrace this teaching as your last, best hope. You should tell yourselves, 'With this teaching I can have everything: I can learn self-mastery, I can become intelligent... everything.' Once you have accepted this teaching, you will be in a position to direct all your energies towards the same goal, and your life will become extraordinarily full, rich, and useful instead of being continually scattered and wasted. I know that this is very difficult. Human beings are not in the habit of mobilizing all their energies in the pursuit of a single goal. Their heads are filled with an untidy jumble of too many different things. But the magic of true power consists in having one goal, one idea, one ideal, and concentrating all one's energies on that ideal. Your energies are like a huge army of millions and millions of soldiers that can be sent out to do battle and come back victorious, their mission successfully accomplished. But human beings go through life without realizing that they have this immense army at their command.

So, keep trying. Work steadfastly for years and years in the same direction, in the direction of light, of the kingdom of God, until all the soldiers in your subconscious, your consciousness, and your superconsciousness fall into line and join forces to help you. Then your army will be so numerous that all the old fortresses will crumble away. Can you not sense the truth of what I am saying? It is true from every point of view—technical, strategic, magic, and cosmic. Even God, all-powerful though he is, is obliged to restrict himself, to concentrate. In order to prevent the energies of the cosmos from being dispersed, he condensed them, and the universe came into being. When he wants it to disintegrate again, he will work with opposite laws, and the whole thing will return to nothingness. If God works with these laws, why should we not do the same when we want to create something? As long as we continue to scatter our energies in all directions, we shall never get results.

You must remember what I have told you today: adopt an idea, an ideal, a goal, a direction, a thought, a god. That is all you need. If you have that, nothing will withstand you; all resistance will melt in the heat of divine fire. The kingdom of God needs workers. I have been talking and calling for help for years and years, but there are very few volunteers because everybody scatters their energies in pursuit of frivolous, futile goals. Ah, if only I could get everybody to work in the same direction, we should soon change the face of the earth. But where are the human beings who are ready to do this? Even you who are listening to me are somewhere else. Even while I am talking to you, you are thinking, 'I must get back home, I am sure I left the gas on... I have to pay my taxes... I must not keep my fiancée waiting... I have not got a thing to put on, I must buy a new dress...' You only pretend to listen to what I am saying.

Sèvres, March 24, 1962

* * * * *

The most important and most glorious activity a disciple can undertake is to bring all the powers of his intellect, heart, and will to converge toward the coming of the kingdom of God on earth. Unfortunately, there are not many candidates for this

The Kingdom of God...

work. Everybody has their own goals, their own ambitions, and the kingdom of God is neglected. This is why it is so important that here in the Brotherhood we should form a vital, potent core working for the realization of the kingdom of God and his righteousness, for that realization embraces everything else. Once we have the whole, it is not necessary to ask for minor details. Besides, an entire lifetime is not enough to obtain even one small detail—and the kingdom of God contains everything.

If we ask consciously for the kingdom of God and his righteousness when we are together, we shall be influencing other minds and souls. One day, when the children of light are all together, united in the same thought and with the same goal, they will tip the balance in their favour and gain the final victory over all those who ask only for destruction and chaos. You will ask, 'But why does heaven not decide to intervene and change the world?' It could do so, of course, but if it were done without the consent and willing collaboration of human beings, they would be no better off, for they would neither understand nor appreciate heaven's handiwork. They would only destroy everything all over again. But if the will to change comes from them, if all they have suffered and all the hard lessons they have had to learn make them sincerely want to improve the situation, the rest will follow automatically. Then the invisible world will release other forces, other currents and energies, and everything will be changed. But the impulse must come from human beings. They must decide to work together to secure the intervention of cosmic forces. They will get nothing if they do not insist. The sublime intelligences of the higher world will never interfere in human affairs for their own pleasure. It is up to human beings to call on them to do so.

If, each time we are together, the brothers and sisters are animated by the desire to draw down these forces from heaven, then their prayers will be extraordinarily powerful. But they do not realize this. Each one brings his own personal problems with him—whether to marry, how to find a house, whether to change jobs, how to supplant a rival, and so on. Obviously, all these unrelated thoughts and desires can never be welded into a single force capable of triggering beneficial energies in the cosmos; they can only scatter and disintegrate without results. In ancient times, when initiates gathered together, it was always for a specific purpose. If there was a serious danger of famine for instance, they would conduct rites in which they concentrated all their thoughts and energies on influencing the growth of the crops, on producing an abundant harvest. As a matter of fact there are still tribes in Africa and America that continue to practise rites of this nature.

There is tremendous power in concentration. You all know that you can start a fire by concentrating the rays of the sun through a magnifying glass. It is even said that this was how Archimedes set fire to the Roman fleet that was laying siege to Syracuse: by concentrating the sun's rays. The initiates know these laws and apply them deliberately and to great effect on the spiritual plane. And when we meet together, it must also be in order to obtain worthwhile results; otherwise it would be stupid and pointless to meet. If we cannot put the forces produced by the collectivity to good use, we should do much better to stay at home. Why spend our lives doing something that is useless? Surely our intelligence is capable of finding methods that will get results? It certainly would be senseless to continue otherwise. My role in all this is to enlighten you and show the way, to guide you so that we may get the best possible results.

Henceforth, when you come up here to see the sun rise, concentrate on the kingdom of God, wish for the kingdom of God; nothing else, only that, for the kingdom of God is a state of perfection and total fulfilment. It embraces everything: health, wealth, beauty, order, freedom, peace, balance, harmony, happiness... everything. Rather than enumerating a long list of requests, it is far more 'economical' to ask for the kingdom of God, the synthesis of all blessings. People say, 'Ah, if only I were rich.... If only I had power.... If only I were beautiful.' Yes, but these things are merely partial aspects of the attributes of the kingdom of God, and when you ask for only one aspect, you unbalance things.

The kingdom of God is, above all, a state of balance and harmony. This is why, once you begin to emphasize one aspect to the detriment of others, you are introducing the seeds of imbalance. Everything that our soul and spirit need, everything that our heart, mind, and physical body need is included in the realization of the kingdom of God. When we are all united in asking for the coming of God's kingdom, therefore, we are like rays of sunshine focused on one point, and everything becomes possible. We can even melt rocks.

I am speaking to you in this way today because of your singing—you sang with such harmony. When the brothers and sisters sing together, the mingling of their voices represents the fusion of the masculine and feminine principles in its most spiritual form. Fusion is a law of the universe: in every domain the two principles, masculine and feminine, must unite in order to create life. In choral singing this fusion takes place on a very high plane, in the world of the soul and spirit, and it produces results in the form of joy, peace, and fulfilment. This is why I tell you that when we sing we can accomplish a work of the purest white magic for the entire world.

The brothers and sisters must become increasingly aware of the great laws that govern the universe. They must work with ever greater ardour to free themselves from all earthly elements while they are singing so as to attain absolute purity, the purity that can make their whole being vibrate with such intensity that everything bursts into flame. Yes, flames and sparks of every colour streaming out into space. When you sing in this way, your vocal chords vibrate differently: they transmit other energies, and those energies unite on a higher level and give birth to celestial beings. God has given great powers to the human voice. It is this faculty more than any other that distinguishes man from the animals. Of course, animals can utter sounds; they possess a certain form of language, but it is not the same thing; they do not possess man's power of speech which is born of the union between the masculine and feminine principles[2].

It is very important, therefore, to be aware of the magical power of song and to learn to sing with the conscious intention of emanating forces and energies of the utmost purity, so that they may join and fuse together on high and achieve divine results. There are days when I can feel everything stirring and vibrating as you sing, when you become like columns of flame. Unfortunately, such days are rare because you are still not fully conscious of the work you are doing, but once you begin to be conscious, we shall be capable of dispersing the clouds and all the negative elements in the world by our singing. Yes, because as reasonable beings, as children of God, we have every right to use these great laws for a good purpose.

As you see, I am leading you to realizations so beautiful and so glorious that many of you will, one day, shed tears of joy and awe at being allowed to participate. So far, you have always been weighed down by such a burden of cares, regret, or despair that you have never even suspected that these new possibilities of the spirit existed. There is only one condition for this to become possible, and it is that you trust me. You must not demand to understand fully before starting to put any of this into practice. It could well be centuries before you understand these things. You must be like children who trust their parents and do what they tell them. Children do not need all kinds of explanations in order to obey their parents. In fact, they would not understand the explanations if they were given them. Trust me, therefore. I will never ask you to do something

---

[2] See *Complete Works*, vol. 32, chap. 11.

The Kingdom of God...

wrong. I have to give an account of myself to the higher spirits who sent me here, and I am well aware of my responsibilities.

From now on, when you come here in the morning, try to push away any thoughts that have nothing to do with the kingdom of God. Concentrate on asking for the kingdom of God to come for the whole world, and if you do this, it will come for you too. Do not ask for it only for yourselves, otherwise the positive aspect of your prayer will be wasted. Your prayer must be impersonal. Its power and efficacy depend, in fact, on its being entirely impersonal. And yet, in reality, there is nothing more personal, for it is you yourself who will be the first to benefit from it. When you ask for the kingdom of God to come for the whole world, it begins by infiltrating into you.

In any case, as I have already said, prayers that are too personal are never answered very rapidly, for the entities on high are constantly besieged by a flood of such requests. They cannot keep up with the demand. But a prayer for the coming of the kingdom of God is such a rare event that they greet it with exclamations of joy and pass it on to the Creator at once, saying, 'Here is one at last.' and the excitement is beyond description. You will say that I am embroidering reality. No, this is nothing but the truth. The higher world is inundated by so many trivial requests from human beings, and when one of them finally decides to ask for the kingdom of God it is as though his prayer arrived by airmail special delivery, and it is processed immediately.

Our meetings must have only one aim, one orientation: the kingdom of God. We must be like a beam of many rays of light all converging on one spot in order to produce fantastic effects in the world. We may never see a trace of those effects from where we are, but in the etheric, astral, and mental worlds you may be sure that quantities of rubbish will be burned in a great bonfire, a great spring-cleaning. You do not believe me? No, but I know that all these possibilities exist. I remember them, for I have already known them in the past. Why should we not be capable of doing such extraordinary work again? Of course, before that is possible, we have to know the laws of the spiritual world, just as physicists have to know the laws of the physical world. In any case, physics is simply a manifestation on the physical plane of the laws of magic; magic is spiritual physics. And mathematics is a manifestation of the Cabbalah on a more material level. The same is true of chemistry and alchemy, or astronomy and astrology.

Physics is the material form or manifestation of magic. This is why we have to know the physical laws, for they are also the laws of magic. I am constantly explaining the principles of transcendental physics to you, but as I have never actually said that I was giving a course in physics, you have never realized it. One of the laws of the physics that we call white magic is that tremendous power is generated by concentrating the sun's rays on one spot. And the words of one of our songs remind us of this: 'Ni sme slanchevi lachi, We are the sun's rays.' And since we are the sun's rays, let us concentrate together so as to burn up all the impurities in the world; let us sing together, knowing what powerful effects our singing can have in other regions. With these songs we can elevate and dilate the hearts of human beings and stimulate them to rise to a higher level of evolution.

For years now you have been in a position to verify the truth of what I tell you. I have told you that each one of you possesses fantastic inner laboratories, in which, like chemical and physical engineers, you can conduct all kinds of experiments. For years, too, you have been conducting your own experiments—some of them highly successful and others less so, no doubt, but at least you have persevered with them— and they have shown you that there really is one science which can give us all the light and all the rules we need. And all this is good, for it is in this way that you advance and become richer. It only remains to thank heaven day and night for the

The Kingdom of God...

privilege of having this teaching, of having so many elements of nature available to work for us. The heavens and the earth, the flowers, water and air, food, our own eyes and hands... all these things are at our disposal and we can use them for the glory of God; for the tremendous work of light which must one day prevail in the world.

Blessed are those who understand me. While we are here we must ask collectively every day for the kingdom of God. Of course, we can also ask for it when we are alone, but when we pray alone our prayer can never be as effective as when we pray with the collectivity—unless, of course, we know other laws. If you are alone, you must realize that you will never produce anything worth while unless, by means of your thoughts, you join that immense collectivity of beings throughout the world who are working ceaselessly for the same end. If you remain alone, you will never achieve anything worth while in this area. Even if you cannot always be with others physically, you can at least be united with them mentally. One day, in Rila, the Master Peter Deunov told me, 'If you really want to reach God, you must unite yourself with all those who are thinking of him.' I was very young at the time, and his words made a deep impression on me; I have thought about them a great deal since. Poor, wretched human beings, why do they always want to isolate themselves? They cannot even bring a child into the world if they are not ready to break out of that stupid, sterile solitude and unite with another being. But they still do not understand. 'I prefer to be alone,' they say. Very well, nobody is going to stop them, but they will reap only sterility, an abundant crop of sterility. What a marvellous prospect.

Even in your quest for God, therefore, you must not remain alone; you must attach yourself to all the highly evolved beings in the universe who are thinking of him. In any case, it is impossible to reach God directly; you always have to go through a whole hierarchy. I know that Protestants are not very receptive to this idea of hierarchy; they imagine that they can go straight into the presence of God. What pride... and what ignorance. They know very well that if they want to talk to a king, or even a Cabinet minister, they have to go through a whole series of intermediaries; but when it comes to the Lord, they think they can just walk up to him and shake hands without more ado. And yet these good people read the Bible, so they know that the angels and archangels exist—the Bible even names some of them: Mikhaël, Raphaël, Gabriel, Uriel, and so on—and yet they still think that they can bypass the hierarchy. But the archangels Gabriel and Raphaël are not at all happy about this; it is a very serious misunderstanding. As though they could barge into paradise without even washing their hands, with dirt still under their nails, and go and shake hands with the Lord. What do they take him for?

The Lord is a consuming fire. This is why they are fortunate not to be allowed direct access to him, for if they were, they would be burned to a cinder. They should be very grateful and thank God for not allowing them to reach him directly and obliging them to go through the angelic hierarchies, for the nine choirs of angels serve as transformers of this mighty energy that is God. It is preferable, therefore, to know how to read and interpret the Bible and, instead of ignoring the angels and archangels, to understand why God created them. The first thing to do before trying to reach God is to study the pattern of the universe he created. If you want to enter the presence of the Lord, start by uniting yourself to all those beings whose gaze is constantly fixed on him, as they sing his praises. There are thousands of them. It is quite possible, of course, that when they see the state you are in and learn that you want to treat the Lord as your chum so that you can make free with all his treasures, they may not let you in, for you would plunder and befoul this great temple on high.

You must work in the Lord's vineyard as new workers, with a new conception of things, a new outlook. In this way, you will soon see that all the things that used to be so difficult, all the things that tormented you and held you back, will fade away and you will feel free. I sense that many of you have already begun to experience this liberation. Great transformations are taking place in all the brothers and sisters. Even those who are not very deeply affected receive a few rays of light, and one day, instead of sitting there scratching their heads and wondering where I am leading them, they will begin to understand. They will even wonder why it took them so long to understand.

I still have many things to say to you, and little by little I will say them. What really matters is the magical dimension. It is this that has always been despised and misunderstood, and yet this is the true science of the initiates. This magic is everywhere: in food, in love, in the way you look at others, in your words, your smiles, your thoughts, and all your gestures. As long as people do not know this, they will continue to destroy and despoil and befoul everything. Nothing works because there is no understanding or respect for the magical dimension; it is simply never used. But it is the magical dimension that obliges you to pay absolute attention to every little thing.

Sèvres, March 25, 1962

IV

However much you explain things to human beings, however many truths you reveal to them, they always think, 'That's wonderful, but how much better it would be if we had a lot of money.' The truth is that if they had nothing but money, they would do all kinds of stupid things with it; whereas with the light, whether they have money or not, they will always know how to behave.

The problem is that people do not want to know the truth; they think that it always leads to disaster. They say: 'Tell the truth and you will have brickbats thrown at your head.' Yes, but who said you had to speak the truth out loud? You should keep it inside you, then it will not lead to disaster. Quite the reverse in fact, for although it is not always good to tell the truth, it is always good to know it. The knowledge of truth can never hurt you. When Jesus said that we should not cast our pearls before swine, he was speaking of the pearls of truth for which human beings are not ready. If you give these pearls to people who are unprepared, not only will they be incapable of appreciating them but they will turn and rend you.

So do not throw truth about haphazardly; treasure it, keep it always within you, for it will make you strong and set you free. It is not truth that causes disaster; it only causes disaster if you

The Kingdom of God...

reveal it to evil people, who live in darkness. If you know truth and guard it inwardly, you can adorn yourself every day with its treasure, as if with necklaces of gold and pearls and precious stones that you take out and contemplate and caress before locking them up again in the depths of your inner treasure chests. How can the truth hurt you if you do this? On the contrary, this contact with truth can only strengthen you and make you capable of helping, supporting, and elevating others.

Why do you suppose that I spend my days revealing these truths to you? Because I consider you as my family; I consider that you are highly evolved and conscious, and I want to help you. In the past I may have been a little imprudent in this respect: I revealed the truth to some swine and they turned and tore me to pieces. But one little atom survived, and that atom has repaired and restored everything. This is why I can be here with you again today. But I found out for myself that it was true, that Jesus was right when he said that we should not give treasures to swine. When I was young, I was very naïve and trusting and full of love. I did not know that even the very best things can bring great misfortune on us if we are not reasonable and prudent. Now I know.

But let us leave all that for the moment. My task is always to explain and emphasize the invisible, divine aspect of things, the aspect that human beings forget or despise. That is why I am here, to highlight and underline this dimension so that you may begin to see the reality and appreciate its proper value once again. I do talk about other things also, of course, but this is the aspect I always insist on. I know that there is a danger that you will be sick and tired of my insistence, that you will consider me a tiresome, poisonous bore. But that does not matter. I am obliged to continue because this is the only dimension worth cherishing and intensifying, the only thing worth cultivating so that it may manifest itself in our lives.

Human beings spend too much time on things that are fated

to fade and disappear. This is why they are always in a void, always poor and destitute. Only when people are rooted in what is eternal, immortal, and infinite can they feel safe. Why, when you meet an initiate, do you have a sense of clarity, of something stable and reassuring, whereas with other people you always have a feeling of something ambiguous, something changeable and unpredictable? Human beings have not had the spiritual masters they needed to mould them and teach them what life is, where they come from and where they should be going. They have allowed themselves to be led by those who are immersed in the material world and who draw their traditions and concepts, their entire philosophy, from that world. And it is a philosophy that leads nowhere, or rather, that leads inevitably to torment, misfortune, and revolt. Whereas the initiates, who have so often been despised and rejected, have always founded their teaching on the essentials, on all that is immortal and all-powerful and capable of creating worlds, new worlds.

If people listened to the initiates, the kingdom of God would come again in the world and all would be abundance, joy, and love—yes, especially love. With things as they are at the moment there is no way out, no solution. You must realize that the world's problems will never be solved unless things change. Here am I, confronting all thinkers, politicians, economists, and so on, and telling them, 'You are all wrong. You will never make things better, never solve anything. You must change your point of view completely and adopt the philosophy of the initiates.'

Look at all the changes and the extraordinary events taking place among young people. If the scientists and philosophers do not bring about change, it is young people who will do so[3].

[3] Three months after this lecture the student unrest that had been simmering in France broke out in violent strikes and demonstrations. See the companion volume to this one (*Complete Works*, vol. 25) for a fuller treatment of the problems of young people in today's society.

The Kingdom of God...

They may not have all the light and guidance they need, but there is something in this revolt of young people against society, against materialism, that we must understand. I am not saying that all their ideas are very reasonable, but their revolt is a sign of the times. It is as though a great tide, a great flood, were sweeping over society and threatening to drown mankind. And young people feel this more keenly than adults, who are firmly entrenched in their old traditions. If adults are unwilling to understand, young people are going to teach them some very harsh lessons, and they will be forced to realize that something must change.

Now I am not saying that you should all become hippies. I do not advise you to wander through the country unwashed and clad in rags, to sleep wherever you find yourselves and never do a day's work. No, none of that is to be recommended. But this phenomenon exists, and since it exists we must think about what it means. All this upheaval comes from the constellation of Aquarius. At the moment, driven as they are by these currents, human beings are not sure of what attitude to adopt. They are in the grip of forces they do not understand, and they go wherever those forces take them, but eventually they will learn to control these forces. Philosophers and writers, indeed all men and women, will be led to change their outlook, to study human nature more closely, and to understand that human beings will never know fulfilment until they learn to satisfy the needs of their souls and spirits.

Why is there so much social unrest these days? Why do so many people have this sense of emptiness and dissatisfaction? They have everything and yet they are never satisfied. The explanation is simple: they do not know themselves. 'Only that?' you will ask. Yes, only that; but it is that that explains everything. Human beings behave as though they consisted only of matter, as though their bellies and genitals were the only parts of them that needed to be satisfied. But there is more to human beings than that; they have souls and spirits. They contain a spark, something of another dimension, another intensity, something divine that vibrates differently; and they must learn to discern the aspirations of this something and understand what it needs. The soul's needs are not those of the physical body, but human beings continually try to give it food that it cannot digest. They never give it what it asks for. The soul asks for infinite space, dazzling light, harmony, celestial music; and humans insist on giving it only material food. This is why their souls are somnolent, why they are sighing and suffocating and dying.

Why are there so many diseases today for which medicine cannot find a cure? For the same reason: medical science does not know what human beings are. When it begins to understand them, it will also begin to heal them, for it will know that it must take care of other dimensions, the inner regions in which illness originates. When human beings know themselves, when they know that they are composed of several principles, of several bodies, and that these bodies are interwoven with each other, that they all need their own particular form of nourishment, and that there must be perfect harmony between them, this knowledge will inspire a different philosophy. And with this new philosophy will come an improvement in all other areas as well—social, political, and economic—and the kingdom of God will reign on earth. As long as human beings do not know themselves, the kingdom of God cannot come, because they are not looking for it in the right place.

The kingdom of God is not what materialists think it is. It is not a material but a spiritual realization; it is a state of consciousness. This means that human beings must be given the knowledge that will change their consciousness. Well, I have my programme, my plan, and if I can apply this plan, the kingdom of God will be the easiest thing in the world to achieve. Of course, this does not mean that it will be established immediately in the minds of every single human being. No, there are some for whom it will come only after thousands of years. But when it comes, it will be in the form of an organization of the whole world, and once that organization is established at the summit, all the 'members' will conform to the order they see at the top. It has to be the summit, the head, that applies this order first, and the arms and legs will follow.

The kingdom of God has to be established first of all as a light, as intelligence in the minds of human beings. Secondly, it will enter the heart as a sensation, as happiness, and finally, it will descend to the physical plane where it will manifest itself as abundance and peace. This is possible. I am working for this. The only trouble is that there are so few people who understand me. Most people cling to their old, antiquated ideas. They say, 'It is impossible. People will never change. Just look at them. Do you need any further proof?' Well of course, I am not blind. I can see what goes on in the world, and I know better than anyone that if this state of affairs endures, the kingdom of God will never come. But I also know that once you accept the philosophy of the initiates, everything becomes possible.

The way in which the intelligence of nature has designed and constructed human beings teaches us an important lesson. If a person is fit and healthy, it is because all his organs are willing to live and work together in an unselfish spirit of brotherhood and generosity. If all the countries in the world did the same, the kingdom of God would be possible. Why do human beings refuse to seek guidance from the intelligence of nature, that sublime intelligence which has foreseen everything and has the solution to all their problems? Why do they continue to look for answers from other human beings? People will listen to you if you quote from this scholar or that scientist, but not if you quote from nature. They say, 'What is all this nonsense? Who ever heard of nature having intelligence? What makes you think that?' It is because of this attitude that they fail to advance. When they are willing to learn from nature, it will be easy to achieve the kingdom of God; until then, they will continue to struggle unsuccessfully with all their complicated problems.

Actually, no undertaking is inherently either difficult or easy; it all depends on who attempts it. Something that is difficult for an animal is easy for a man; and something that is difficult for a man is easy for an initiate. The difficulty of any enterprise depends on who undertakes it. Many people moan and groan at something that makes others smile. It is very difficult for someone who has never smoked and who hates the smell of tobacco to start smoking; while others find it all too easy to smoke... and so terribly difficult to give it up. It would be impossible for an honest man to pick somebody's pocket; but it is equally impossible for a pick-pocket to refrain from doing so. For some people, therefore, it is very difficult to establish the kingdom of God, but for me it is very easy. Give me people who are really capable of understanding me and you will see what I shall do.

Human beings will find no solutions to their problems without a knowledge of their own nature. So far, the only thing they understand about themselves is their physical dimension, and this is why the solutions they apply are no more than palliatives. They often have the impression that they have solved a problem, only to find shortly afterwards that the solution itself has caused other problems. Medicine is a case in point: very often the treatment for one illness causes another. And in the field of education it is the same thing: with all the improvements in the material equipment of schools, do children learn to lead better lives? No, education is deficient because it is not based on an understanding of the nature of human beings.

This is why I have always maintained that the only science worth studying in depth is the science of human nature. Yes, at the centre of everything should be this science, and all the other sciences—physics, chemistry, astronomy, biology, and so on—should be at its service. You will say, 'But surely anatomy and physiology are valuable fields of study.' Yes, they are a necessary foundation, but they do not concern the whole human being, only the physical framework. You would be seriously misguided to study a car in the belief that you were studying the man driving it. And this is exactly what human beings are doing: they talk about the car as though it were its owner. No, the body of the car is not the owner of the car; you are going to have to look for him elsewhere. In such deplorable conditions human beings cannot blossom and manifest themselves as they truly are.

Henceforth, all this must change, and the whole human being—including the Godhead within—must be at the centre of all our study and research; and the other sciences, instead of being seen as independent disciplines, must contribute to this central science. For a human being is in fact the synthesis of all that exists; he contains all sciences within himself. Once scientists adopt this changed point of view, the world itself will be transformed; for instead of giving priority to what is no more than a lifeless and inert shell, they will give it to what is alive, to life itself. And I assure you that when the kingdom of God comes, even poets will shut up shop, for the lives of human beings will be so poetic, so full of wonder, that they will have no time to waste on books of poetry. Yes, poets will have nothing more to say because everybody will live in a state of true poetry.

There is so much more I should like to tell you, but today I want to insist on this one thing, on this point of view which alone is capable of restoring everything to its rightful place. For years and years I studied and searched for the central point that brings everything together, and I found it: it is mankind. Human beings still need to be enlightened, they still need to know their true nature, but once they know themselves, the attitude of scholars and students of all disciplines—medicine, education, economics, religion, politics, and so on—will have to change. And not only their attitude but their behaviour, and the way they work as well. Yes, they will be forced to change because the centre will have changed. Once the centre is restored to its rightful place, once all human beings begin to know themselves and to know what is important and what is not, the rest will revolve around this divine centre within, and all other problems will be easily resolved.

This is why I always insist so much on the divine centre within, for the organization of all the cells and particles of our being depends on this centre; it is the focal point around which they must revolve. This then is the secret: to gather up all the various elements that fly off in different directions and bring them back into orbit around this centre, like planets around the sun. Only when there is a centre, a hub around which each element slips into place and follows its own orbit without conflict or interference with others, can we speak of order, health, and happiness; only then can we speak of the kingdom of God.

My trust in the philosophy of the initiates is absolute. Yes, absolute, for when you examine it closely and compare it to all the other philosophies that exist, you see that it is the only one that is left standing; all the others are disqualified. You see how simple it is: take away the centre of a human being—the spirit, the soul—and all you have left is a cadaver. The physical body decomposes when its centre is removed. So each of us has to find that living, vibrant atom at the centre of our being and make everything else converge toward it, for it alone is capable of keeping things in order.

You often hear people say: 'I lost my head.' Yes, you lose your head; you lose control of yourself and no longer know what you are saying or doing. And when you are not in control, you inevitably do something stupid and have to undo it later. Of course, the head is only a symbol; you could equally say, 'I lost my heart,' since the heart is also the centre. So whether you call it the heart or the head, what you actually lose is your divine centre, and it is when you lose this that everything goes awry and disorder gets the upper hand. When your cells learn that the head, the boss, is no longer there, they feel free to do whatever they please; you become the enemy and they are a threat to you. When your centre was in place, all the cells of your heart and lungs and arms and legs were obedient and docile and served you well; but now they threaten your very life. You are ill in bed, and they are delighted. They say, 'Aha, that is good. Now perhaps you will understand.' But when you reinstate the centre, the spirit, they immediately calm down and work harmoniously again. There is something that human beings are going to have to learn one day, and it has nothing to do with either microbes or the stars; it is how to maintain the spirit at the centre of all their activity.

Today, my dear brothers and sisters, you have suddenly become richer, and from now on, if you trust me, you will find yourselves more and more able to overcome your difficulties by having recourse to the power slumbering within you. You always forget this power; you look for solutions outside yourselves, and then the balance is lost. If you want your scales to balance perfectly, you have to put as much weight on one side as on the other. You have often seen children swinging up and down on a see-saw. Even animals are trained to do the same at the circus. Everybody enjoys and applauds the performance, but they never see that it is a portrait of life itself, of the balance without which no life is possible. So you must not rely exclusively on external means; you must also call on the inner spirit in order to achieve perfect balance.

Sèvres, January 21, 1968

V

Question: It says in the Gospels: *'Seek first the Kingdom of God and his justice.'* If the Kingdom of God represents the fullness of all qualities and virtues, why did Jesus add *'and his justice'*?[4]

That is a good question. If Jesus added 'and his justice' it is precisely because the kingdom of God has nothing to do with justice. If justice came into it, it would not be the kingdom of God. The kingdom of God is exclusively a world of love, generosity, and kindness. Justice belongs to the physical, human order, and it becomes necessary only when the kingdom of God descends and manifests itself on earth. Justice excludes love. It is a kind of barter, an exchange: you give something, and you have a right to expect the exact equivalent, neither more nor less, in exchange. Whereas love is an injustice: to love is to give someone more than they deserve.

You could say that love is grace. The love of God for

[4] Most modern English translations of the Bible use the word righteousness in preference to justice. There is a sense in which the two are virtually synonymous—moral integrity or rectitude—but in this lecture the word justice is used as it refers explicitly to the more common meaning of the word—impartiality, retribution, the administration of civil and criminal law. (Translator's note)

The Kingdom of God... 213

humanity is a grace that human beings do not deserve; it is given to them in place of the justice they deserve. Grace exists above and justice exists below. As human beings are not very enlightened, are not lit from within, either by the spirit or by love, they are unwilling to give more than absolutely necessary, so they base their actions on justice. This whole question will be clearer perhaps if we look at the implacable laws laid down by Moses: an eye for an eye, a tooth for a tooth. The least little fault had to be punished; there was no question of indulgence or forgiveness. At the time this was normal, for it corresponded to the stage of evolution human beings had reached: they had to learn justice before they could go any further. Justice in fact represented a considerable step forward at the time, but the reign of justice could not last for ever. God is indulgent and merciful, and human beings had to learn to be like him, to be indulgent and merciful too. This is why Jesus came to teach forgiveness, and his treatment of the woman taken in adultery, whom the Pharisees wanted to stone, was an example of this attitude—an attitude that transgressed the law of justice but obeyed the law of love.

There is another world, and it is governed by other laws—the laws of heaven—which do not include justice. Since there are no crimes in heaven, what need is there for justice? Heaven is ruled only by light and love; whereas justice is needed in places where laws are broken. So this is why we speak of the kingdom of God and his justice. When the kingdom of God arrives on earth, there will still be some men and women who are not sufficiently enlightened to embrace the rule of love. Yes, you must not think that all human beings will automatically be transformed as soon as the kingdom of God is established on earth. The kingdom of God will be formed only by an elite, by the most intelligent, most sensitive, and most highly evolved human beings. All the others will have to follow the example and accept the authority of this elite. There will have to be justice, therefore, because it is impossible to live on earth without laws; laws not only to punish wrongdoers but also to guide and point the way.

You must not believe that as soon as the kingdom of God arrives, all men without exception are going to be shining lights, suns in the heavens. Far be it from me to mislead you with any such idea. Anyone who believes this would have to be blind to the way the history of mankind unfolds. Even if the kingdom of God is achieved on earth, human beings will not be perfect just like that, from one day to the next. That is impossible; it is a process that takes time. To begin with, there will be a small minority of highly evolved beings who understand and accept the ideas of the Universal White Brotherhood, of the kingdom of God on earth, of the golden age. Government will be in the hands of this minority, and all others will be obliged to follow, just as the tail follows the head. The masses will be given every opportunity to collaborate and join forces with the minority that forms the kingdom of God, and when they see the new life offered to them and the new social order that will be so tremendously beneficial to all, they will have no hesitation in doing so. When that day comes, we shall no longer see what we see today—each country wanting to be the most important, the greatest, the most powerful. Unattainable as it is, this ambition still fascinates and captivates the minds of many. Yes, 'Deutschland, Deutschland über alles'... and we all know how that ended. But the Germans are not the only ones who cherished this ambition for their country. Mankind can never live in happiness until all countries are united. Even if the kingdom of God is established on earth, therefore, justice will still be needed. But it will be another kind of justice, not the justice of ignorant men who make laws that are not even sensible.

Now, I want to add a few words to what I said in the beginning about justice and grace. Imagine that you are looking at a pyramid. A pyramid is a cube surmounted by four

The Kingdom of God...

triangles, and you can spread out the four triangles to form a Maltese cross. Similarly, if you develop the cube you get another kind of cross. The cross derived from the cube is the cross of justice, whereas that derived from the four triangles is the cross of grace. This is because the cube is a symbol of matter, which imprisons; whereas the triangle is a symbol of the spirit, which liberates. And the pyramid too is a symbol, a symbol of the human being, who is both body and spirit.

And now, how does grace manifest itself? Why is it given only to a few and not to everyone? Grace, of course, is an injustice, and yet it works in conformity with another kind of justice, one which is beyond human justice. Suppose someone starts to build a house, and when it is only half finished he finds that his capital has run out. He asks the bank for a loan, but before giving him the money the bank manager, who is no fool, makes sure that he will be able to pay it back. If the answer is affirmative, the loan will be granted. And this, symbolically speaking, is grace. If grace gives to some people rather than to others, it is because it has made enquiries about them and found out that although they are short of cash in this life, they have worked well in previous incarnations. Thanks to their good record they will be given some capital to help them on their way. Grace is neither stupid nor blind, as so many people imagine, and if it is given to you, it means that you have worked long and well to earn it.

It is impossible to understand the laws of destiny if you do not accept the fact of reincarnation. Ask any priest, for instance, why one of your friends is so heavily handicapped in life and meets with nothing but failure, while another meets with nothing but success. Instead of saying, 'There must be a reason; everything happens for a reason, because life is just,' he will say, 'It is the will of God.' But if God's will is so arbitrary, how can anyone trust him? It is very bad to present God in this light, for if you never know what he is liable to do or why, you will always be afraid of him; you can never feel safe. And then they tell us that God is a shield, a refuge, a fortress. How can we believe two such contradictory notions? Explanations of this kind can only undermine religion and morality. For my part, I never accept without question what I read or what people tell me; I always compare it with what I know of the laws of nature and the way in which God created the world.

For instance, when I hear clairvoyants and others declaring that thirty or forty years from now mankind will be wiped out, that there will be a third world war, and so on, I agree with them, and at the same time I disagree. Of course, anything can happen: world war, revolutions, natural cataclysms... But if the light continues to increase in the world—and that is what we are working for—mankind will escape destruction. The course of events is not irrevocably predetermined; it can be altered by the way human beings behave. God is not a cruel, relentless tyrant. If he decrees cataclysms, it does not mean that once decreed they are irrevocable and unavoidable; neither does he do so for his own amusement. No, I reject any such philosophy. Nothing is absolutely pre-ordained; there is no such thing as an irrevocable destiny, either for individuals or for the world as a whole. Human beings have been created with free will, and their future is in their own hands. If they trigger adverse currents by spending their lives in disorder and frivolity, then of course the laws of nature—which are the laws of justice—come into play, and as certainly as two and two make four, the outcome will be devastating. But if they reform and mend their ways, if they project other, more harmonious forces into the environment, the balance of nature will not be disrupted and there need be no devastation.

I too can predict the future: I can tell you that in thirty years from now things will be thus and so. It is not difficult to foresee certain things, but no one can do so with absolute certainty, because human beings can change; their aspirations can change. Even a prophet cannot say with absolute certainty that such and such will happen—or if he does, it means that he is not a very clear-sighted prophet. Absolute predictions are possible, but only for the future of animals, plants, or inanimate objects—and for a class of human beings who are no better than animals and consequently incapable of transforming themselves. But you can make no reliable predictions for intelligent, conscious human beings, because they have the power to escape all predictions. If they mend their ways, they can alter whatever was decreed. This is the philosophy of the Universal White Brotherhood, and it is this philosophy you need, for it can make you conscious and powerful children of God, capable of controlling your own destiny.

It is written: 'Seek first the kingdom of God and his justice, and all these things shall be added to you.' The kingdom of God is a world of harmony, delight, and joy, and such a world could not exist on earth if there were no justice; for even when it is established on earth, not all human beings will be sufficiently evolved to appreciate divine grace and abundance and use them for good. On the other hand, the justice of the future will not be the justice we know today, which consists mainly in punishing people and sending them to prison. Society will be organized in such a way that this will no longer be necessary. I shall say no more on the subject today (although what I have said is necessarily incomplete), but if you reflect and meditate on this from time to time, you will begin to see with your spiritual eyes what life will be like in the future. For this ability to see how events will turn out in the future is there, within yourselves. No one on this earth can really explain it to you.

This is the goal that we are working for: to increase the light and heighten the consciousness of human beings. Unfortunately, there are not many men and women who understand the value of this work. A few thousand follow this teaching, but that is not a great number. Nobody realizes that this science is capable of preventing future catastrophes. I feel as though I were all alone in a desert. Human beings have all kinds of other plans, other desires and occupations, and I am still alone. If I had a few hundred thousand with me... Ah, that would mean the end of war and suffering. But human beings fail to see the importance of this light. And yet all initiates would tell you the same thing: the world will not be saved by money, or tanks, or atom bombs, or missiles, or any other human invention; but by light, spiritual light. Human beings need to be enlightened.

'Seek first the kingdom of God and his justice.' What treasures you will discover in these words if only you work with them. And there are other passages in the Gospels to which you should also pay particular attention. Passages such as 'Be perfect, therefore, as your heavenly Father is perfect,' and, 'My Father is still working, and I also am working.' And you must work with light, work to identify with light, so that you may be able to say, 'I am the light of the world... I am the resurrection and the life.' Yes, for all this will be true one day. So, as I say, pick out the passages in the Gospels that express the highest and most sublime ideal and work with them. Some people choose one of the commandments ('You shall not covet your neighbour's goods,' for instance—or his wife.), but this does not amount to much. They do not steal or commit adultery perhaps, but what do they really gain in the spiritual world? You must wish for nothing less than the coming of the kingdom of God, for it is this state of total perfection that contains all other virtues and qualities. And you must not be content to wish for it; you must do everything in your power to bring it about.

Sèvres, November 11, 1964

* * * * *

Capital punishment is a subject that always arouses heated debate. There are often programmes on radio or television in which judges, psychiatrists, and sociologists present their observations and draw differing conclusions, and public opinion is deeply divided. Some think that criminals should be punished as an example to others, and the death penalty is seen as a deterrent. Others argue that fear of the death penalty has never prevented anyone from committing a crime and, more importantly, that no human being has the right to sentence another to death. The discussion never ends, but I have never heard anyone on the radio or television saying what I am going to say to you today. Why not? Because human beings have no knowledge of initiatic science; they can only solve their problems in the light of the events that take place around them and in conformity with the ideas or prejudices in which they have been brought up. They do not know what really goes on in the invisible world.

The law of retaliation—an eye for an eye, a tooth for a tooth—has never solved anything. The proof of this is all around us; you only have to see the extent to which crimes are increasing rather than diminishing in spite of the application of this kind of law. The statistics are there to confirm what I say. But above all—and this is a very important truth—it is a great mistake to think that you can get rid of a criminal by killing him. People do not realize that once a criminal's physical body is dead he moves to the astral and lower mental planes and becomes capable of even greater evil. When he is on that level, he can poison the minds and hearts of the living and influence them to commit his crimes for him. He has even more scope for his evil designs than when he was alive, for he is no longer confined to the limits of his own physical body; he can use any number of people as intermediaries. As long as a foul-smelling liquid is corked up in a bottle, the stench cannot spread; but once the bottle is opened and the liquid poured out, the stench spreads far and wide. In the same way, as long as a criminal is alive, the demonic being that inhabits him is confined to his physical body, but as soon as he dies, this being is released and his astral body spreads out and reaches and influences the minds of a great many people.

Does this astonish you? These are truths that are unknown to the majority of people. Even the specialists who debate these questions on television are very far from being in a position to solve the great problems of life, because they base their arguments exclusively on their narrow, earth-bound point of view. The real solutions can be found only by rising to a much higher plane and learning about the structure of the universe and of man. Suppose a criminal is executed, what then? His physical presence is no longer a problem, of course, but he remains alive on the subtler planes, and his thirst for revenge and destruction is as virulent as ever. You cannot kill a man's desires by killing his body, because his desires are not physical, they do not belong to the physical plane. People imagine that their hunger and thirst, their need for love, or the pain they feel exist on the physical plane. No, these things are suffered on the astral plane. If you cause a man's astral and etheric bodies to leave his physical body, you can cut his body up in little bits and he will not feel a thing. Sensation does not belong to the physical plane.

Those who think that capital punishment is a solution to the problem of crime do not realize that the spirit of a criminal continues to be active on the other side. They think that just because his body is no longer there he will commit no more crimes. But have they never thought about the phenomenon that occurs when a prophet or a great master is assassinated? Have they never wondered why his ideas, far from fading away, spread and take an even stronger hold on men's minds? This too remains inexplicable.

As a matter of fact, there are a few political leaders today who seem to have a little more understanding of the question. For instance, if they want to get rid of a popular religious or political figure who is an embarrassment to them, they say to themselves, 'Careful now. If we kill him he will be seen as a martyr; his followers will be even more fanatical, and we shall have done ourselves more harm than good.' They understand that you cannot kill the ideology by killing the man, because others take it up and give it a new and even stronger impetus. You will say, 'But that is because his disciples and followers are so infuriated by the assassination of their leader that they are even more ardently determined to spread his ideas.' Yes, there is some truth in that of course, but what people do not know is that in the other world the spirit of a prophet or martyr continues to harbour the same convictions and the same desire to enlighten human beings and help them to evolve. He goes on with his work, therefore, and not only does he go on with it but his ability to propagate his ideas is greater than before. While he lived on earth he could not actually meet every man and woman who was ready to embrace his ideas, for they were scattered throughout the length and breadth of the world. But once he is in the astral world he is free; he can go and find them in order to influence them. This is why it was often better that an initiate should die so that his ideas might spread. Look at the phenomenal growth of Christianity after the death of Jesus.

While a spiritual master is on earth, of course, he can work actively and be an example to others, but the number of people reached by his activity is necessarily restricted to a few close followers who are constantly with him. Once he is freed from his physical body, however, he is able to reach and influence many more minds. Now you must not misunderstand me; I am not saying that a master should allow himself to be killed so that his influence may be greater. No, I am simply explaining how things work in the invisible world.

So as I say, in view of the consequences on the invisible plane, criminals should not be executed. The only solution is for human beings to organize conditions in the world in such a way that there will be no more criminals. Yes, but as long as society is not founded on spiritual principles it will continue to resemble a swamp, and swamps can only produce mosquitoes, that is, criminals. In these conditions it is pointless to hope for justice. Besides, if you always act in accordance with justice you will never solve any vital problems. You must not be just. Ah, I see that that makes your hair stand on end. But it is true: I am for injustice. Now wait, do not be in too much of a hurry to criticize; you will soon understand what I am saying.

One of the symbols of justice is a pair of scales, and if you study what human beings do when they use scales you will understand many things. You go to the market and ask a merchant for a pound of cherries. The man weighs out the cherries, and if there is one too many he removes it from the scales. Yes, because he is just. The owner of the next stall has tinkered with his scales, and if you go home and weigh the fruit and vegetables you buy from him, you will be very angry to find that you are always an ounce or two short. You are ready to accept the justice of the first merchant, even if you are not particularly enchanted by it (at least he is just), whereas you are furious with the man who gave you less than he should. Finally, you go and buy from yet a third stall, and when the man weighs out your pound of cherries, he throws in a few more for good measure. Is this justice or injustice? It is injustice, of course, but it is an injustice that you appreciate enormously. How is it that you are so full of admiration for someone who is unjust?

There are two kinds of injustice, therefore, and only one kind of justice. Injustice can be either good or bad; whereas justice is neither good nor bad... it is simply just. That is why I recommend injustice. But which kind? If someone hits you once and you respond by hitting him twice, not only are you being unjust, but you are also being unkind. You should at least limit your response to one blow. If someone else hits you and you respond with a hug, a kind word, or a gift, you are again being unjust, but this is the injustice I recommend: the injustice that is called love. Yes, love is very unjust. It is an injustice to love, and help, and give to someone who does not deserve it, but this is the injustice we should practise. Of course it is not wrong to want to apply the rule of justice. If everyone were just, there might not be very much love about in the world, but at least there would be less crime and fewer wars. Yes, but even so I advocate the injustice that alone can save the world.

The Bonfin, April 14, 1977

Chapter Six

The New Jerusalem

I

Today I am going to read you the twenty-first chapter of the Book of Revelation of St John[1].

Then I saw a new heaven and a new earth; for the first heaven and the first earth had passed away, and the sea was no more. And I saw the holy city, the new Jerusalem, coming down out of heaven from God, prepared as a bride adorned for her husband. And I heard a loud voice from the throne saying,
      'See, the home of God is among mortals. He will dwell with them as their God; they will be his peoples, and God himself will be with them; he will wipe every tear from their eyes. Death will be no more; mourning and crying and pain will be no more, for the first things have passed away.'
      And the one who was seated on the throne said, 'See, I am making all things new.' Also he said, 'Write this, for these words are trustworthy and true.'Then he said to me, 'It is done! I am the Alpha and the Omega, the beginning and the end. To the thirsty I will give water as a gift from the spring of the water of life. Those who conquer will inherit these things, and I will be their God and they will be my children. But as for the

---

[1] *The Book of Revelation* is discussed in detail in vol. 230 in the *Izvor Collection*.

cowardly, the faithless, the polluted, the murderers, the fornicators, the sorcerers, the idolaters, and all liars, their place will be in the lake that burns with fire and sulphur, which is the second death.'

Then one of the seven angels who had the seven bowls full of the seven last plagues came and said to me, 'Come, I will show you the bride, the wife of the Lamb.' And in the spirit he carried me away to a great, high mountain and showed me the holy city Jerusalem coming down out of heaven from God. It has the glory of God and a radiance like a very rare jewel, like jasper, clear as crystal. It has a great, high wall with twelve gates, and at the gates twelve angels, and on the gates are inscribed the names of the twelve tribes of the Israelites; on the east three gates, on the north three gates, on the south three gates, and on the west three gates. And the wall of the city has twelve foundations, and on them are the twelve names of the twelve apostles of the Lamb.

The angel who talked to me had a measuring rod of gold to measure the city and its gates and walls. The city lies foursquare, its length the same as its width; and he measured the city with his rod, fifteen hundred miles; its length and width and height are equal. He also measured its wall, one hundred forty-four cubits by human measurement, which the angel was using. The wall is built of jasper, while the city is pure gold, clear as glass. The foundations of the wall of the city are adorned with every jewel; the first was jasper, the second sapphire, the third agate, the fourth emerald, the fifth onyx, the sixth carnelian, the seventh chrysolite, the eighth beryl, the ninth topaz, the tenth chrysoprase, the eleventh jacinth, the twelfth amethyst. And the twelve gates are twelve pearls, each of the gates is a single pearl, and the street of the city is pure gold, transparent as glass.

I saw no temple in the city, for its temple is the Lord God the Almighty and the Lamb. And the city has no need of sun or moon to shine on it, for the glory of God is its light, and its

The New Jerusalem

lamp is the Lamb. The nations will walk by its light, and the kings of the earth will bring their glory into it. Its gates will never be shut by day—and there will be no night there. People will bring into it the glory and the honour of the nations. But nothing unclean will enter it, nor anybody who practices abomination or falsehood, but only those who are in written in the Lamb's book of life.

* * *

From earliest antiquity there has always been one great initiatic centre on earth which commanded all others. All the lesser centres were branches of this unique centre, whose light has never ceased to shine throughout the centuries.

To guarantee the continuity of this flame, there had to be a being who possessed all powers and all knowledge, a being who could be God's representative on earth, a being who would never die. And such a being actually exists. He is mentioned in the Bible and, under different names, in all the spiritual traditions of the world; there can be no doubt as to his existence. In the Hebrew tradition he is known as Melchizedek. In Genesis Moses tells us that Melchizedek brought bread and wine to Abraham and that Abraham gave him the tenth part of his spoils of war. St Paul also speaks of Melchizedek in his Epistle to the Hebrews:

This King Melchizedek of Salem, priest of the Most High God, met Abraham as he was returning from defeating the kings and blessed him; and to him Abraham apportioned one-tenth of everything. His name, in the first place, means 'king of righteousness'; next he is also king of Salem, that is, 'king of peace.' Without father, without mother, without genealogy, having neither beginning of days nor end of life, but resembling the Son of God, he remains a priest forever.

You will ask, 'But if he had no father or mother, how was

he created?' A being who is God's representative on earth is all-powerful in respect to matter. He can form an etheric body that is capable of lasting until the end of time, and he can also disintegrate it at will. Of all God's representatives it is Melchizedek—whose name means 'king of justice'—who has the most important role to play on earth. He is the judge of the living and the dead, and all decisions concerning the destiny of mankind come from him. All the high initiates received instruction from him: Hermes Trismegistus was an aspect of Melchizedek, and Orpheus, Moses, Pythagoras, Plato, Buddha, and Zoroaster. All the greatest initiates were taught by him— even Jesus. It was Melchizedek who delegated the three Magi to represent his kingdom in paying homage to Jesus, because Jesus was the incarnation of the Divine Principle, of the Word made flesh. But Melchizedek, representative of the living God, who has neither beginning nor end, has a different role to play.

Jesus took the flesh and blood of a man, and this means that he had a mother and a father. But he spent the eighteen years of his life about which the Gospels are silent (from the age of twelve to the age of thirty) in the kingdom of Melchizedek, king of justice and of peace; and there, in the company of all the highest initiates, he did tremendous work for the whole world. He was about thirty when he returned to Palestine to accomplish his mission and extend to his own disciples his close relationship with the kingdom of Melchizedek. There is a tradition common to all religions that a mysterious kingdom exists in an inaccessible region known as the 'land of the immortals' or 'land of the living'. This mysterious kingdom is the kingdom of Melchizedek, but only a few initiates with close links to Melchizedek have firsthand knowledge of it.

No initiate can reach the summit without going through the school of Melchizedek. It is he who gives human beings access to the Sephirah Kether, for he possesses the knowledge of all the angelic hierarchies; he moves freely from one to the other and has millions of angels at his service. He watches over the evolution of mankind, guiding it according to God's plan and intervening to restore order when human beings stray from the path laid down for them. And as the four elements—earth, water, air, and fire—are at his service, he has all powers. This, then, is the being whom St John saw and whom he describes at the beginning of Revelation: 'In his right hand he held seven stars, and from his mouth came a sharp, two-edged sword.' This communication between St John and Melchizedek came about because Jesus put them in touch with each other. Of course, details of this kind are never mentioned by the established religions, but anyone who is capable of doing some research in the archives of initiatic science will find them recorded there.

The being whom St John saw in his vision, therefore, the being who declared, 'I am Alpha and Omega... the beginning and the end,' was none other than Melchizedek. He is called by different names according to the cycles of the ages because his name is magic. And behold, the first seal of the Apocalypse is open. It is very important that you should know who this great being was, for St John was transported to his kingdom of Salem so that he should be capable of writing the Apocalypse. It was there that he was shown the depths of the earth and of the seas; it was there that he saw how the spirits do their work in nature by means of the four elements; and it was there that he contemplated the angelic hierarchies. It was at the orders of Melchizedek, therefore, that he wrote the Apocalypse, which will be deciphered in the last days.

Today, I want to talk to you about the New Jerusalem. What did St John mean when he spoke of 'the new Jerusalem, coming down out of heaven from God?' It is true that it will come down from heaven, but great upheavals and transformations must take place before this can come about. You yourselves will witness all this, for it will happen in our times. St John speaks of a 'New Jerusalem' because there was another Jerusalem, which was destroyed. Why was the first Jerusalem given a name similar to Salem, the city of which Melchizedek was king? Because those who named it knew about Melchizedek. They had been initiated by Moses, who had himself received initiation from Jethro, his father-in-law. When Moses fled from Egypt he took refuge in the land of Midian, where he married Zipporah, the daughter of the high priest of the land. For years, Moses studied under the guidance of Jethro, his father-in-law. It was he who put him in touch with Melchizedek, and it was Melchizedek who gave Moses the mission to take to the world that great and terrible religion of the one true God, and to impose it by force.

In Genesis, Moses tells the story of Abraham, and it is in this context that he mentions Melchizedek. He does not say very much about him, but later, when he gave the key to his five books to the seventy Ancients of Israel, he revealed the existence of that initiatic centre that controls everything from the unknown place that represents the lost paradise, or *Pardes*, as it is called. This great science, in which Abraham and Jacob had been initiated before Moses, was also known to David and Solomon, whose name in Hebrew, *Shlomo*, has the same root as *shalom*, peace—which is also found in *Yerushalaim*, the Hebrew name for Jerusalem.

Solomon was told to build the temple of Jerusalem, the dimensions and architectural design of which, as well as all the objects it contained, corresponded to a science handed down by tradition. But this first temple was destroyed by the armies of Titus in order to punish the Jews for breaking the law. The temple was destroyed and the Jewish people scattered to the ends of the earth, because at that time the Jews had abandoned the spirit of their religion and refused to recognize Jesus as the Messiah. The old Jerusalem was the initiatic centre that contained the seed of the humanity of the future, but this centre failed in its mission. This is why a new one must now be created to take its place. The New Jerusalem will be built on the pattern of Salem, the city in which Melchizedek dwells

The New Jerusalem

surrounded by all those extraordinary beings of history and legend who are still alive and who, it is said, will one day return to the world. Many cabbalists and alchemists dwell there. Even Nicolas Flamel, the famous alchemist who never died, is there in the kingdom of the initiates, the kingdom of Melchizedek.

The New Jerusalem—what it is and how it will come to the world—this is what I have to reveal to you today. The picture of the New Jerusalem as St John describes it—its dimensions, its gates, its foundations of precious stones—is quite clear, and it can be understood in different ways: as a city, as a way of life, and as a human being. The New Jerusalem cannot come until there are enough human beings built on the same pattern, symbolically speaking, for the twelve gates of pearl and the foundations of precious stones symbolize virtues and qualities. You will perhaps ask why the city has twelve gates. Because it is an image of the universe and also of a human being, for a human being possesses twelve gates or doors.

Let us have a look at these gates and see where they are. There are the two eyes, two ears, two nostrils and the mouth; that makes seven (and it is no coincidence that they are all in the head). Then there are five more: the two breasts, the navel, and two more which I will leave you to find for yourselves... So, twelve gates—not eleven, not thirteen: exactly twelve. It is amazing to see how intelligent and exact it all is, and how full of meaning. Human being were built in the workshops of the Lord in such a way as to be capable of communication and exchange with heaven and earth and the whole universe. This is why their gates must be kept open so that the currents may circulate.

Every detail of St John's description of the New Jerusalem is symbolic. He speaks of it as a cube, for instance, because the cube symbolizes something stable, something complete. It is also the symbol of justice, and Melchizedek is the king of justice. By developing a cube you get a cross, and the cross represents a human being with outstretched arms. I am sure that you can see the correspondences.

It is no good expecting to see the New Jerusalem coming down as a ready-made city from heaven. No such city will fall on us from heaven. The New Jerusalem will 'come down' only when human beings are new. Yes, the New Jerusalem is the new human being; it is all the 'new' men and women who have undertaken a gigantic work of transformation in themselves. And this work of transformation is nothing less than the transformation of the old Adam into Christ, of the old man into the new, or, to put it in alchemical terms, the transformation of the red into blue. The parallel is very clear in Hebrew: Adam is the red man *(adom,* red), who was taken from the earth *(adamah,* earth), and the red man of earth must transform himself into Christ, the blue of heaven, the symbol of peace. For anyone who is familiar with the language of symbolism these correspondences are very clear. As red is the colour of the spectrum that has the lowest vibrational frequency, it represents man's physical impulses: vitality, sensuality, anger, aggressiveness, even drunkenness. But each colour has different shades (love has hundreds of different shades; life also). All these tendencies represent thousands of different shades of red.

Jesus made it very clear that it was possible for the physical body to be transformed into light; he showed us this in his transfiguration on Mount Thabor. The Gospels tell us that his face shone like the sun and his clothes became as white as light, and Moses and Elijah appeared and talked with him. Why were Moses and Elijah there? Their presence at this moment in Jesus' life was highly significant. It means that their spirit entered into him. Moses came to give him strength, for he was the master of strength; and Elijah came to give him his foremost quality, knowledge. The teaching and prophecies of Elijah are so highly renowned and esteemed that, even today, it is said that he never died and that he will come again in the last days. At the moment of his transfiguration, therefore, Moses and Elijah took up their abode in Jesus. Jesus was not a single spirit; he was a collective being. All the great initiates before him had given him something of themselves, something that he needed in order to accomplish his mission.

At this point, you might begin to wonder whether it is possible for all human beings to be transfigured in this way, and the answer is yes. Such a transfiguration is possible for all those who succeed in purifying and sublimating their physical body. For it is not only in our souls and spirits that Christ must be born, but in our physical bodies as well. This is the symbolism of the manger, which I explained to you on Christmas Day[2]. When human beings work consciously for a long time with faith, hope, and love, their body becomes so pure and so sublimated, and all their particles vibrate with such intensity, that transfiguration becomes possible for them, just as it was possible for Jesus. And this is the New Jerusalem. The New Jerusalem is the perfection of an initiate, a master, in whom Christ is born, in whom Christ lives and breathes and manifests through those twelve gates, those twelve openings.

The New Jerusalem is preparing to come into the world; it is on its way from heaven. Angels are already active in the world, working to perfect human beings and make them truly beautiful. Every day and every night the ponderous, dark, discordant particles of our beings are swept away and replaced by particles that are light, supple, and luminous. Thousands of new Jerusalems are getting ready to unite in forming the one great New Jerusalem in which God himself will dwell, in which there will be no more tears and no more suffering.

The New Jerusalem embraces all the children of God, all those in whom Christ is born. This means, of course, that it is a perfect society in which all human beings live as brothers and

---

[2] See chap. 1 of *Christmas and Easter in the Initiatic Tradition*, Izvor Collection, N°. 209.

sisters. And, finally, the New Jerusalem is this initiatic centre that has always existed just as St John described it, with all its gold, and pearls, and precious stones. For all this already exists in the world above, and all the truths, all the elements that exist above must one day exist materially on earth.

If you study the earth you will, of course, find that it is made up of layers of dark, dull matter, but a multitude of creatures is working to purify that matter from within. Indeed, gems and precious metals are earth, but earth that has been transformed and sublimated to an extraordinary degree. A precious stone is the quintessence of all that is purest in the earth, and the initiates are the precious stones of mankind, the quintessence of the human race. The custom of adorning the crowns of kings or the sacred vestments of priests with gems stems from the knowledge that they represent the qualities and virtues of the most highly evolved beings, and that each stone symbolizes a particular virtue. A wise and intelligent man for instance is a topaz; a man of peace is a sapphire; someone who is enthusiastic and ardent is a ruby, and so on. If human kings wear jewels in their crowns, it is because there are jewels in the crown of the Almighty. God wears a crown, and in that crown are archangels and divinities, the jewels of creation.

The New Jerusalem is the perfect man, perfect universal life; it is Melchizedek's kingdom of justice and peace. This New Jerusalem is coming into the world. All those who have spoken of its coming say that it will come before the end of the century, and the reality will be something you cannot even imagine. In it will be a temple with the twelve precious stones described by St John. These precious stones—mountains of precious stones—are being kept for this age in the dwelling place of the king of justice and peace. Believe me or not as you please, it is all the same to me, but I tell you that you will see all this. Some of you will see it.

First and foremost, however, it is we ourselves who must become the New Jerusalem with our twelve gates in perfect working order, so that there may be an uninterrupted flow of exchange, and we may be transfigured. For, as I have already explained, the most important thing to understand is the symbolism of the New Jerusalem.

St John says that the heavenly city was surrounded by a great and high wall. A wall is a protection; the symbol of a powerful aura that surrounds and protects man. Those who possess a powerful aura are protected by the radiance of their own light.

This city had twelve gates. 'And at the gates twelve angels, and on the gates are inscribed the names of the twelve tribes of the Israelites.' These twelve tribes represent the twelve functions, for behind each gate (the eyes, the ears, the mouth, and so on) stands an angel. And now I ask you to listen in a spirit of great purity to what I have to tell you. Each of the twelve gates of every man and woman who is sufficiently purified to become a New Jerusalem is guarded by an angel whose function is to receive and transform all that enters through that gate. This means that when a woman who has really purified herself wishes to conceive a child, the angel at the gate works on the sperm she receives, and the child that is born to her will be genius or a divinity. But if a woman is impure, a demon, an angel of darkness lurks behind that gate, and her child will be an idiot or a monster.

So many truths still remain hidden. But they will all be revealed in time. Be patient! You still have no real understanding of what men and women are—of their structure, of the forces at work in them, or of the way they must live in order to be true tabernacles of the living God, New Jerusalems. It is toward this that I have been leading you for years and years: that you become New Jerusalems. And those who refuse to understand today will be obliged, whether they like it or not, to understand in the long run, but by then it will be too late. Human beings are completely indifferent to what might be happening behind their gates. A man is satisfied as long as he has a woman who will let him enter. He neither knows nor cares whether what goes in is demonic or not. And the woman neither knows nor cares whether what she lets in is received by a demon or by an angel. But one day they will be obliged to take the question seriously, for it is very important.

'I saw no temple in the city, for its temple is the Lord God the Almighty and the Lamb.' Once again we have the confirmation that the New Jerusalem is a temple, and this means that each human being is a temple. As St Paul says, 'You are the temple of the living God.'

The New Jerusalem is the new human being in whom all is gold, pearls, and precious stones. And the light shines within. Each one of you must become the New Jerusalem. For two thousand years there has been a succession of occult groups that claimed to be the New Jerusalem—and there are still some today. But how can anyone delude themselves that they are the New Jerusalem when these things are still so far beyond their comprehension, when they are still prisoners of the old forms, still looking for the keys to the book of life? Only those who have these keys, the seven seals—those who have a profound understanding of the Scriptures—can be the New Jerusalem. To be the New Jerusalem it is not enough to be able to trot out a few scraps of initiatic science while continuing to be as puny, fearful, weak, irresolute, and vicious as ever. No, we can all become the New Jerusalem, but only with the help of this new light which opens all doors, and which must produce visible results. If you possess knowledge, there must be results to show for it. If there are no results, it means that your knowledge does not amount to much.

'And the city has no need of sun or moon to shine on it...' The sun symbolizes the intellect and the moon the heart. Those in whom divine light and divine love dwell will need neither the sun nor the moon; that is, they will need neither philosophy nor religion.

'Its gates will never be shut by day—and there will be no

night there.' When someone is illuminated there is no night in him. The light is always shining in those who are illuminated; even when they are asleep, there is no night for them. Whereas, others fluctuate constantly between night and day; at one moment they are in the light and at the next they are in darkness. But when illumination comes, the Holy Spirit is their light and they are no longer in darkness. Night is the lack of understanding. You must not take the phrase, 'there will be no night' literally. Use your imagination: if there were no night it would mean that the cosmic order was disrupted; the earth would no longer spin on its axis; one half of the world would be in perpetual light and the other in perpetual darkness. That is not possible. In another chapter of Revelations we read, 'To the one who conquers I will also give the morning star.' The morning star is Venus. Does this mean that the celestial harmony of the heavens must be disrupted so that one who conquers may be given the planet Venus? What could he possibly do with it? Where would he put it? And suppose there were several who conquered—where could they find several other planets? No, it is obvious that all this has to be understood symbolically. So there is no need to worry; day and night will continue to exist. In this context, night symbolizes all that is negative. As long as night exists you will be full of hope one minute and in the depths of despair the next, full of faith one minute and full of doubts the next, and so on.

The New Jerusalem, therefore, is, first and foremost, the individual human being. Secondly it is a magnificent society, and thirdly it is the true Church of God, the Church of St John, the Church of the Spirit and of Truth, the Church of all the great initiates. No one can prevent this Church from coming, and when it comes all these things will be explained; everything will become clear, for Scripture tells us that God will dwell in human beings and write his law in their hearts. When this day comes, people will not need anyone to preach religion or morals to them; they will all know inwardly what to do, how to love, how to serve, and how to work. When a woman has a child she has no need of anyone to tell her how to feed and care for her child, to tell her that she must get up and look after it if it cries in the night; she knows all that because she has love in her heart. The Lord has written his laws in the hearts of mothers; they do not need rules or recipes from others. It is only when there is no love that we need rules. And even then they do not do much good.

As long as there is no love, there will continue to be religions, but the religions will never lead humanity to God. When love reigns there will be no more need for the religions. Religion will develop inwardly and express itself as kindness, radiance, sacrifice, sweetness, and light. I teach you as I have been taught. It was when love no longer dwelt with mankind that religion appeared and tried to make up for the loss. But when love returns, religion as we know it today will disappear again, for it will live once more in the hearts of men.

Sèvres, January 4, 1959

II

I can feel that you are beginning to be in less of a hurry to cut short these moments of meditation and silence. Little by little you are learning to live in eternity; you are learning to be more open, and the beneficial forces of nature are beginning to dwell within you.

Yesterday, I decided with some of the brothers that we should install a microphone and some loud-speakers up here on the Rock so that you could hear me better. You will say, 'That is wonderful. But what a pity we cannot hear you from far away, from the various towns and villages we live in.' And do you know why you cannot hear me? Because there are so many waves and currents that come between us and disrupt communications and prevent my words from reaching you. The same applies to your relations with the invisible world: if you have allowed too many things to come between the divine world and your soul and spirit, it is no use hoping to pick up and understand the messages it sends you. Between yourselves and God you can put Christ, the Holy Spirit, the Twenty-four Elders, Melchizedek, the angels and archangels, the sun, or a truly great master, for they will not disrupt your lines of communication; on the contrary, they can even serve as amplifiers. But be very careful about putting anything or anyone else between you and God.

If you put a pane of absolutely clear glass between yourself and the outside world, light will be able to pass through it. This is why people value precious stones so highly, because they allow light to pass through them. And if women, in particular, love to wear rings, necklaces, and pearl tiaras, it is because they know a great deal about such things. The only trouble is that they do not know that they know. They need an instructor who can reveal to them what they already know. A woman loves jewels because she has the intuition that they possess extraordinary powers.

The earth, which possesses intelligence, a soul, and a spirit, works on raw matter, and by dint of patience and great skill, it has managed after several million years to transform this crude mineral matter and bring it to maturity in the form of gems and precious metals. Yes, this is the science that the earth possesses in such abundance, and it is based on a science that belongs to the world above, to heaven; for earth is continually in communication with the sun by means of its etheric body. It receives its instructions from above, and slowly, patiently, and with passion, it works on the raw material that has been entrusted to it, fashioning it into geometrical forms of the most perfect beauty. From this vile, opaque matter it extracts a quintessence which it sublimates and condenses into gold, rubies, turquoises, emeralds, sapphires, diamonds, and other precious stones too numerous to mention.

The earth perfects all these treasures in its workshops, because it aspires to give material form to the qualities and virtues of the celestial sphere; it seeks to reflect them and show them to us here below in concrete, tangible forms. This is why women, who know this intuitively, think that by appropriating the beauties of the earth for themselves they will acquire the virtues and qualities of heaven. They still do not understand that precious stones are no more than a material manifestation of heavenly riches, and that the external aspect of things is there to be transformed and refined. In other words, all these

The New Jerusalem

symbols in which the virtues, qualities, and properties of heaven are condensed must be given back to heaven. The virtues they contain must be allowed to permeate the hearts and souls of the women who wear them. A woman's jewels are no more than material symbols; they have to be brought to life and transformed into virtues in her soul. When a woman succeeds in bringing her precious stones to life within herself, she becomes a divinity.

The earth has succeeded in drawing down into itself the qualities, powers, and virtues of heaven. It has succeeded in making them visible in the form of crystals and precious stones, and this is a tremendous achievement. But the work is not finished, and it is up to human beings to carry it on. Esoteric science tells us that initiates have always attributed a particular virtue to each kind of precious stone, for the material particles of each stone are organized in such a way as to allow the passage of a particular vibration of the solar spectrum while excluding all others. This is why each stone specializes, as it were, in allowing a specific quality of light to pass through it. But as white light is the synthesis of all the different colours, you need only to have a prism in order to contemplate the seven colours, which are the manifestation of all the virtues and forces of heaven.

There is nothing wrong with loving precious stones; on the contrary, it is normal. In fact we should love them. Why not? In this area, as in so many others, I have to correct the errors that have crept into the minds of so many spiritual people who continually despise or underestimate elements in which God himself has placed immense treasures of knowledge and virtue. Why are these people so ignorant? Why do they despise such magnificent creations that have been produced and fashioned by the combined efforts of the earth and the stars? Is it right for man to condemn and disdain the work of the whole cosmos? No, on the contrary, he should understand and appreciate these things at their true worth; he should give them the place they deserve in his esteem, and while admiring them and rejoicing in their beauty, continue on his upward path.

The fact that you admire the glorious treasures of the earth does not mean that you have to give in to selfishness and greed and steal them for yourself, in the way of ordinary human beings. Both those who are ready to resort to any means, however criminal, in order to get their hands on precious stones and those who despise them have the wrong attitude. And this wrong attitude has a very negative effect on their minds and hinders their evolution.

What is the best attitude? The best attitude is to study and understand and keep everything in its proper place, and, above all, to use all things as a means to evolve, to elevate yourself, and to achieve something useful for the kingdom of God on earth. Yes, as I say, instead of trying to gratify your greed and give yourself the sensual pleasure of possessing as many precious stones as possible, you would do far better to begin by understanding the meaning of what God has created; and then, without dwelling on the pleasure it gives you, make up your mind to reproduce the same work in yourself. In other words, make up your mind to create within yourself the same qualities and virtues. In this way you will receive an impetus of enthusiasm, joy, and wonder that will help you to understand divine beauty and wisdom; to understand how God works throughout the universe. But if you throw yourself greedily on precious stones for the sake of the wealth they represent, or in order to seduce others, or simply for the satisfaction of your vanity, you will be depriving yourself not only of this science, but also of the extraordinary joy that comes from doing this spiritual work.

The work of a disciple is precisely this: to become a precious stone, a stone so beautiful, pure, and transparent that, seeing it, God himself will be astonished and will send his servants to bring it to him so that he can put it in his crown. For as I have already told you, God too has a crown, and his crown is embellished with all the most beautiful precious stones—the archangels and divinities. Just imagine what ignorant people turn their backs on: the angels and archangels that grace the crown of the Almighty. How could the fifty Gates of Binah, the fifty Gates of Understanding open for such dullards who plunder and defile everything? They still have not understood the science of symbols, they have not understood that everything on earth is a reflection of what is in heaven.

Hermes Trismegistus said, 'That which is below (that is, in the depths of the earth) is like that which is above (that is, in the heavenly regions).' Everything that happens below is an exact reproduction, a faithful reflection of what exists above. No one has ever stated this as well as Hermes Trismegistus. His Emerald Tablet is still the most perfect monument that any intelligence has ever bequeathed to mankind. Only one text can compare with the Emerald Tablet (can even be said to surpass it), and that is the prayer that Jesus gave us, the Lord's Prayer. As a matter of fact, the Lord's Prayer is a variation of the Emerald Tablet. Although they are expressed differently, the truths it contains are the same. Instead of speaking of 'that which is below' and 'that which is above', Jesus says, 'Your will be done, on earth as it is in heaven.' The words are different but the truth is the same. Another difference between them is that Hermes Trismegistus speaks in the present tense of a situation that already exists; whereas Jesus expresses a wish for the future. Hermes takes note of something that exists, and Jesus asks for it. These two passages, therefore, concern different regions, different worlds. What worlds are they referring to? That which is below in the mineral, vegetable, and animal worlds is already like that which is above, because minerals, plants, and animals are loyal subjects of nature. They obey its laws meticulously and never feel the urge, constantly felt by human beings, to flout God's will. Only human beings refuse to live in harmony with nature and try to impose their own will on it. The world of human beings is not yet organized. It is the only region about which we cannot yet say, 'That which is below is like that which is above, and that which is above is like that which is below.' This is why Jesus expressed the wish, 'Your will be done on earth as it is in heaven.' But the three other worlds faithfully reflect the laws of nature.

Hermes Trismegistus said that he possessed 'the wisdom of the three worlds', and commentators have interpreted these three worlds as being the divine world, the astral world, and the physical world. This is true, but Hermes Trismegistus was also referring to the mineral world from which he obtained the philosophers' stone, the vegetable world which gave him the elixir of everlasting life, and the animal world in which he found the power of the magic wand. It was left to Jesus to take care of the world of human beings; for the fact that human beings are not in harmony with the natural order puts them in a world apart, a world in which the will of God is continually defied. They have a will of their own (which is something that neither animals nor plants nor minerals have), and it was for their sake that Jesus came and brought a new element into their world, an element that was destined to create the future. Hermes brought knowledge, science, but Jesus came to teach men to do the will of their heavenly Father. The perfect accomplishment of the kingdom of God will come about only when all creatures want the will of God to be done on earth as it is in heaven—that is, when all creatures want this order, harmony, and splendour to reign not only in the world around them but in themselves, in their own physical bodies as well.

Unfortunately, this is not the interpretation that Christians have given to these words. They continue to repeat them, but they feel no obligation to establish the kingdom of God in their own beings. They would like it to come by itself, from outside, so that they can enjoy all its advantages. But it is no good just wishing for the kingdom of God to appear on earth; that will never make it come. Or rather, if it has not yet come, it is because human beings do not know how to wish for it, how to ask for it. If they knew this, it would have come by now. Do you want to know how to ask for it? Exactly as I have already said: each individual must begin by achieving it inwardly. Only then will it be achieved outwardly as well. This is the only way to bring the kingdom of God into the world; it cannot come any other way. How can it be established in the world when the minds and hearts of men are still in a state of disorder, selfishness, and wickedness? A genuine transformation on the external plane can take place only to the extent to which it has already taken place on the inner plane, because the external world is a reflection, a materialization, a tangible realization of the spiritual world. Nothing can exist outwardly that does not already exist inwardly. How can stupid people produce anything intelligent? Intelligence is not in them.

The kingdom of God cannot exist outwardly if it does not first exist inwardly. A whole is composed of parts; take away those parts and the whole disappears. The kingdom of God is a social order composed of enlightened human beings. If human beings are not enlightened, how can that social order exist? It can only exist and endure thanks to its individual components, thanks to their characters, their qualities, and virtues. The astonishing thing is that human beings have never understood this. They want the kingdom of God to be established in the world, but they do nothing to make it so. They need to be shaken out of their lethargy, for it is they who prevent the coming of the kingdom of God on earth.

Jesus said, 'Your will be done on earth as it is in heaven.' He did not say 'is done' but 'be done,' and this form of the verb indicates that it concerns the future. But if we want that future to come, we are going to have to join forces and work for it. What could be simpler? Some will perhaps object, saying that they are Catholics and are reluctant to work with us for that reason. My response is that if they want to be perpetually bogged down in their problems, then, indeed, they might as well stay as they are. In the long run they will see whether it does them any good to be Catholics. I am a Catholic too, you know—people gape at me when I say that. But it is true: I was born in the Orthodox Church, but I am more catholic than the Catholics because I understand the word differently. I put it into practice differently too. I am sure you all agree that the word 'catholic' means universal? Well, show me what your catholicity has done for you so far. Nothing. You are still ignorant creatures who understand nothing of the great laws of the cosmos, and I cannot say that I find this sort of catholicism very attractive. It is time Catholics became truly universal. They are still wrapped in swaddling clothes; it is time they grew up and left the shelter of the cradle. They still have no idea what real spiritual work is.

But let us get back to the question of precious stones. We were saying that we must understand them and have the right attitude towards them. We must not see them only as something we like to possess; we must also transform ourselves into precious stones so that we may be an ornament in God's crown. The intuition of women helps them to understand that precious stones can lend them beauty, and that beauty is linked to love. Men are more inclined to seek power, but women are inclined to seek vanity, beauty, pleasure... and perdition. These things are strung together like a necklace—and it is not a necklace of pearls.

Even sadhus in India who have elected to live in poverty like to have a necklace, a necklace of flowers or small seeds. When I was visiting India, several of them gave me necklaces of that kind, and I still have them. A sadhu's necklace often has 108 beads, because the number 108 is sacred for them; it is the number they attribute to Babaji. All the elements of the occult are contained in this number, for it is formed by adding together several highly significant numbers: 1 for the Creator; 7 for the archangels and for light; 10 for the Sephiroth; 12 for the signs of the Zodiac; 22 for the elements of the Cabbalah;

24 for the Twenty-four Elders, and 32 for the 32 Paths of Wisdom. $1 + 7 + 10 + 12 + 22 + 24 + 32 = 108$. And when you are here in a circle round the fire, you are like the beads (pearls or precious stones) of a necklace. At the moment, perhaps, many of these beads are paste, but one day they must be transformed and become genuine precious stones and real pearls.

When you understand the profound meaning of the geometrical figures that form the structure of crystals and precious stones, you will be in possession of true knowledge. In fact, you will certainly visit the bowels of the earth one day and see for yourselves how the spirits work on minerals. This is an obligatory stage on the path of evolution of every human being, and if you do not reach it in this life it means that it is still ahead of you, waiting for a future incarnation. When you visit the underground workshops you will see how the spirits of nature work with billions of intelligent spirits. So far as it is possible, they strive to reproduce on earth the beauty and perfection of heaven. But stones and metals can never really be a faithful reflection of heaven, for the beauty of heaven is unique, matchless. Nothing on the physical plane can equal heaven, but it can at least suggest heaven to us. Plants, flowers, precious stones, the beautiful things of nature are so many distant reflections of the celestial sphere; they suggest the purity, transparency, limpidity, and geometrical perfection of the divine world.

There, that is all I have to say to you today. Be content with these few words, and thank the Lord for the blue sky, the brilliant sunshine, the pure air, and this brotherly ambience so full of love. I repeat, open yourselves and try not to be in too much of a hurry. If you want to achieve any real, tangible transformation, you must not be in a hurry. Those who are impatient and cannot wait to see the results of their spiritual work always end by being discouraged and are even tempted to turn back to the world of tumult and chaos. But perhaps you think that it is not enough to spend one life contending with difficulties and problems of all kinds? You need not worry, God is very generous, and he will give you another incarnation in which you can continue in the same way. In the long run, when you feel that your difficulties have lasted too long, you will be more inclined to draw closer to the Lord and spend a little more time contemplating him.

It is true that human beings are always in a hurry to meet suffering. You take someone to a pure, natural spring or waterfall, or to look at some beautiful flowers or trees, and he looks at his watch and says, 'Oh heavens, my wife will be waiting for me.' (to berate him no doubt), or 'I have a business appointment at the pub on the corner.' And that is the end of his appointment with the spring and the waterfall. Perhaps in ten or twenty years from now the same opportunity will arise... but how magnificent it would be if you could understand me today.

And now I wish you all a very good morning.

The Bonfin, August 14 1962

* * * * *

I should like to add a few words to what I was saying this morning. In the Bible, both in the Old and New Testaments, we find many indications that the initiates considered precious stones to be symbols of virtues and qualities. The High Priest of the Jews, for instance, wore a breastplate adorned with twelve precious stones, the twelve symbolical stones that correspond to the twelve signs of the Zodiac and the twelve tribes of Israel.

From earliest antiquity, men have valued precious stones. Even St John shows this same appreciation, for in Revelation he names the precious stones that form the foundations of the

The New Jerusalem

New Jerusalem: jasper, sapphire, agate, emerald, onyx, carnelian, chrysolite, beryl, topaz, chrysoprase, jacinth and amethyst. And Christians are still waiting for that New Jerusalem to come down from heaven. Well, I have no objection to their spending their days looking up at the sky and waiting for the New Jerusalem to appear... but they will not see it. Why should a city descend from heaven? One city for three billion people would be a bit too small anyway. And what kind of cables could be used to lower it to earth without crushing everybody under it? No, instead of waiting for the New Jerusalem to descend from heaven, you must work to become New Jerusalems yourselves. What we have at the moment is not the New Jerusalem; it is the old Jerusalem in ruins, and we must do something to improve the situation.

St John speaks also of twelve gates, the twelve gates that are twelve pearls: each gate is one pearl. Who has ever heard of an oyster capable of forming such a gigantic pearl? No, no, the New Jerusalem must be you, your perfected selves. The New Jerusalem is the new human being. So, let all these new men and women with new minds and new hearts come together. Let them march as one, as brothers and sisters united in love and with a common, divine goal, and there we shall have this city, this New Jerusalem. And this city does, indeed, come from heaven, because all that is new and luminous comes from heaven. The extraordinary thing is that each one of the beings that make up this city, each one of you, possesses twelve gates. We have counted them, and not one is missing. It is important that you know and understand these twelve gates—which I have already identified for you—because all kinds of beneficial forces, entities, and energies seek to come in and out of you, and if you keep your gates, closed they will be unable to enter you. It is never very beneficial to have something that is blocked up.

The great question, now, is to understand things in a new way so that you may do work that you have never done before.

And for this you must open yourselves to the four points of the compass. The four points form a cross, and each arm of the cross has three gates. And there you have the twelve signs of the Zodiac, the twelve angels, and the twelve precious stones. In this way, you are in communication with the luminous forces of the universe, thanks to which you may transform the nature of your being. Once you are regenerated, purified, sanctified, and illuminated, you will be the New Jerusalem, and the sun will shine within you. Night will no longer exist; all darkness will disappear, and God will reign, the God of love, wisdom, and truth.

It is no use waiting for the New Jerusalem to be delivered to you at home. Christians are comfortably ensconced in their armchairs, smoking their pipes, with the radio going full-blast and their children swarming round them, waiting for the New Jerusalem to arrive. No, it is up to them to do something about it; otherwise, even when it comes, they will continue to smoke and drink and fritter away their time in amusements. Yes, even in the New Jerusalem there will be men who cling to their tobacco and women who cling to their powder and paint. If they cannot go anywhere today without their make-up kit, they are not likely to give it up in the New Jerusalem. Seeing how bright and beautiful it is, they will say, 'Oh, what fun! Look at all those people!' And then they will put on their scent and powder their faces and go and dance.

So you must not just sit there and wait for the New Jerusalem. Get to work, and with the means and methods of this new teaching you will transform your own matter so completely that it becomes flexible, expressive, and radiant. In this way you will be opening your doors and letting in the light, and God himself will come to dwell within you. Is that possible? It is indeed. All initiates have always taught that it was possible, and some of them have achieved it. There have been at least eighteen great masters who have fully achieved the New Jerusalem, who have truly become the New Jerusalem.

The New Jerusalem

One day perhaps the eighteen will unite in one being and come to create the New Jerusalem in the world. And this nineteenth being will be the nineteenth major trump of the Tarot, the Sun.

The New Jerusalem is a universal symbol. It can be interpreted from several different but compatible points of view: alchemical, astrological, magical, and geometrical. The New Jerusalem is a collective realization, in which each individual stone will be a marvellous, luminous, enlightened being; for every individual element that contributes to its construction must be in total harmony with the whole. Any stones that want to do things 'their own way' will be rejected; only precious stones, that is, stones that vibrate in harmony with the whole, will be accepted. Precious stones always vibrate in harmony with the forces of nature. It is precisely because they are docile and obedient that they are transparent, that light can pass through them. Ordinary stones are opaque because they refuse to let light penetrate them, with the result that it abandons them. It can neither enter nor pass through them; it can do no more than illuminate the surface. But a precious stone is a stone that has understood. It says to itself, 'I must hasten to let light shine through me so that all its subtle shades may be seen; this is what will make people love and appreciate me; this is what will make them cherish me. Instead of being left to lie in the mud and be trodden underfoot by anybody and everybody, I shall be given a splendid setting and displayed for all to see.' Yes, this is how a precious stone reasons. And disciples of the new life are precious stones who understand that in order to become beautiful and radiant they must allow God, the light, to dwell in them and shine through them.

Years ago, when I first realized the importance of the twelve precious stones St John talks about, I acquired some for myself. Of course they are not as big as those mentioned in the Apocalypse, but they are the same stones. Would you like to have some too? Why not? It is not too late. You should find some, for they can really help you. Something material can be the starting point for spiritual work, and a stone can serve as a visible link with the corresponding reality in the invisible world. It is a great mistake to say, 'Oh, I attach no importance to material, physical things. I am only interested in the spirit, in abstract things.' You will not get very far with such an attitude. Nature works with matter, and man has no right to neglect it; it is there for our instruction, to point the way. A precious stone, however tiny, is a particle of this valuable matter and as such is capable of containing cosmic forces. It is important to understand this and know how to make use of it.

However, it is no good pinning all your hopes on a gem and expecting it to heal you and communicate all its virtues to you. No, if you do not do the spiritual work required, it is no use counting on a precious stone; it will do you no good at all. A stone is like an antenna, an aerial: you have to tell it what messages to transmit, and if you do this it will obey you and carry out your orders faithfully, because behind that stone is a current, a whirlwind of vibrant forces. If you want positive results, you must really understand how things work. To carry out the gestures without knowing what they mean is nothing more than superstition.

People rely on talismans and pantacles, on roots or plants... or on relics such as a length of rope that was once used to hang a man. Even today, you can see advertisements for mandragoras which, you are told, cost almost nothing and are guaranteed to open the treasure houses and palaces of the world. Above all, if you are a man, they are reputed to make every woman swoon with love for you. You can imagine how the appetites of many foolish people are roused to boiling point by such promises. 'I shall buy a mandragora and then money, freedom, and love will be mine.' And do you know what these gullible wretches receive? A tiny wooden doll carved in the shape of a mandragora root. How can people be so naïve? But enough of that; it is really of no interest.

As I was saying, it is important both to understand how things work and to have the right attitude. Your precious stone will not do your work for you. Even if nature has designed it to be an aerial capable of picking up and transmitting certain cosmic energies, that does not mean that you can go to sleep and leave it to do all your work. No, it means that you can use it for a particular kind of work. If you have the twelve stones, you can use them to link you to the virtues they represent. The twelve stones must enter into your being; this is where they must germinate and grow, as pearls grow.

A pearl is not something that appears spontaneously in nature; it is manufactured by a pearl oyster. It starts life as a tiny speck which grows bigger and bigger with time. You would be amazed if you knew the secret of a pearl, the reason for its existence. A pearl is the fruit of the will-power of an oyster. A tiny grain of sand falls into the oyster's shell and causes an irritation, and as an oyster has neither hands nor feet—nor a broom—it cannot just sweep it out again, and it remains a source of discomfort. But an oyster is a philosopher at heart, so it thinks about its problem and discovers that it can secrete a substance in which to wrap the grain of sand and make it smooth and iridescent... and quite bearable. This is how pearls are born.

The pearl oyster has a very important lesson for us: it teaches us that we must make our own pearls and our own precious stones out of the difficulties and obstacles we encounter in life. We can neither climb over them nor push them out of the way, so we have to work on them in order to transform them. It is possible to project particles of oneself, particles of one's intelligence and one's heart on to each difficulty and wrap it in a pure, luminous substance. What wealth can be ours in this way! How many pearls we can make thanks to our intelligence and patience; to the strength and tenacity of our will; thanks, above all, to an unchangeable ideal. This is why we can say that the pearls of the twelve gates represent the fruits of all the work that the saints, martyrs, and prophets have done in order to overcome the obstacles and difficulties of their lives.

Do not expect the kingdom of God to come, or the New Jerusalem to descend from above, therefore, if you do not work for it, if you make no effort to produce your own twelve pearls and precious stones. It is all very well to wear pearls and gems on your person, but they cannot help you if you do not understand the spirit of this teaching and learn to create them inwardly. A physical stone should be no more than a model. Just as a sculptor or painter works from a model, so a gem can inspire you and show you how to reproduce it inwardly. You can enjoy looking at it, but above all it should inspire a desire to create a living gem within yourself. It is wonderful to possess the twelve stones if you understand things in this way; otherwise it is simply superstition. Each thing that exists can teach us a great deal.

The New Jerusalem is in reality the symbol of the spiritual work that each human being must accomplish within himself. When all human beings have accomplished this work, the New Jerusalem will descend into the collective body of the Universal White Brotherhood, in which all philosophical and religious tendencies will eventually merge. The very name Universal White Brotherhood shows that it embraces all religions and all initiatic orders; it brings us the means best suited to our era. And what will come after this era? The same Universal White Brotherhood, with the same divine principles, but with means appropriate to the next new era. For everything evolves, and forms constantly have to be changed and adapted.

But let us get back to the question of precious stones; there is still so much to say about them. For example, it is dangerous to wear a precious stone if you do not know who its previous owner was and what influences it carries with it. For if a human being can influence a stone, the reverse is also true; a stone can influence its wearer. The power of precious stones is often weakened by the way of life of those who own them. Human beings continually produce emanations and vibrations both positive and negative, and their negative vibrations can influence and impregnate a stone to such a degree that its powers can be destroyed or even turned to evil.

History has many examples of precious stones that brought disaster on their owners. If a gem had decorated the handle of a dagger that had been used to murder someone, for instance, it could be so deeply impregnated with the influence of ghosts and elementals that its new owner would also be driven to commit crimes. There have been many such stones that have passed through the hands of a succession of owners, causing one tragedy after another, until they came into the possession of someone who was sufficiently clairvoyant to be able to read their story. Then this clairvoyant would either neutralize the evil influences in them or simply get rid of them by burying them or throwing them into the sea.

You must be careful, therefore. Some people collect antiques, old furniture, jewellery, or statuettes, without realizing that this is a very dangerous hobby. You must always study such objects carefully and not buy them rashly and impetuously. I can well understand that you admire precious stones, but you must choose stones that are pure and unsullied, that have never belonged to anyone else. Even then they should be exorcized, that is, you must remove the impurities left on them by those who cut and polished them.

A tremendous work is awaiting you, my dear brothers and sisters. You must get rid of all your superstitions and begin working at your own transformation. There is no more beautiful, no more glorious work for disciples than this work of transforming themselves, for it reflects on every other being and helps them to evolve also.

The Bonfin, August 14, 1962

By the same author
'Complete Works' Collection
TABLE OF CONTENTS

VOLUME 1 - THE SECOND BIRTH
1. The Second Birth - 2. 'Ask, and it Shall be Given to You. Seek, and You Shall Find. Knock, and it Shall be Opened to You.' - 3. Truth is Hidden in the Eyes - 4. Wisdom is Hidden in the Ears - 5. Love is Hidden in the Mouth - 6. Love, Wisdom and Truth - 7. The Master of the Universal White Brotherhood - Peter Deunov - 8. The Living Chain of the Universal White Brotherhood.

VOLUME 2 - SPIRITUAL ALCHEMY
1. Gentleness and Humility - 2. 'Except Ye Die Ye Shall Not Live' - 3. Living in Conscious Reciprocity with Nature - 4. The Unjust Steward - 5. Lay Up for Yourselves Treasures - 6. The Miracle of the Loaves and Fishes - 7. The Feet and the Solar Plexus - 8. The Parable of the Tares - 9. Spiritual Alchemy - 10. Spiritual Galvanoplasty - 11. The Mother's Role During Gestation.

VOLUME 5 - LIFE FORCE
1. Life - 2. Character and Temperament - 3. Good and Evil - 4. Pitting Oneself Against the Dragon - 5. Presence and Absence - 6. Thoughts are Living Entities - 7. Unwanted Guests - 8. The Strength of the Spirit - 9. Sacrifice - 10. A High Ideal - 11. Peace.

VOLUME 6 - HARMONY
1. Harmony - 2. Medical Science Must be Based on Initiatic Science - 3. The Future of Medicine - 4. A Disciple Must Develop His Spiritual Senses - 5. What Can We Learn From a House ? - 6. How Thought is Materialized on the Physical Plane - 7. Meditation - 8. The Human Intellect and Cosmic Intelligence - 9. The Solar Plexus and the Brain - 10. The Hara Centre - 11. The Initiatic Heart - 12. The Aura.

VOLUME 7 - THE MYSTERIES OF YESOD
Yesod reflects the Virtues of All the Sephiroth - Part I. Purity : Purity is a Question of Nourishment - Sorting and Selecting - Purity and the Spiritual Life - Purity in the Three Worlds - The River of Life - Purity and Peace - The Magic of Trusting - Purity and Speech - To Find Purity - Blessed are the Pure in Heart - The Gates of the New Jerusalem - Part II. Love and Sex - Part III. Realization - The Spring - Fasting - Washing - The Real Baptism - The Angels of the Four Elements.

VOLUME 10 - THE SPLENDOUR OF TIPHARETH

1. Surya-yoga - The Sun, Centre of our Universe - 2. Obtaining Etheric Elements from the Sun - When We Gaze at the Sun Our Soul Begins to Resemble it - 3. Our Higher Self Dwells in the Sun - 4. The Creator Sows Seeds in Us and the Sun Makes Them Grow - The Sun Reflects the Blessed Trinity - 5. Every Creature Has a Home - The Seven Beads of the Rosary - 6. The Master and the Seven-bead Rosary - Every Creature Needs to Own and Protect its Dwelling Place - The Aura - 7. The Heliocentric Point of View - 8. Love as the Sun Loves - 9. A Master Must be Like the Sun and Remain at the Centre - Some Prayers to Say at Sunrise - 10. Rise Above the Clouds - The Sephirah Tiphareth - 11. The Spirits of the Seven Lights - 12. The Prism, Symbol of Man - 13. A New Heaven and a New Earth - Spiritual Grafting - 14. The Sun Has the Solution to the Problem of Love - Telesma - 15. The Sun is in the Image and Likeness of God - 'In Spirit and in Truth' - 16. Christ and the Solar Religion - 17. Day and Night - Consciousness and the Subconscious - 18. The Sun, Originator of Civilization - A Disciple's Clairvoyance Must Begin on the Highest Levels - 19. The Sun Teaches Unity - The Power of Penetration - 20. The Sun Teaches by Example - The Sun, Heart of our Universe - 21. Three Kinds of Fire - 22. Making Everything Converge Towards One Goal.

VOLUME 11 - THE KEY
to the Problems of Existence

1. The Personality - 2. Jnana-yoga - 3. Giving and Taking - 4. Evil is Limited, Good is Limitless - 5. Eternal Happiness - 6. Fermentation - 7. Which Life ? - 8. The Image of the Tree - The Individuality Must Consume The Personality - 9. Working on the Personality - 10. The Personality Keeps You from Reflecting the Sun - 11. Identify with the Individuality - 12. The True Meaning of Sacrifice - 13. The Balance Restored - 14. Render Therefore Unto Caesar - 15. The New Philosophy - 16. The Personality Devoured by The Individuality - 17. Call On Your Allies - 18. The Further Down, The Less Space - 19. Your Inner Animals - 20. But Which Nature ? - 21. Sexual Sublimation - 22. Toward Universal Brotherhood.

VOLUME 12 - COSMIC MORAL LAW

1. 'As You Sow, So Shall You Reap' - 2. The Importance of Choice - Work not Pleasure - 3. Creative Activity as a Means of Evolution - 4. Justice - 5. The Law of Affinity : Peace - 6. The Law of Affinity : True Religion - 7. The Laws of Nature and Moral Law - 8. Reincarnation - 9. Don't Stop Half-Way - 10. Know How to Use Your Energies - 11. How to Distil the Quintessence - 12. The Moral Law Exemplified in a Spring - 13. Why Look for Models in the World Above - 14. Man

Creates in the Invisible World by Means of his Thoughts and Feelings - 15. We must not Sever the Link Between the World Below and the World Above - 16. If You Are Light You Will Seek the Company of Light - 17. Duplicates - New Recordings - 18. Morality Comes into its Own in the World Above - 19. Example ist the Best Teacher - 20. Turn the Other Cheek.

VOLUME 13 - A NEW EARTH
Methods, Exercices, Formulas and Prayers

1. Prayers - 2. A Daily Programme - 3. Nutrition - 4. Actions - 5. Overcoming the Evil Within - 6. Methods of Purification - 7. Human Relations - 8. Man's Relations with Nature - 9. The Sun and the Stars - 10. Mental Work - 11. Spiritual Galvanoplasty - 12. The Solar Plexus - 13. The Hara Centre - 14. Methods for Working with Light - 15. The Aura - 16. The Body of Glory - 17. Formulas and Prayers.

VOLUME 14 - LOVE AND SEXUALITY - PART I

1. The Masculine and Feminine Principles - The Love of God, the Love of Others, Self Love - 2. Taking the Bull by the Horns - The Caduceus of Mercury - 3. The Serpent -Isis Unveiled - 4. The Power of the Dragon - 5. Spirit and Matter - The Sexual Organs - 6. Manifestations of the Masculine and Feminine Principles - 7. Jealousy - 8. The Twelve Doors of Man - 9. From Yesod to Kether : The Path of Sexual Sublimation - 10. The Spiritual Screen - 11. Nourishment and Love - 12. Woman's Role in the New Culture - 13. The Initiatic Meaning of Nudity - 14. Exchanges and Relationships - 15. Wealth and Poverty - 16. To Love is the Work of the Disciple - 17. Love in the Universe - 18. A Wider Concept of Marriage I - 19. The Twin-Soul - 20. Everything Depends on Your Point of View - 21. A Wider Concept of Marriage II and III - 22. Analysis and Synthesis - 23. Like the Sun, Love Brings Order to Life - 24. Mother Love - 25. The Meaning of Renunciation - 26. The Bonds of Love - 27. Youth and the Problem of Love - The New Currents - Marriage - Why Self-Control - The Need for a Guide - Give Your Love to God First.

VOLUME 15 - LOVE AND SEXUALITY - PART II

1. A Question of Attitude - 2. True Marriage - 3. The Sun is the Source of Love - 4. The Goal of Love is Light - 5. The Manifestations of the Masculine and Feminine Principles - 6. Master or Mistress ? - 7. Vestal Virgins ; the New Eve - 8. Materialism, Idealism and Sexuality - 'On Earth as in Heaven' - 9. Heart and Mind ; the Universal White Brotherhood - 10. Seek the Soul and the Spirit - 11. Restoring Love to its Pristine Purity - 12. Love Transforms Matter - 13. Love and Identification - 14. The Task of a Disciple - 15. Open Yourself to Others and

They Will Love You - 16. Tantra-Yoga - 17. Emptiness and Fullness : the Holy Grail - 18. Love is Everywhere - 19. Look for Love at its Source - 20. Know How to Use Your Powers of Love - 21. A Broader Concept of Marriage, Part IV - 22. It Rises from Earth and Descends from Heaven - 23. The Secret of Happiness is in an Expanded Consciousness - 24. 'Whatever you Bind on Earth' - 25. Love God so as to Love Your Neighbour Better - 26. Live Lovingly - 27. Our Only Weapons: Love and Light - 28. Never Stop Loving - 29. Towards a Broader Concept of the Family.

VOLUME 17 - 'KNOW THYSELF' JNANA YOGA - PART I

1. 'Know Thysel" - 2. The Synoptic Table - 3. Spirit and Matter - 4. The Soul - 5. Sacrifice - 6. Food for the Soul and the Spirit - 7. Consciousness - 8. The Higher Self - 9. Truth - 10. Freedom.

VOLUME 18 - 'KNOW THYSELF' JNANA YOGA - PART II

1. Beauty - 2. Spiritual Work - 3. The Power of Thought - 4. Knowledge: Heart and Mind - 5. The Causal Plane - 6. Concentration, Meditation, Contemplation and Identification - 7. Prayer - 8. Love - 9. The Will - 10. Art and Music - 11. Physical Gestures - 12. Respiration.

VOLUME 25 - A NEW DAWN:
Society and Politics in the Light of Initiatic Science - Part I

1. The Age of Aquarius - 2. The Dawn of Universal Brotherhood - 3. Youth and Revolution - 4. Communism and Capitalism - 5. True Economics - 6. Wealth - 7. Aristocracy and Democracy - 8. Politics in the Light of Initiatic Science.

VOLUME 26 - A NEW DAWN:
Society and Politics in the Light of Initiatic Science - Part II

1. Forms and Principles - 2. The Religion of Christ - 3. The Idea of a Pan-World - 4. The Cosmic Body - 5. The Kingdom of God and His Righteousness - 6. The New Jerusalem.

VOLUME 29 - ON THE ART OF TEACHING
from the Initiatic Point of View

1. Spiritual Work - 2. On Responsibility - 3. On Building the New Life - 4. On the Living Knowledge - 5. On Perfection - 6. On the Reality of the Invisible World - 7. On Participation in the Work of the Universal White Brotherhood.

VOLUME 30 - LIFE AND WORK IN AN INITIATIC SCHOOL
Training for the Divine - Part I

1. The International Day of the Sun - 2. The Bonfin - 3. Training for the Divine - 4. Hrani-Yoga and Surya-Yoga - 5. The Spirit of the Teaching - 6. Matter and Light - 7. Purity and Light - 8. The Meaning of Initiation.

VOLUME 32 - THE FRUITS OF THE TREE OF LIFE
The Cabbalistic Tradition

1. How to Approach the Study of the Cabbalah - 2. The Number Ten and the Ten Sephiroth - 3. Structure and Symbols of the Tree of Life - 4. The Tetragrammaton and the Seventy-Two Planetary Spirits - 5. The Creation of the World and the Theory of Emanation - 6. The Fall and Redemption of Man - 7. The Four Elements - 8. Evening Vigils Round the Fire : I. The Power of Fire - II. Fire and the Sun - III. The Fire of Sacrifice - 9. Water and Fire - 10. A Bowl of Water - 11. The Living Logos : I. The Alphabet and the Twenty-Two Elements of the Logos - II. The Universal Language of the Logos - III. The Power of the Logos - 12. The Esoteric Church of Saint John - 13 Binah, the Realm of Stability - 14. The Human Spirit is Above Fate - 15. Death and the Life Beyond - 16. Human and Cosmic Respiration - 17. The Cardinal Feasts - 18. The Moon and its Influence on Man - 19. The Glorified Souls - 20. The Land of the Living - 21. A Magic Wand - 22. Nature Spirits - 23. Objects are Receptacles of Life - 24. The Holy Grail - 25. Building the Inner Sanctuary.

By the same author

Izvor Collection
TABLE OF CONTENTS

201 – TOWARD A SOLAR CIVILIZATION
1. The Sun, Initiator of Civilization – 2. Surya Yoga – 3. Seeking the Centre – 4. The Sun our Provider – 5. The Solar Plexus – 6. Man is Made in the Image of the Sun – 7. The Spirits of the Seven Lights – 8. The Sun as our Model – 9. The True Solar Religion.

202 – MAN, MASTER OF HIS DESTINY
1. The Law of Cause and Effect – 2. You will Separate the Subtle from the Gross – 3. Evolution and Creation – 4. Two Justices: Human and Divine – 5. The Law of Correspondences – 6. Natural and Moral Law – 7. Nature's Records – 8. Reincarnation.

203 – EDUCATION BEGINS BEFORE BIRTH
1. The First Priority: Educating Parents – 2. Education Begins before Birth – 3. A Blueprint for the Future of Mankind – 4. Don't Neglect Your Children – 5. A New Understanding of a Mother's Love – 6. The Magic Word – 7. Never Let Your Children be Idle – 8. Prepare Your Children for Adult Life – 9. Protect Your Children's Sense of Wonder – 10. Love without Weakness – 11. Education versus Instruction.

204 – THE YOGA OF NUTRITION
1. Eating: An Act which Concerns the Whole Man – 2. Hrani-Yoga – 3. Food: A Love-Letter from God – 4. Choosing Your Food – 5. Vegetarianism – 6. The Ethics of Eating – 7. Fasting: I – Means of Purification. II – Another Form of Nutrition – 8. Communion – 9. The Meaning of the Blessing – 10. The Spirit Transforms Matter – 11. The Law of Symbiosis.

205 – SEXUAL FORCE OR THE WINGED DRAGON
1. The Winged Dragon – 2. Love and Sexuality – 3. The Sexual Force is Essential for Life on Earth – 4. Pleasure: I – Do not Seek Pleasure for it Will Impoverish You – II – Replace Pleasure with Work – 5. The Dangers of Tantric Yoga – 6. Love without Waiting to be Loved – 7. Love is Everywhere in the Universe – 8. Spiritual Love is a Higher Way of Feeding Ourselves – 9. A High Ideal Transforms Sexual Energy – 10. Open Your Love to a Higher Path.

206 – A PHILOSOPHY OF UNIVERSALITY
1. What is a Sect? – 2. No Church is Eternal – 3. The Spirit Behind the Form – 4. The Advent of the Church of St. John – 5. The Foundations of a Universal Religion – 6. The Great Universal White Brotherhood – 7. For a Universal Notion of the Family – 8. Brotherhood, a Higher State of Consciousness – 9. The Annual Conventions at the Bonfin – 10. The Universal Dimension of All Our Activities.

207 – WHAT IS A SPIRITUAL MASTER?
1. How to Recognize a True Spiritual Master – 2. The Necessity for a Spiritual Master – 3. The Sorcerer's Apprentice – 4. The Exotic Should not be Confused with Spirituality – 5. Learn How to Balance the Material and Spiritual Worlds – 6. A Master is a Mirror Reflecting the Truth – 7. A Master is There Only to Give Light – 8. The Disciple and His Master – 9. The Universal Dimension of a Master – 10. The Magical Presence of a Master – 11. Identification – 12. 'Except Ye Become as Little Children...'

208 – THE EGREGOR OF THE DOVE OR THE REIGN OF PEACE
1. Towards a Better Understanding of Peace – 2. The Advantages of Unity amongst Nations – 3. Aristocracy and Democracy – 4. About Money – 5. The Distribution of Wealth – 6. Communism and Capitalism – 7. Towards a New Understanding of Economics – 8. What Every Politician Should Know – 9. The Kingdom of God.

209 – CHRISTMAS AND EASTER IN THE INITIATIC TRADITION
1. The Feast of the Nativity – 2. The Second Birth – 3. Birth on the Different Planes of Being – 4. 'Except Ye Die Ye Shall not Live' – 5. The Resurrection and the Last Judgment – 6. The Body of Glory.

210 – THE TREE OF THE KNOWLEDGE OF GOOD AND EVIL
1. The Serpent of Genesis – 2. What Good is Evil? – 3. Beyond Good and Evil – 4. Until the Harvest – 5. The Philosophy of Unity – 6. Into the Wilderness to Be Tempted – 7. The Undesirables – 8. Suicide is not the Answer – 9. The Real Weapons – 10. The Science of the Initiates, or the Inner Lamps.

211 – FREEDOM, THE SPIRIT TRIUMPHANT
1. Man's Psychic Structure – 2. Mind over Matter – 3. Fate and Freedom – 4. Freedom through Death – 5. Sharing in the Freedom of God – 6. True Freedom: a Consecration of Self – 7. Freedom through Self-Limitation – 8. Anarchy and Freedom – 9. The Notion of Hierarchy – 10. The Synarchy Within.

212 – LIGHT IS A LIVING SPIRIT
1. Light : Essence of Creation – 2. The Sun's Rays, their Nature and Activity – 3. Gold is Condensed Sunlight – 4. Light Enables us to See and be Seen – 5. Working with Light – 6. The Prism : a Symbol of Man – 7. Purity Clears the Way for Light – 8. Living with the Intensity of Light – 9. The Spiritual Laser.

213 – MAN'S TWO NATURES, HUMAN AND DIVINE
1. Human Nature or Animal Nature? – 2. The Lower Self is a Reflection – 3. Man's True Identity – 4. Methods of Escape – 5. The Sun Symbolizes the Divine Nature – 6. Put the Personality to Work – 7. Perfection Comes with the Higher Self – 8. The Silent Voice of the Higher Self – 9. Only by Serving the Divine Nature – 10. Address the Higher Self in Others – 11. Man's Return to God, the Victory.

214 – HOPE FOR THE WORLD : SPIRITUAL GALVANOPLASTY

1. What is Spiritual Galvanoplasty? – 2. Reflections of the Two Principles – 3. Marriages Made in Heaven – 4. Love Freely Given – 5. Love on the Lower Plane – 6. Love on the Higher Plane – 7. Love's Goal is Light – 8. The Solar Nature of Sexual Energy – 9. Mankind Transformed – 10. The Original Experiment and the New One – 11. Replenish the Earth! – 12. Woman's place – 13. The Cosmic Child.

215 – THE TRUE MEANING OF CHRIST'S TEACHING

1. 'Our Father Which Art in Heaven' – 2. 'My Father and I Are One' – 3. 'Be Ye Perfect, Even as Your Father Who is in Heaven is Perfect' – 4. 'Seek Ye First the Kingdom of God and His Justice' – 5. 'On Earth as it is in Heaven' – 6. 'He That Eateth My Flesh and Drinketh My Blood Hath Eternal Life' – 7. 'Father, Forgive Them, For They Know Not What They Do' – 8. 'Unto Him that Smiteth Thee on the One Cheek...' – 9. 'Watch and Pray'.

216 – THE LIVING BOOK OF NATURE

1. The Living Book of Nature – 2. Day and Night – 3. Spring Water or Stagnant Water – 4. Marriage, a Universal Symbol – 5. Distilling the Quintessence – 6. The Power of Fire – 7. The Naked Truth – 8. Building a House – 9. Red and White – 10. The River of Life – 11. The New Jerusalem – Perfect Man. I – The Gates. II – The Foundations – 12. Learning to Read and Write.

217 – NEW LIGHT ON THE GOSPELS

1. 'Men do not Put New Wine into Old Bottles' – 2. 'Except Ye Become as Little Children' – 3. The Unjust Stewart – 4. 'Lay up for Yourselves Treasures in Heaven' – 5. The Strait Gate – 6. 'Let Him Which is on the Housetop not Come Down...' – 7. The Calming of the Storm – 8. The First Shall Be Last – 9. The Parable of the Five Wise and the Five Foolish Virgins – 10. 'This is Life Eternal, that they Might Know Thee the Only True God'.

218 – THE SYMBOLIC LANGUAGE OF GEOMETRICAL FIGURES

1. Geometrical Symbolism – 2. The Circle – 3. The Triangle – 4. The Pentagram – 5. The Pyramid – 6. The Cross – 7. The Quadrature of the Circle.

219 – MAN'S SUBTLE BODIES AND CENTRES
the Aura, the Solar Plexus, the Chakras...

1. Human Evolution and the Development of the Spiritual Organs – 2. The Aura – 3. The Solar Plexus – 4. The Hara Centre – 5. Kundalini Force – 6. The Chakras: The Chakra System I. – The Chakra System II. Ajna and Sahasrara.

220 – THE ZODIAC, KEY TO MAN AND TO THE UNIVERSE

1. The Enclosure of the Zodiac – 2. The Zodiac and the Forming of Man – 3. The Planetary Cycle of Hours and Days – 4. The Cross of Destiny – 5. The Axes of Aries–Libra and Taurus–Scorpio – 6. The Virgo–Pisces Axis – 7. The Leo–Aquarius Axis – 8. The Fire and Water Triangles – 9. The Philosophers' Stone : the Sun, the Moon and Mercury – 10. The Twelve Tribes of Israel and the Twelve Labours of Hercules in Relation to the Zodiac.

221 – TRUE ALCHEMY OR THE QUEST FOR PERFECTION

1. Spiritual Alchemy – 2. The Human Tree – 3. Character and Temperament – 4. Our Heritage from the Animal Kingdom – 5. Fear – 6. Stereotypes – 7. Grafting – 8. The Use of Energy – 9. Sacrifice, the Transmutation of Matter – 10. Vainglory and Divine Glory – 11. Pride and Humility – 12. The Sublimation of Sexual Energy.

222 – MAN'S PSYCHIC LIFE: ELEMENTS AND STRUCTURES

1. Know Thyself – 2. The Synoptic Table – 3. Several Souls and Several Bodies – 4. Heart, Mind, Soul and Spirit – 5. The Apprenticeship of the Will – 6. Body, Soul and Spirit – 7. Outer Knowledge and Inner Knowledge – 8. From Intellect to Intelligence – 9. True Illumination – 10. The Causal Body – 11. Consciousness – 12. The Subconscious – 13. The Higher Self.

223 – CREATION: ARTISTIC AND SPIRITUAL

1. Art, Science and Religion – 2. The Divine Sources of Inspiration – 3. The Work of the Imagination – 4. Prose and Poetry – 5. The Human Voice – 6. Choral Singing – 7. How to Listen to Music – 8. The Magic Power of a Gesture – 9. Beauty – 10. Idealization as a Means of Creation – 11. A Living Masterpiece – 12. Building the Temple – Postface.

224 – THE POWERS OF THOUGHT

1. The Reality of Spiritual Work – 2. Thinking the Future – 3. Psychic Pollution – 4. Thoughts are Living Beings – 5. How Thought Produces Material Results – 6. Striking a Balance between Matter and Spirit – 7. The Strength of the Spirit – 8. Rules for Spiritual Work – 9. Thoughts as Weapons – 10. The Power of Concentration – 11. Meditation – 12. Creative Prayer – 13. Reaching for the Unattainable.

225 – HARMONY AND HEALTH

1. Life Comes First – 2. The World of Harmony – 3. Harmony and Health – 4. The Spiritual Foundations of Medicine – 5. Respiration and Nutrition – 6. Respiration: I. The Effects of Respiration on Health – II. How to Melt into the Harmony of the Cosmos – 7. Nutrition on the Different Planes – 8. How to Become Tireless – 9. Cultivate an Attitude of Contentment.

226 – THE BOOK OF DIVINE MAGIC

1. The Danger of the Current Revival of Magic – 2. The Magic Circle of the Aura – 3. The Magic Wand – 4. The Magic Word – 5. Talismans – 6. Is Thirteen an Unlucky Number – 7. The Moon – 8. Working with Nature Spirits – 9. Flowers and Perfumes – 10. We All Work Magic – 11. The Three Great Laws of Magic – 12. The Hand – 13. The Power of a Glance – 14. The Magical Power of Trust – 15. Love, the Only True Magic – 16. Never Look for Revenge – 17. The Exorcism and Consecration of Objects – 18. Protect Your Dwelling Place.

227 – GOLDEN RULES FOR EVERYDAY LIFE

1. Life: our most precious possession – 2. Let your material life be consistent with your spiritual life – 3. Dedicate your life to a sublime goal – 4. Our daily life: a matter that must be

transformed by the spirit – 5. Nutrition as Yoga – 6. Respiration – 7. How to recuperate energy – 8. Love makes us tireless – 9. Technical progress frees man for spiritual work – 10. Furnishing your inner dwelling – 11. The outer world is a reflection of your inner world – 12. Make sure of a good future by the way you live today – 13. Live in the fullness of the present – 14. The importance of beginnings... etc.

228 – LOOKING INTO THE INVISIBLE
Intuition, Clairvoyance, Dreams

1. The Visible and the Invisible – 2. The Limited Vision of the Intellect, The Infinite Vision of Intuition – 3. The Entrance to the Invisible World: From Yesod to Tiphareth – 4. Clairvoyance: Activity and Receptivity – 5. Should We Consult Clairvoyants ? – 6. Love and Your Eyes Will be Opened – 7. Messages From Heaven – 8. Visible and Invisible Light: Svetlina and Videlina – 9. The Higher Degrees of Clairvoyance – 10. The Spiritual Eye – 11. To See God – 12. The True Magic Mirror: The Universal Soul – 13. Dream and Reality – 14. Sleep, an Image of Death – 15. Protect Yourself While You Are Asleep – 16. Astral Projection While Asleep – 17. Physical and Psychic Havens – 18. The Sources of Inspiration – 19. Sensation is Preferable to Vision.

229 – THE PATH OF SILENCE

1. Noise and Silence – 2. Achieving Inner Silence – 3. Leave Your Cares at the Door – 4. Make Your Meals an Exercise in Silence – 5. Silence, a Reservoir of Energies – 6. The Inhabitants of Silence – 7. Harmony, the Essential Condition for Inner Silence – 8. Silence, the Essential Condition for Thought – 9. The Quest for Silence is the Quest for the Centre – 10. Speech and the Logos – 11. A Master Speaks in Silence – 12. The Voice of Silence is the Voice of God – 13. The Revelations of a Starry Sky – 14. A Silent Room.

230 – THE BOOK OF REVELATIONS: A COMMENTARY

1. The Island of Patmos – 2. Introduction to the Book of Revelations – 3. Melchizedek and Initiation into the Mystery of the Two Principles – 4. Letters to the Church in Ephesus and Smyrna – 5. Letter to the Church in Pergamos – 6. Letter to the Church in Laodicea – 7. The Twenty-Four Elders and the Four Holy Living Creatures – 8. The Scroll and the Lamb – 9. The Hundred and Forty-Four Thousand Servants of God – 10. The Woman and the Dragon – 11. The Archangel Mikhaël Casts Out the Dragon – 12. The Dragon Spews Water at the Woman – 13. The Beast from the Sea and the Beast from the Land – 14. The Wedding Feast of the Lamb – 15. The Dragon is Bound for a Thousand Years – 16. The New Heaven and the New Earth – 17. The Heavenly City.

231 – THE SEEDS OF HAPPINESS

1. Happiness: A Gift to be Cultivated – 2. Happiness is not Pleasure – 3. Happiness is Found in Work – 4. A Philosophy of Effort – 5. Light Makes for Happiness – 6. The Meaning of Life – 7. Peace and Happiness – 8. If You want to be Happy, Be Alive – 9. Rise Above your Circumstances – 10. Develop a Sensitivity to the Divine – 11. The Land of Canaan – 12. The Spirit is Above the Laws of Fate – 13. Look for Happiness on a Higher Level – 14. The Quest for Happiness is a Quest for God – 15. No Happiness for Egoists – 16. Give Without Expecting Anything in Return – 17. Love Without Asking to be Loved in Return – 18. Our Enemies are Good for Us – 19. The Garden of Souls and Spirits – 20. Fusion on the Higher Planes – 21. We are the Artisans of Our Own Future.

232 – THE MYSTERIES OF FIRE AND WATER
1. The Two Principles of Creation, Water and Fire – 2. The Secret of Combustion – 3. Water, the Matrix of Life – 4. Civilization, a Product of Water – 5. The Living Chain of Sun, Earth and Water – 6. A Blacksmith Works with Fire – 7. Water is Born of Mountains – 8. Physical and Spiritual Water – 9. Feeding the Flame – 10. The Essential Role of Fire – 11. The Cycle of Water: Reincarnation –12. The Cycle of Water: Love and Wisdom – 13. A Candle Flame – 14. How to Light and Tend Fire – 15. Water, the Universal Medium – 16. The Magic Mirror – 17. Trees of Light – 18. The Coming of the Holy Spirit – 19. A Treasury of Pictures.

233 – YOUTH: CREATORS OF THE FUTURE
1. Youth, a World in Gestation – 2. The Foundation Stone of Life: Faith in a Creator – 3. A Sense of the Sacred – 4. The Voice of our Higher Nature – 5. Choosing the Right Direction – 6. Knowledge Cannot Give Meaning to Life – 7. Character Counts for More than Knowledge – 8. Learning to Handle Success and Failure – 9. Recognize the Aspirations of Soul and Spirit – 10. The Divine World, Our Own Inner World – 11. Did you Choose Your Own Family? –12. Benefit From the Experience of Older People – 13. Compare Yourself to Those Who Are Greater – 14. The Will Must be Sustained by Love – 15. Never Admit Defeat – 16. Never Give Way to Despair – 17. Artists of the Future – 18. Sexual Freedom – 19. Preserve the Poetry of Your Love – 20. Members of One Universal Family (I) (II).

234 – TRUTH: FRUIT OF WISDOM AND LOVE
1. The Quest for Truth – 2. Truth, the Child of Wisdom and Love – 3. Wisdom and Love; Light and Warmth – 4. The Love of a Disciple; the Wisdom of a Master – 5. Truth, the Kernel of Life –6. 'I am the Way, the Truth and the Life' – 7. The Blue Ray of Truth – 8. Three Levels of Truth – 9. Be Faithful to the Truth – 10. There is no Arguing about Tastes – 11. Reality: Objective and Subjective – 12. The Primacy of Subjective Reality – 13. Scientific Progress v. Moral Progress – 14. Scientific Truth and the Truth of Life – 15. A Fresh View of Reality – 16. Dreams and Reality – 17. Truth Transcends Good and Evil – 18. 'The Truth shall Make you Free'(I) (II).

235 – 'IN SPIRIT AND IN TRUTH'
1. The Framework of the Universe – 2. The Divine Office of Weights and Measures – 3. The Link with the Centre – 4. Reaching for the Top – 5. From Multiplicity to Unity – 6. Building the Edifice – 7. Contemplating the Truth: Isis Unveiled – 8. Garment of Light – 9. The Skin – 10. The Perfume of Eden – 11. 'In Spirit and in Truth' – 12. An Image Can Be a Support for Prayer – 13. The Spirit is not Held Captive in Relics – 14. Speak to the Spirit of Those You Love – 15. The Sun, the Quintessence of Religion – 16. The Truth of the Sun is in Giving – 17. The Kingdom of God is Within.

236 – ANGELS
and other Mysteries of The Tree of Life
1. From Man to God, the Notion of Hierarchy – 2. Introduction to the Sephirotic Tree of Life – 3. The Angelic Hierarchies – 4. The Names of God – 5. The Sephiroth of the Central Pillar – 6. Ain Soph Aur, Unlimited Light – 7. Light, the Substance of the Universe –

8. 'When God Drew a Circle on the Face of the Deep' – 9. The Kingdom of God is like a Mustard Seed – 10. The Cosmic Family and the Mystery of the Trinity – 11. The Body of Adam Kadmon – 12. Malkuth, Yesod, Hod, Tiphareth, Archangels and Seasons – 13. The Sephirotic Tree, Symbol of Synarchic Order – 14. Yesod, Foundation of the Spiritual Life –15. Binah: I The Laws of Destiny - II The Realm of Stability – 16. Chokmah, the Creative Word – 17. Yesod, Tiphareth, Kether, the Sublimation of Sexual Energy – 18. The Prayer of Solomon.

237 – COSMIC BALANCE
The Secret of Polarity

1. Cosmic Balance and the Number Two – 2. Oscillation of the Scales – 3. One and Zero – 4. The Role of The Masculine and The Feminine - Adam and Eve : Spirit and Matter - Adam and Eve : Wisdom and Love - The Mental and Astral Planes - Man and Woman – 5. God Transcends Good and Evil – 6. The White Head and the Black Head – 7. Alternation and Antagonism - The Law of Opposites – 8. 'To Work the Miracles of One Thing' - The Figure of Eight and the Cross – 9. The Caduceus of Hermes - The Astral Serpent – 10. *Iona*, Principle of Life - *Horeb*, Principle of Death – 11. The Triad *Kether-Chesed-Geburah* - Sceptre and Orb - Mind and Heart - A Straight Line and a Curved Line – 12. The Law of Exchange – 13. The Key and the Lock – 14. The Work of the Spirit on Matter - The Holy Grail – 15. Union of the Ego with the Physical Body – 16. The Sacrament of the Eucharist – 17. The Androgynes of Myth – 18. Union with the Universal Soul and the Cosmic Spirit.